FASHIONING MEMORY

FASHIONING MEMORY

Vintage Style and Youth Culture

Heike Jenss

Bloomsbury Academic
An imprint of Bloomsbury Publishing Plc

BLOOMSBURY
LONDON · OXFORD · NEW YORK · NEW DELHI · SYDNEY

Bloomsbury Academic
An imprint of Bloomsbury Publishing Plc

50 Bedford Square	1385 Broadway
London	New York
WC1B 3DP	NY 10018
UK	USA

www.bloomsbury.com

BLOOMSBURY and the Diana logo are trademarks of Bloomsbury Publishing Plc

First published 2015

British Library Cataloguing in Publication Data
A catalogue record for this book is available from the British Library.

ISBN:	HB:	978-1-4725-7396-4
	PB:	978-1-3500-2436-6
	ePDF:	978-1-4742-6198-2
	ePub:	978-1-4742-6199-9

Library of Congress Cataloging in Publication Data
Jenss, Heike, 1970-
Fashioning memory : vintage style and youth culture / by Heike Jenss.
pages cm
Includes bibliographical references and index.
ISBN 978-1-4725-7396-4 (hardback : alk. paper)– ISBN 978-1-4742-6198-2 (ePDF)– ISBN 978-1-4742-6199-9 (ePub) 1. Clothing and dress. 2. Youth--Clothing. 3. Fashion--Social aspects. 4. Subculture. I. Title.
GT596.J46 2015
391–dc23
2015016053

Series: Dress and Fashion Research, 2053-3926

Typeset by Fakenham Prepress Solutions, Fakenham, Norfolk NR21 8NN

To my mother Ursula Jenβ

CONTENTS

FIGURES

PREFACE

I n 2012 *Showstudio* released a short film titled *The New Faces*, photographed by Dean Chalkley. The film is shot in crisp black and white, capturing in slow motion against a white seamless studio backdrop the dance moves, poses and appearances of eight twenty-first-century modernists—six men and two women—dressed in sharp suits, polished shoes and meticulous hair styles. The viewer hears no music to this scene of dancing bodies, but the voices of three men talking about their passion for modern, timeless clothing and style. The camera zooms in on the details of clothing and appearance: on the covered buttons of suit jackets, the side vents of neatly ironed trousers, the women's eye make-up, the tassel and woven loafers, the heels that leave dark traces of the dancing bodies on the white vinyl studio backdrop. The immaculate old-fashioned clothes, the bodies dancing to mute music, the slow motion and monochrome photography create a scene that accentuates and aestheticizes a material absence and presence of time. The twenty-minute documentary gives a glimpse into the endurance of mid-twentieth-century fashion and style that is picked up, worn, enacted, remembered and reimagined by a new generation of youth or young adults, whose looks and moves are material testimony of the "affective force" (see Thrift 2010) of former fashions, or how past aesthetics "move" present bodies.

In this book I seek to explore the experience and allure of past fashions to new wearers, bringing together different times and places of research. Empirically the book builds and expands on research I began to pursue in Germany in the early twenty-first century, culminating in my German book *Sixties Dress Only: Mode und Konsum in der Retro-Szene der Mods* (Jenss 2007). Early stages of this research also appeared in some English publications (Jenss 2004, 2005a). This work is based on an ethnographic study of the sixties scene in Germany, with a particular focus on how clothing of the 1960s is used, refashioned and forms a material part of practices and processes of identification and social relationships in the context of youth culture.

My research evolved as part of a collaborative project located at the universities of Dortmund and Frankfurt am Main (funded by The Volkswagen Foundation 2002–5) that investigated dynamics of uniformization and seriality in diverse clothing contexts, from corporate dress codes to everyday fashion, the rise of fast fashion, and mass-individualization (see Mentges and Richard 2005; Mentges, Neuland-Kitzerow and Richard 2007).

After I had moved to take on a new position in the US, the work on this book, *Fashioning Memory: Youth Culture and Vintage Style*, initially began to evolve as a project of translation. Yet with the dynamics of time and place, the process of writing and further research, this project started to crystallize its own focus on the intersection of youth, vintage, fashion time and cultural memory—with the latter offering a productive methodological angle to explore how time or the cross-temporal dynamics of fashion and youth cultural style come to be experienced and enacted through dress practices. While such an interest was to an extent inherent in the original field research and interviews, it is the bringing together of fashion and memory as an "operative metaphor," and the understanding of remembering as a "performative act," as it is conceptualized in more recent research in the field of memory studies, as I will outline in the introduction to this book, that shed new light on my material. In addition, it is the role of language itself and the thinking about shifting terminologies, for example from retro to vintage, and what these shifts may entail, as well as the impact of time and change itself—including the developments of new technologies and the fostering of vintage aesthetics, as well as experiences of nostalgia through media over the last decade (see Jenss 2013) and the observation of changing preferences, aesthetics and perceptions of "the sixties" and sixties style—that led me to reflect on and expand my research through perspectives on time, memory, fashion and modernity.

This book brings then different phases of research together, with insights—and hindsight—emerging from each that inform the chapters in this book, including historical research on the rise of vintage in fashion, and on the allure of the new and the old in youth culture, empirical explorations of the materialities of second-hand consumption and the performance of vintage style, and their framing through perspectives and theories on the dynamics, mediation and experience of cultural memory, modernity and the temporalities of fashion.

ACKNOWLEDGMENTS

This book evolved through the course of several phases and places of research. Much of the empirical material informing the discussion in this book, especially in Chapters 4 to 6, is grounded in field research I conducted on vintage and sixties enthusiasts in Germany, without whom this book would not exist. I am indebted to anyone who participated in the original ethnographic research: those who took me along to sixties events, who spoke with me informally, who hung out with me and who let me participate. I am particularly grateful to my interviewees who took the time and generously let me into their homes, allowed me to look through their wardrobes and talked with me about their clothes, and who provided me with insights into their experiences and feelings about clothing and vintage shopping and their discoveries of, and affinity for, sixties style. I want to express my thanks to The Volkswagen Foundation for funding this research from 2002 to 2005 at Dortmund University, and for the travel support to meet interviewees and participate in sixties events in Germany, Italy and Spain, as well as to pursue archival research at the Archiv der Jugendkulturen e.V. in Berlin. Thanks also to Campus Verlag, in particular to Judith Wilke-Primavesi, for the permission to work off selected material from my German book *Sixties Dress Only: Mode und Konsum in der Retro-Szene der Mods* (Jenss 2007).

The more recent work on this book began most productively with a pre-sabbatical leave I was awarded by Parsons The New School for Design in the academic year 2012/13 that enabled me to immerse myself in the research and early writing stages of this book. I want to express my gratitude to Dean Sarah Lawrence for all her support. My special thanks go also to my colleagues and friends at Parsons' School of Art and Design History and Theory and beyond: particularly to Hazel Clark, Jilly Traganou, Miodrag Mitrasinovic, Clive Dilnot, Pascale Gatzen, Christina Moon, Francesca Granata, Rachel Lifter, Marilyn Cohen, Todd Nicewonger, Janet Kraynak and David Brody for opportunities to speak about my research in classes or in conversations, and for their interest, comments or encouraging nods along the way. I am thankful for the generous funding I received from Parsons to help with research expenses, including travel to conferences to present and discuss my work in various international and interdisciplinary contexts—and for the funding of research assistants: Stephanie E. Herold has been truly incredible with her sharp thinking, wit and multitasking skills, from library and image research to proofreading and thoughtful commentary. Without her diligent work and assistance, this book would not have made the deadline. I also thank Cayla O'Connell for her work on the book cover.

My thanks also go to my former research assistants Laura Snelgrove, Molly Rottman and Nicole Rivas who supported me in early stages of this book and helped me to carve out research time while serving as founding director of Parsons' MA Fashion Studies program. Leilah Vevaina was incredibly supportive with her research assistance during my sabbatical, including the reading of early draft materials for this book. Big thanks also to Philip Schauss for helping with the translation of parts of my German material, especially for finding the right voice in the diverse interview excerpts. I am also grateful to the graduate students in my Fashioning Time and Memory course whose various interests in and perspectives on the intersections of fashion and memory were truly inspiring.

My heartfelt thanks go to the scholars, mentors and friends who gave their input during varied stages of this book: Susan B. Kaiser for her continuous support and for fostering my interest in fashion, time and place, urging me to expand a paper on fashion and nostalgia, now published in the journal *Critical Studies in Fashion and Beauty*. Janet Hethorn for her input during the shaping of the book proposal and for being such a generous source of good spirit and support. Elke Gaugele and Gudrun König for thoughtful comments on my early outline for this book. Carol Tulloch and Alexandra Palmer for helpful conversations around my ideas for this project. Viola Hofmann for the ongoing exchange and for being a wonderful friend, despite any distance in time and place. I also thank Regina Henkel for the friendship and stimulating conversations. I want to express my gratitude especially to Gabriele Mentges, a brilliant scholar and supportive doctoral adviser and mentor, who has been an important source of inspiration. My thanks go also to Birgit Richard for her invaluable feedback and support during my time as her doctoral advisee, and beyond.

Joanne Eicher has been wonderful and I want to thank her for her interest early on in this project. At Bloomsbury, Anna Wright's enthusiasm for the idea of this book has been continuously reassuring. My thanks also to Hannah Crump, Ariadne Godwin, and in the early stages Emily Ardizzone, for their assistance, patience and for seeing this project through.

Finally I want to express my deepest gratitude to Markus Geisler, my partner and best friend, for the companionship and for the support on the path towards this book: for the patience and ongoing interest and curiosity, for the many walks, conversations and insightful commentary on my thoughts and ideas, and for bringing the music in our life.

1 INTRODUCTION: FASHION AND CULTURAL MEMORY

Memory is in fashion. The reevaluation of used, aged and discarded clothes, making their way through the second-hand clothing circuits back onto the bodies of new wearers as "vintage," is an example for the appeal of fashion and clothes as forms of material memory. A century ago the word vintage was used in the context of high fashion to describe last season's clothes, whose age or "datedness" should ideally be hidden by updating them in fresh combinations or by modifying any season-revealing details. Today, however, the word vintage refers to clothes of a certain age: clothes that are precisely valued for their materialization of time and "datedness" and their capacity as memory modes through which new wearers can feel in touch with a former fashion time.

The rise of old clothes to the rank of vintage and the incorporation of the sartorial past in contemporary appearance making has become one of the major developments across fashion and popular culture in recent decades, tying in with the promotion of ideas of individuality and authenticity. This popularity of the past as vintage occurred alongside an increasing acceleration of fashion production and communication, leading to the global expansion of fast fashion, but yet equally along an expanding memory culture propelled through the accumulation and circulation of the past in material and visual culture. The use and valuing of second-hand clothing as vintage, a kind of reversal of the idea of "newness" in fashion by dressing in outmoded clothes, has been particularly popular among youth, raising questions with regard to the intersections of fashion, time, age/generation and cultural memory. Building on ethnographic fieldwork in Germany, this book sets out to explore how these intersections play out in everyday dress and consumption practices—focusing in on youth and young adults, who through clothing and style recollect "the sixties" in the early twenty-first century.

As part of a youth cultural scene that bridges past and present, contemporary sixties enthusiasts form a particularly interesting case study for an exploration of vintage style and cultural memory. They are remembering a decade intricately bound up with ideas of modernity, the expansion of fashion and consumer culture, and the generation of a powerful memory culture. By immersing themselves into the fashion and music of the 1960s, hunting for old clothes and modeling themselves on past styles as closely as possible, "the sixties" are here not distant history but come to enter their own memory, even though they were not even born in the time they now recall with their bodies.

Despite the fashionability of vintage and retro styles in varied youth cultures, the everyday practices and experiences that are part of their use and performance through the material and visual culture of fashion have so far been only little explored. This may be in part due to the conception and expectation of both fashion and youth culture as sites of innovation and eternal renewal. Through its apparent ephemerality and its continuous production or intriguing narration of the "new," fashion is understood to immerse us in the now by generating distance to the past and a desire to forget: "Every new Fashion is a refusal to inherit, a subversion against the oppression of the preceding Fashion," noted Roland Barthes (1990: 273). In this sense fashion has been conceived as a promise of future and modernity, liberating from the past as a cultural burden. This idea of working against the past, the "refusal to inherit," can be extended to the understanding of youth, or youth culture, as motor and metaphor for modernity. From its conception in the late nineteenth century and even more so with the expansion of consumer culture from the mid-twentieth century onwards, "youth" has been conceptualized as an innovative force (see Savage 2007), feeding into the development of fashion styles, brands and markets. From this perspective, the ongoing aesthetic immersion into the past among younger people may read as a sign of cultural regress or as indicating a lack of, or even inability for, cultural inventiveness. Such a tendency is evident in the discourse that has evolved since the 1970s and 1980s around the meaning, or rather the lack of meaning, associated with "retro" in the context of media and consumer culture, seen as a random, "cannibalistic" or ironic ransacking of history. This perspective has been formulated most forcefully by Fredric Jameson, who argued that "the producers of culture have nowhere to turn but to the past: the imitation of dead styles, speech through all the masks and voices stored up in the imaginary museum of a now global culture" (see Jameson 1984: 65; see also Baudrillard 1993). This postmodern reading of retro as an all-encompassing phenomenon continues to inform contemporary views of the engagement with the past among youth. Music writer Simon Reynolds reflects in his book *Retromania* (2011a) on a wide range of examples of "pop culture's addiction to its own past" and expresses concern about the impact that the expansion of media and its apparently endless storage capacities have on youth:

What seems to have happened is that the place that The Future once occupied in the imagination of young music-makers has been displaced by The Past:

that's where the romance now lies, with the idea of things that have been lost. The accent, today, is not on discovery but on recovery. (Reynolds 2011b)

Reynolds sees a "compulsion to relive and reconsume pop history" as evidence of an "unhealthy fixation on the bygone" (Reynolds 2011b). His worry is that the omnipresence of the past in images, videos and websites suffocates the present, and results only in a "total recall" and exact replication of the past; a process that suppresses in his view any innovativeness, originality or "imaginary reworkings" of the past (Reynolds 2011b). Inherent in these readings is to a certain extent the continuation of a narrative of modernity that idealizes ideas of "newness" and "progress;" promoting a perspective on time or temporality that tends to undermine the dynamic role of the past—for example in the form of cultural memory or remembering—as constitutive to the present, and an integral part in the experience of time or temporality, and identity or subjectivity.

Many scholars have critiqued the postmodern discourse on retro (see Wilson 1990; McRobbie 1994; Evans 2000; Baker 2013), for its generalizing and also essentializing tendencies that overshadow the varied ways in which forms of the past are used in diverse contexts, and with quite different meanings or effects. With a perspective on fashion, Elizabeth Wilson already questioned in 1990 if retro is in fact "exclusively *de nos jours*" (Wilson 1990: 224), giving examples for a range of preceding style-revivals in the history of fashion (see also Burman-Baines 1981). For Wilson the generalizations inherent in the postmodern discussion of retro across all forms of visual and material culture have more to do with the "creation of a cultural myth about 'our times'" (1990: 231)—they remain anchored in the "*project* of defining a *Zeitgeist*" (1990: 232), "which flattens out the contradictory, refractory nature of contemporary existence and seeks to create a stereotype of the present in the present" (1990: 231).

It is likely due to the stereotyping tendencies and overuse of the term retro as an all-encompassing label to define a particular late-twentieth-century disposition, a "retro-mood" (Horx 1995), that the term vintage started to see more frequent use in the early twenty-first century. According to the statistics of a search in *The Vogue Archive* on Proquest, which is based on the American edition, the magazine's use of the term "vintage" almost tripled in the first decade of the twenty-first century, compared to the preceding 1990s (rising from 571 to 1,448 mentions). The term vintage is itself a kind of throwback to the time when the wearing of old, second-hand clothes emerged as an alternative to new fashion in the 1960s, and thus works as a kind of distinction from the word retro, or rather from what the term retro has been associated with, such as cultural regress, lack of innovativeness, pastiche, irony, or an "unsentimental nostalgia for the past" (Guffey 2006: 17; for a discussion see Baker 2013). Yet, as with any label, vintage as well is a term that has attracted negative critique, especially for its "branding" of old clothes, and for inflating their price. However, in what way vintage constructs a certain value around old clothes, and around the idea of age in fashion, is open for further exploration and will be part of the discussion in this book. While I have used the term retro in my previous work, and retro and vintage interchangeably (Jenss 2005a), I am using vintage (and vintage style) in this book because it is the term that has come to name a specific form of using old clothes for their age or anachronism that has emerged as a practice among youth at least since the 1960s (McRobbie 1994). As I will further discuss in this book, it is a term, or concept, that describes a specific value related to or constructed around the age of clothes, including an idea of rarity associated with them. Overall it seems to be a word that has its origin in material culture (as an old word for "antique"), rather than in visual culture (like the word retro, emerging in the context of film).

Newer academic research, and in particular work engaging with the actual forms and practices in which objects of the past are used, has moved beyond the postmodern retro discourse, opening up more nuanced perspectives on how objects, images and styles of the past are used in a variety of practices and contexts ranging from film (Sprengler 2009), fashion (Evans 2000, 2003; Gregson, Brooks and Crewe 2001; DeLong, Heinemann and Reiley 2005; Clark 2008; Aronowsky Cronberg 2009; Granata 2010), to interior design (Baker 2013). Especially the research of scholars working on second-hand markets, both in historic and contemporary contexts, has been invaluable to illuminate the circulation of objects and their investment with new meanings and values in the context of a highly diversified market, that caters to a wide range of consumers (see Hansen 2000; Gregson and Crewe 2003; Palmer and Clark 2005; Hawley 2006; Norris 2012; Lemire 2012; Botticello 2012). Contributing to this body of research are also ethnography and interview based studies that explore the consumption of vintage clothing in the early twenty-first century (DeLong, Heinemann and Reiley 2005; Reiley and DeLong 2011; Cassidy and Bennett 2012). These studies offer insightful explorations contextualizing vintage with wider developments in the fashion market, most notably with a move towards more sustainable practices and ecological awareness among consumers. Building on this work, and to establish a context to understand the use of old clothes with a perspective on youth culture— as well as the values produced around "old" or discarded clothes—it is useful to consider here further how vintage clothes and practices are bound up with the dynamics of fashion and style, consumer culture and the fashioning of memory.

Fashion and/as memory

It is only through our ability to remember that we experience "being" or "becoming" in time, experiences through which we develop a sense of self in time and place and in relation to others (see Olick, Vinitzky-Seroussi and Levi 2011: 37). Or in other words, the activating, sharing and shaping of memories together with others is crucial to the formation of identities, the generation of social relationships and our experience of time and change. Memory, engaging with the past in the present, informs our understanding of who we are; it can provide us with feelings of belonging. Although remembering, as Edward Casey notes, is continually going on with "every fiber of our bodies, every cell of our brains," and even "inanimate objects bear the marks of their past histories upon them" (Casey 2000: xix), remembering is at the same time an exception (Assmann 2011: 334). Because the act of remembering is always ongoing, in constant flux, and the capacity of memory is limited, we tend to forget more than we remember—or as Alaida Assmann notes, there is a "perpetual interaction between remembering and forgetting … forgetting is part of social normality" (2011: 334). Due to its temporariness and its dynamic situatedness in time, remembering is then an inevitably selective process, focusing on what is relevant in a current moment (see Assmann 2011, 2013). Its temporariness and selectiveness mean also that memory produces the past as we engage with it in the now: "There is no past, no present and no future as such; the relation between the past, the present and the future is always made from some point of view and must be *expressed* or *enacted* for the past, the present or the future to emerge" (Kontopodis 2009: 6).

This understanding of the past builds on Walter Benjamin's thesis on the concept of history as "the subject of a structure whose site is not homogenous, empty time," but one filled by now-time (*Jetztzeit*) (Benjamin 1968: 263), highlighting history not as something that is given or fixed (see also Lehmann 1999). Where both terms, history and memory, can be understood to describe processes that are ongoing, continually under construction, methodologically the term memory has come to draw attention to the personal, subjective dimension of the engagement with, or making of, the past (Macdonald 2013: 234). Where history in the sense of the development or narration of events implies a certain chronology, and tends to be oriented towards an establishment of "facts," even if history is also something that is rewritten (see Lehmann 1999: 298), memory as an ongoing process and practice is not sequentially organized. Memory does not fix events to specific moments of time, but it recalls or engages with time more in a form of snapshots, fragments, and flashes (Kuhn 2000: 190). In this sense, as Annette Kuhn puts it, we can understand memory to be primarily "the language of images" (Kuhn 2000: 188). Kuhn notes in her thesis on the workings of memory, and memory texts such as autobiographies, that there is "a sense of synchrony, as if remembered events are somehow pulled out of a linear time-frame, or refuse to be anchored in real historical time" (Kuhn 2000: 190).

In its nonlinearity, partiality and revisionary capacity the workings of memory, or remembering, not only share similarity with the visual and material culture of clothing and fashion, but clothing and fashion can be understood as constitutive components of personal and cultural memory, or remembering. The costume book of Matthäus Schwarz (1496–1564), in which the Renaissance man documented his personal clothing history in 137 portraits from age 19 (and retrospectively from his birth) until close to his death, is a manifest of the importance of clothing in biography, not only as a mnemonic device but also as a tool for exploring or making sense of time (see the discussion in Mentges 2002; also Rublack 2010). Emma Tarlo has used the term "sartorial biography," which highlights the prominent role of dress in personal memory, which Tarlo draws on as a methodology to explore in her study of three Muslim women living in London, "the complexity and transformative potential of personal experience in the creative and symbiotic relationship between people and their clothes" (Tarlo 2007: 145). In her ethnographic study on women's relationships to clothing, Sophie Woodward has also closely investigated the role of clothing as a bearer of memory. She describes how in its "physical sensuality and tactility ... clothing is able to hold former aspects of the self" and conceives for example of the wardrobe sort-out as a form of editing memory, through the disposal of former sartorial selves (Woodward 2007: 57). The wearing of a retro-look or vintage style is a further example of the relation between fashion and memory: they are fashioned by recalling, or remembering, fashion styles from the past, such as the sixties. The remembering through wearing or seeing vintage styles may here not necessarily be connected to one's own experienced past, or "lived" memory of wearing these clothes, but they are usually more widely connected to fashion as a form or part of cultural memory. When worn and enacted in one's appearance, vintage clothes or styles come to embody and perform memory, and can also stimulate memories of others. Yet they recall a past not "exactly," like memory they are situated in time: the contemporary context and (wearer) shapes or revises the past style in the sartorial recollection.

Ulrich Lehmann, in his analysis of Walter Benjamin's engagement with fashion, discussed the capacity of fashion to reference and quote as a form of "sartorial remembrance—an ability to create an intricate temporal relation as well as chart a metaphysical experience" (Lehmann 1999: 308). Further utilizing the perspectives of Benjamin in the exploration of 1990s experimental fashion design Caroline Evans (2000, 2003) has shown that, while the history of fashion has a vast repertoire of forms and styles, the recall in fashion revivals is not random but something of the past must resonate with the present—it must be recognized. She argues that "contemporary fashion has an unerring eye for the topical in its choice of historical imagery" (Evans 2000: 99). Or in the words of Benjamin: "every image of the past that is not recognized by the present as one of its own concerns threatens to disappear irretrievably" (Benjamin 1968: 257). This emphasis on the timeliness of memory also informs the way Alaida Assmann refers to memory as exception, as an effort, necessitated by its limited capacity: not everything has a place in memory, only what is meaningful, that is what resonates with recalling subjects in the now (Assmann 2011).

Building on Maurice Halbwachs' (1992) research on "collective memory" in the 1920s, in which he highlights that memory—even if it feels deeply personal and intimate—is never solely individual but always shaped in and through social relationships with others, the term "cultural memory" has come to refer more broadly to the "interplay of present and past in socio-cultural contexts" (Erll 2010: 2). Scholars in the field of memory studies use it as an "operative metaphor," where "the concept of 'remembering' (as a cognitive process which takes place in individual brains) is metaphorically transferred to the level of culture" (Erll 2010: 2). As such the term "cultural memory" is used to highlight that "much of what is done to reconstruct a shared past bears some resemblance to the processes of individual memory, such as the selectivity and perspectivity inherent in the creation of versions of the past according to present knowledge and needs" (Erll 2010: 5).

In a broader sense the engagement with the past, or cultural memory, must not be focused on the past, or make sense *of* the past, but cultural memory opens up an avenue to explore how the past forms a part of meaning-making in and of the present. Astrid Erll and Ann Rigney describe this with an emphasis on the dynamics of memory as "remembering," conceived as an "active engagement with the past, as performative rather than reproductive. It is as much a matter of acting out a relationship to the past from a particular point in the present as it is a matter of preserving and retrieving earlier stories" (Erll and Rigney 2009: 2). The emphasis here is not only on what is remembered, but also on the how, opening up perspectives on the varied modes of remembering in culture, including more implicit, non-narrative ways that include visual, material and bodily practices (see Erll 2010: 2). The term cultural memory includes the material dimension of memory in objects, or things, in images and practices. This is based on an understanding that images and objects take on a constitutive role in the formation of or engagement with memory. As pointedly noted by Marius Kwint, in the introduction to the edited volume *Material Memories*, "human memory has undergone a mutual evolution with the objects that inform it; … in other words, the relationship between them is dialectical" (Kwint 1999: 4). He highlights the interrelations of material objects and memory by referring to Susan Stewart's emphasis on the sensation of touch that bridges the threshold between self and other or subject and object, since the "act of touching, she observes, exerts pressure on both toucher and touched" (Kwint 1999: 5–6). Or as Sherry Turkle puts it: "Objects help us make our minds, reaching out to us to form active partnerships" (Turkle 2007: 308). This is perhaps nowhere more evident than in the material culture of clothing, which imprints itself in all its materiality on the human body, molding its physical shape, affecting corporeality or subjectivity, and the embodiment of dress and style through the wearer.

The English word fashion is derived from the Latin verb *facere*, meaning to do, to make, to give shape, as in fashioning an appearance, fashioning a style, or self-fashioning. In this active understanding, fashion can be conceived of as a complex cultural practice, presupposing agency. This active understanding of fashion as making and shaping can also be related to memory or remembrance, conceived of as an "act" (see Bal, Crewe and Spitzer 1999). Liedeke Plate and Anneke Smelik highlight this as "doing memory," memory as something we perform or enact: "if memory is social and cultural, it is also performative, making the past present in ways that can be experienced" (Plate and Smelik 2013: 3). Building on Judith Butler's concept of gender and identity as performative acts (Butler 2007), this conception of memory as performative foregrounds the embodied dimension of memory, and its temporality (see Plate and Smelik 2013). This understanding of memory is alluded to in this book's title, "fashioning memory," referring to both fashion and memory as practices that are material, embodied, enacted. The use of "fashioning memory" highlights the role of fashion—and linked to that, body and dress—in the experience and performance of memory. Fashion can be understood as a complex cultural practice and form of visual and material culture, which involves shopping in stores, getting dressed, putting together an outfit, as well as acquiring fashion information, for example, by browsing through online images. For Sophie Woodward, fashion as an everyday practice is a practice of assemblage, including "knowledges over what is in fashion as well as cultural competences about 'how' to wear clothes" (Woodward forthcoming). The wide reaching dimension of fashion—stretching from the garment to the body, from production to consumption, and across space and time, is mapped out in Christopher Breward's comprehensive definition of fashion as:

> a bounded thing, fixed and experienced in space—an amalgamation of seams and textiles, an interface between the body and its environment. It is a practice, a fulcrum for the display of taste and status, a site for the production and consumption of objects and beliefs; and it is an event, both spectacular and routine, cyclical in its adherence to the natural and commercial season, innovatory in its bursts of avant-gardism, and sequential in its guise as a palimpsest of memory and tradition. (Breward 2004: 11)

Fashion is also conceived of as "a flux in time" (Riello and McNeill 2010: 1). This emphasizes, as does Breward's definition, how fashion is bound up with time and change, which is usually understood to be felt by recognizing and differentiating the new from the old: experiences that are only possible through memory, as the faculty through which we experience time. Here "fashioning memory" refers then also to the fashionability of the past and memory, including the popularity and commodification of old clothes as "vintage," and also of experiences of memory (and sometimes nostalgia) through the use of old clothes or through new clothes that look old, and through putting together and embodying a "vintage style" based on objects and images of the past. In their close proximity to the body clothes are in a prominent position to "fashion memory," on a very personal level, where clothing becomes part of a person's material or sartorial biography and remembering, as well as in a broader social and cultural sense in the way that former fashions and discarded clothes form the visual and material memories of past seasons, years, decades or generations. It is the latter on which this book will specifically concentrate, through an in-depth investigation of the dress, style and consumption practices of young sixties enthusiasts in Germany.

Methodology—Exploring dress practices in the sixties scene in Germany

Clothes, due to their distinct material qualities and immediacy to the human body—molding its shape and movement, appealing to the senses—can enable a particularly intimate engagement with the past. Yet, like the "work of memory" (Kuhn 2000), sartorial remembering is fragmentary, revising and personalizing the past in the present. In using "fashioning memory" here as a methodological angle, informed by the conception of cultural memory as "operative metaphor" (Erll 2010: 2), this book explores how a group of youth and young adults—who immerse and fashion themselves with minute attention to detail in the style of the sixties—come to use, select, purchase, wear and enact this fashion style and invest it with meaning in a new context. What kind of relationships to the past, and what kind of experiences of time and memory, do fashion and clothes open up to their wearers? What is the appeal of the past fashion style to the new wearer? What kind of practices are developed in order to sartorially "remember" the sixties in the now? Which material and visual resources from the past are incorporated in the style? How does the sixties styler's use of old clothes and a former fashion style as vintage relate to the temporality and ephemerality associated with current fashion? These are some of the guiding questions throughout this book, which focuses on context-specific ways and modes of using old (and new) clothes as vintage. In other words, vintage or vintage style is here not understood as an overarching or coherent phenomenon (for example in the way "retro" has sometimes been conceived). Instead the underlying assumption of this book is that fashion and dress—including the use of old clothes or vintage styles—are as part of everyday practices and material in the performance of bodies and identities, always embedded or situated in specific spatio-temporal or cultural contexts (see Mentges 2004, 2005b; also Entwistle 2000; Craik 1994; Kaiser 2012). As Gabriele Mentges puts it, cultural meanings of clothes are not simply inherent in them, but they become produced or emerge through uses and complex networks of relationships between material things, here clothes, and their wearers (Mentges 2004: 73–4). Both—clothes and the wearer—can then be understood as agents (see Miller 2009a; see also Miller 2005), which in the material context of wearing and embodiment come together with their own histories, and own capacities of "doing" or enacting memory (see Turkle 2007; Kwint 1999; Korff 1991).

In order to focus in on the way clothes are used and become meaningful for their wearers, this book takes a material culture based approach informed by cultural anthropology, with a particular concentration on fashion, dress, style and performance practices (see Mentges 2004; Jenss 2005b and 2007; Woodward 2007). This includes a focus on the buying or making of clothes, their wearing with the body, as well as the interest in and development of "the sixties" as vintage style. The focus also centers on the interplay of clothing and style practices between past and present, and in current social and material interaction; that is the dynamics of clothing and vintage in the context of a youth cultural scene as well as more widely in the context of fashion and consumer culture. The approach draws on the methods of interpretive ethnography (Denzin 1997; Amit 2000; Stellrecht 1993), involving direct participation and observation in the field of the social actors, here with participants in the sixties scene, including their scene-specific events.

The use of the term "scene" is based on the common use of the term as a reference to the "sixties scene" by those participating in it, as well as oriented on German academic research on youth cultures, where the term "scene" tends to be more commonly used than the Anglo-American concept of subculture. The term "scene" has been defined by sociologist Ronald Hitzler as a theme centered, cultural network of persons, who share specific material and/or mental forms of style practices and who collectively and interactively form and maintain social relations and commonalities in the context of specific times and places (Hitzler 2001: 20). My research involved participation in the activities of the sixties scene, which is also a music-centered scene, thus meaning to go to concerts and clubs. In Germany the sixties scene began to evolve with the revival of the British mod style of the 1960s in the context of late 1970s and 1980s pop and youth culture. Since that time the style has been taken up by following generations of youth or young adults, with some maintaining their interest in the style over many years and even decades, for example from the 1990s until today, when some are reaching their forties. Etymologically the term scene, derived from the Latin word *scena* for stage, carries a connotation of temporality. For example in a theatrical sense the term scene describes an act of performance: a time-based, embodied act. This gives an indication of the role of embodiment and people acting (together) making scenes, including youth cultural scenes, formed by social relationships that can stretch across time and place, as long as people maintain or share an interest in them (and enact them through diverse practices).

I started my initial research on the sixties scene in the beginning of the 2000s in the Ruhr area in the northwest of Germany, where I lived and worked, and where I had the opportunity of meeting sixties stylers at music clubs and concerts, and from where I expanded my research. The Ruhr area is historically the "industrial heart" of Germany consisting of several larger cities in close proximity to each other, with a total population of 5 million. Efficient public transport makes these cities, including Bochum, Dortmund and Essen, well connected to each other and to cities nearby, such as Düsseldorf and Cologne, which together have a vibrant concentration of clubs, concerts and diverse music and youth scenes.

In order to understand the dress practices of people in the sixties scene—and the practice of doing a "vintage style" recalling a fashion from the past and specifically the sixties—my research included ethnographic fieldwork as well as a historical study of the scene. Further, to gain an in-depth understanding of the actual practices of dress and the performance of vintage style, I conducted qualitative interviews with sixties stylers at their homes, whom I selected based on their notable performance of and immersion into sixties style in their everyday dress practices. The interviews focused on the use of clothing, the particular interests in wearing second-hand dress and the self-fashioning in the style of the 1960s. The interviews also in many cases included a show and tell about clothing in their wardrobes, during which sixties stylers talked about where they purchased clothes, or how they incorporated newly produced clothing into their vintage style. The interviewees, ten men and ten women, were between 15 and 35 years old. The majority of the interviewees were students or early in their careers (including a notable number of them in creative professions such as design), living in the Ruhr area, Cologne and Berlin. In addition to the longer interviews, I also had many informal conversations with sixties stylers as part of my field research at events in Germany, as well as in the context of international events in Rimini in Italy and in Gijon in Spain reflecting the transnationality of this scene. I will situate the sixties scene in Germany further when I begin the discussion based on my interview material in Chapter 4—after establishing a broader context in Chapters 2 and 3: first on the meaning of vintage in fashion, and second on the history and memory of the sartorial point of reference, that is fashion and youth in the sixties.

Outline of the book

Vintage is an old-fashioned term for "year," "aged" or "old." Etymologically it is an Anglicized French word that has roots in wine culture, and is from there transferred to other commodities. In the context of fashion it has been used as a word to describe old clothes, and more recently the old clothes that become again fashionable. In this sense vintage describes a form of "fashioning time," turning time or age into a value and a commodity. This fashioning of "age" is related to the broader relationship between fashion and time, and in particular to the concepts of modernity and newness, on which fashion thrives. The first chapter draws on writing in the fields of fashion and cultural studies, as well as on encyclopedia entries and an excursion into wine culture, to discuss the meaning and value of vintage in fashion, which will form a context for the discussion in the following chapters.

Memories are shaped by their cultural, national and generational contexts, as well as by global media and consumer culture. Chapter 3 looks to "the sixties" and the youth culture of British mods, which forms a sartorial reference point for the current sixties scene in Germany. Highlighting the intersection of fashion, time and place, the chapter locates the emergence of mods in late 1950s and 1960s "Swinging London" as a new, consumption centered youth culture that evolved in synthesis with new consumer or market structures. In their style practices the mods embraced modernity and change, yet the chapter maps out how it is also in the context of the 1960s youth market that the use of old clothes and fashion styles begins to emerge more widely as a "vintage" fashion practice.

Following a first wider revival in the context of 1970s punk culture the mod style, charged with a certain image or imaginary of Britishness, has become an important reference point for youth internationally. Chapter 4 describes how the style of the British 1960s mods was adopted and adapted by German youth, starting out with a discussion of the experience of cultural memory through the intersection of music and style. Drawing on my fieldwork and interviews with sixties stylers, this chapter then focuses on the "beginnings" of getting into the aesthetics of the sixties, a process involving the seeing, learning, embodying and internalizing of sixties fashion as vintage style—as well as on the scene-specific dynamics of style.

Original clothes surviving from the 1960s are the most valued ones among the sixties stylers I interviewed. As aged objects, materializing time, they are appreciated as witnesses of the 1960s with material qualities that enable a sensual, imaginary and bodily exchange with the past. Their temporality makes these clothes scarce, imbuing them with symbolic value. Chapter 5 shows that as much as the aesthetic qualities of 1960s clothes are important to sixties enthusiasts, so are the actual practices of purchasing and collecting them. Hunting for the past on flea markets and in vintage stores, on websites like eBay, or seeking out hidden sources of rare old stock, involve the investment of conscious effort and time, that open up experiences of material intimacy, difference and uniqueness associated with old or original sixties clothing.

Chapter 6 explores how the temporalities of objects intersect with the temporalities of images, and the bodily performance of the sixties as vintage style. While the sixties stylers I interviewed prefer original clothes from the 1960s, their clothing repertoire is made up of a hybrid temporal mix of clothes due to the scarcity and rising prices of original old clothes. Dealing with the "now-time" of contemporary fashion includes blending new with old, historicizing or changing clothing details. Old movies and TV series, or images on record covers, and their re-mediation online, blended with layers of retrospective images and sixties revivals, constitute some of the mediated memories impacting the performance of the sixties as vintage style. The chapter asks how "the sixties" are remembered and remade through fashion and clothing, what gets focused and what gets blurred in the sartorial remembrance of the past.

Through sartorial remembrance, the past becomes integrated with experiences and subjectivities of present wearers as they invest the past style with new meanings. The past is not cut off from the present; instead, making sense of temporality and memory is a constitutive part of the experience of modernity. Fashion as material/visual/embodied memory provides an intimate material for this, especially since sartorial memories survive in greater scale through the mass-production of fashion and the image producing industries, stimulating engagements with mediated pasts. The final chapter provides concluding thoughts on the cross-temporal dimensions of the use of sartorial memories and on the ambiguities of the commodification of memory and time.

2 VINTAGE: FASHIONING TIME

(Disguising) time in fashion

An early usage of the word vintage in the context of clothing can be found in American *Vogue*. In the rubric "Smart Fashions for Limited Incomes" in the September 1913 issue, the writer offers "Several Ruses for Disguising the Vintage of Last Year's Wardrobe," to make an up-to-date appearance with clothes that survive from past seasons. This includes hands-on advice on updating the "tailor suit of last year's vintage" with a "new, upsloping belt" so the suit may make its "second début" ("Smart Fashions for Limited Incomes" 1913). In this early context the word vintage is used in the sense of "year," or more precisely, it refers to the year something was made—as in the German translation of the English term vintage as *Jahrgang*. Distinct from the word *Jahr* (year) *Jahrgang* refers not only to the year someone is born, to an age-group or cohort, or in the context of commodities to the year of manufacturing, but *Jahrgang* carries also a connotation of movement and development over time, as the noun *Gang* means "walk," "gait" or "course of action." According to the entry on vintage in the *Oxford English Dictionary* (2014) the English language adapted vintage from the French *vendange* to refer to the "date or period when a person was born or flourished," which eventually came to be replaced simply by "year." The word vintage, when it was transferred to objects in the first part of the twentieth century, took on a connotation of dated or datedness: "Denoting an old style or model of something, esp. a vehicle." The *Oxford English Dictionary* (2014) provides a reference from 1939: "... a rattling car of ancient vintage." It also gives an example of the use of vintage in the context of clothing from 1946: "His pointed tan buttoned shoes, faded pink shirt and bright tie belong to the same vintage."

While vintage in the context of cars takes on a meaning of "collectable" (as in a 1928 reference "[y]ou should see mine in London—a vintage Buick"), the dictionary definition does not provide evidence for such a meaning in relation to garments. This indicates how age or datedness in the context of clothing—tied to fashion and embodiment—might not have been seen as a highly valued quality in comparison to other material goods that are expected to be longer lasting investments over time, such as cars or furniture.

Clothes, as the 1913 *Vogue* advice on disguising the vintage of the items in one's wardrobe indicates, should be "up to date." The past, or rather anything triggering a memory of past seasons, should be absent as it disrupts the articulation of—and one's belonging to—the present moment, the now. That this advice in the *Vogue* rubric is targeted at women who are on a low budget, and thus restricted in their ability to buy the latest styles, can be contextualized with the importance placed on new clothes: not only for signifying that one is up to date with the time, but combined with that, also with the importance of the possession of new clothes in signifying one's social standing; the belonging to (at least in appearance) or ability to keep up with the leading social circles. Looking up to date, by wearing new clothes or by concealing the continued use of previous fashion purchases, can prevent the pitfall of being socially stigmatized in a context where dress and keeping up with the changing styles of fashion through continuous consumption of new clothes is seen to function "as an evidence of [the] ability to pay" (Veblen 2004: 340). In his *Theory of the Leisure Class*, Thorstein Veblen describes the "principle of novelty" as a consequence of the "law of conspicuous waste" that he sees at the heart of pecuniary culture in the late nineteenth century (Veblen 2004: 342).

The importance of social class in relation to the temporality of fashion and the social value of newness are also discussed by sociologist Georg Simmel in his early-twentieth-century writing on fashion. Simmel mapped out a sophisticated model that implicitly naturalizes fashion's privileging of the present and the need to distance itself from its past. He conceptualizes fashion as a field in which the social dynamics between "adaptation to society and individual departure from its demands," which drive for him the "whole history of society," manifest themselves most evidently (Simmel 2004: 290). He writes, "whether they be grounded in practical conflict representing socialism on the one hand or individualism on the other, we have always to deal with the same fundamental form of duality which is manifested biologically in the contrast between heredity and variation" (Simmel 2004: 290). Drawing an analogy with biology or evolution theory, the driving force of fashion is for Simmel a natural, yet class bound struggle between differentiation and imitation; leading in the circuit are the members of the upper social ranks who are the first to initiate or embark on the latest fashion to mark an advanced and distinguished position at the top of society. Yet, "as soon as the lower classes begin to copy their style, thereby crossing the line of demarcation the upper classes have drawn and destroying the uniformity of their coherence, the upper classes turn away; and thus the game goes merrily on" (Simmel 2004: 293). Entangled with or driven by this social dynamic, Simmel describes fashion as a naturally transitory phenomenon. A new fashion loses its value to secure its wearer a position of distinction as soon as it spreads, tying social dynamics together with the nature of time or temporality; as fashion aids in establishing a sartorial boundary between social classes, it also does so by drawing a line between present and past. Or, as Simmel puts it, fashion "always occupies the dividing-line between the past and the future, and consequently conveys a stronger feeling of the present, at least while it is at its height, than most other phenomena" (Simmel 2004: 295).

In heightening attention to the now and privileging the present, the dynamic of fashion appears as an inevitable struggle with or against time. The up-to-date appearance in new clothes can elevate the wearer through what Simmel describes as a "peculiar attraction of limitation, the attraction of a simultaneous beginning and end, the charm of novelty coupled to that of transitoriness" (Simmel 2004: 295). At the same time the struggle with fashion time can be cause for anxiety and shame, where datedness in clothing and appearance is felt or used as a measure of exclusion. Using tricks then to give old clothes a new look, so as not to stand out of fashion time but blend in with the moment, as one could read into the *Vogue* advice, turns fashionable clothes into a security blanket, protecting "against those painful reflections which the individual otherwise experiences when he becomes the object of attention" (Simmel 2004: 302): for example, if the un-timeliness of one's clothes is recognized as dated or "so last season" (see van de Peer 2014). According to this narrative of fashion as newness, the "vintage" of one's clothes, their evident date-ability or coming of age in the context of the production and promotion of the new, is then nothing that should be foregrounded, or that is valued. This is not to say last seasons' clothes are out of use; the fact that *Vogue* includes this advice section in its pages indicates that they certainly are not. But in order for them to qualify socially for a "second début," they have to be disassociated from the past seasons and updated in details or in new arrangements, to be made new and to come to feel modern.

Narratives of fashion and modernity

Writing in the early twentieth century Georg Simmel sees fashion in its privileging attention to the present symptomatic of the emergence of a new temporality that has been produced by the "break with the past, which, for more than a century, civilized mankind has been laboring unceasingly to bring about" (Simmel 2004: 296). Fashion or more precisely an accelerated tempo of fashion changes is here inherently tied to modernity, a process or concept deeply interwoven with the industrialization and economization of time (see Urry 2000), changing patterns of production and consumption, and the value dynamics of newness and obsolescence on which modernity comes to thrive.

Numerous writers have commented on fashion in relation to the experience or concept of modernity, which is terminologically anchored in many European languages' words for fashion (see Wilson 2005a and 2005b; Lehmann 1999 and 2000; Breward and Evans 2005; Steele 2005). The French term *la mode* refers to a "prevailing fashion, custom, practice, or style, esp. one characteristic of a particular place or period" (*Oxford English Dictionary* 2014). Other than the word fashion (derived from Latin *facere*, to make), the word *mode* derived from *modus* has already etymologically a temporal connotation. As in music the classical Latin word *modus* is used for rhythm and melody or in its ancient Greek sense for music style. In this context *mode* refers to the "ratio of the duration of a long or a large to that of the next longest note, which determines rhythm" (*Oxford English Dictionary* 2014). This musical and temporal meaning dimension also connects the word *mode* to *mood*. Connotations of *mood* include "disposition," "feeling," "mind," "thought," "will," and also another reference to time: "prevailing but temporary state of mind or feeling; a person's humour, temper, or disposition at a particular time (later also applied to a crowd of people or other collective body)" (*Oxford English Dictionary* 2014). These references to time, temper, manner and state of mind inform the way fashion, or rather *la mode*, has been conceived as a "vibrant metaphor for modernity itself" (Breward and Evans 2005: 3).

Characterizing modernity as an experience of ephemerality and fleetingness, Charles Baudelaire has perhaps most famously commented on the alliance between fashion and modernity in his 1863 essay "The Painter of Modern Life" (2004). Fashion is an articulation of the now, it gives each time its distinct appearance, with every age having "its own gait, glance and gesture" (Baudelaire 2004: 217). Fashion is absolute nowness, yet its former appearances can have staying power, as their survival as objects or images will transmit something about their time to future generations. For Baudelaire, the task of the painter of modern life is therefore to pay attention to the "special nature of the present," which he sees materializing in the manufacture of new fabrics or in a new arrangement of pleats: "for any 'modernity' to be worthy of one day taking its place as 'antiquity,' it is necessary for the mysterious beauty which human life accidentally puts into it to be distilled from it" (Baudelaire 2004: 217). Baudelaire describes the experience of time—or more precisely the experience of transience—as the main characteristic of modernity. This experience of temporality is for him markedly felt through a fleetingness of fashion: through the experience of an apparent distinctiveness between fashion in the now and in the past. Living in mid-nineteenth-century Paris, Baudelaire perceives the temporal dynamics of history and modernity intimately in the urban fabric, when the city was in its early transformation stages into the "modern city," developed between 1853 and 1870 by George-Eugene Haussmann and commissioned by Napoleon III. As Richard Terdimen notes, in "such moments memory of the 'time before' is still active; the ideological density of developing reality has not yet obscured the contingency of this new reality and rendered its structures opaque" (Terdimen 1993: 119). Or in other words, change itself "still seemed like change, it had not yet become routinized ... the remaking of the city had not yet demolished the memory of the city remade" (Terdimen 1993: 119). Baudelaire notes this in his earlier 1859 poem "The Swan" (Le Cygne): "Old Paris is no more (the form of a city Changes more quickly, alas! than the human heart)" (see Terdimen 1993: 119). Writing on the painter of modern life, Baudelaire then warns:

> Woe to him who studies the antique for anything else but pure art, logic and general method! By steeping himself too thoroughly in it, he will lose all memory of the present; he will renounce the rights and privileges offered by circumstance—for almost all our originality comes from the seal which Time imprints on our sensations. (Baudelaire 2004: 218)

While the past can be studied for the development of technique for example, a too thorough engagement with it gets in the way of experiencing the distinctiveness of one's own time. Baudelaire points here to the dichotomy between past and present in relation to notions of originality and innovativeness that are also anchored in the modern conception of fashion, as well as in the conceptualization of history (see Koselleck 2004; Lowenthal 1985).

If originality is rooted in the "modern sensibility," then it must be seen as the consequence of an attentiveness to being in the now; of an embrace of change and temporal orientation towards the future. Underlying this conception of modernity is an understanding of time, in which the present is constantly evolving forward in a linear mode, transforming the forthcoming into the past (Grossberg 2010: 269; Assmann 2013). In her writing on the production of the fashion present, Aurelie van de Peer makes use of Johannes Fabian's (2002) concept of the politics of time to elaborate on this idea. She describes how the present as it is experienced or narrated through fashion:

> requires a relational self-fashioning in which fashion seeks to pin down its present momentum by allocating the passé outside the boundaries of the present; hence into fashion history ... The past and present of fashion, its history and modernity, are thus mutually excluding and mutually dependent notions. (van de Peer 2014: 323)

This co-dependency is implied in Lawrence Grossberg's elaboration on euro-modernity's institutionalization of change requiring at the same time an institutionalization of "tradition;" an "other" against which modernity can come to be defined: "Most frequently, the chronotope of modernity is assumed to be History: modernity is the invention of History, and the acceptance, even the celebration and institutionalization of change, it stands against stasis (as tradition)" (Grossberg 2010: 269). The distancing of new from old, of present from past, and along with this the opposing of the temporalities of change versus continuity, or alternatively the "fashion-able" versus the "fixed-in-time," are intimately entwined with the conception of euro-modernity and its narrative of *la mode* or fashion. This is exemplified in Simmel's writing, when he describes changes in fashion as an indicator for the advancement of European civilization thereby utilizing the notion of time to fashion one of modernity's others. Where "primitive conditions of life favor … infrequent change of fashions" (Simmel 2004: 294), civilization has an affection for novelty: "The removal of the feeling of insecurity with reference to all things new was accomplished by the progress of civilization" (Simmel 2004: 294). Changing fashions are for Simmel a natural symptom of modern (seen as urban and Western) "nervous impulses: the more nervous the age, the more rapidly its fashions change" (Simmel 2004: 295).

According to this narrative, embarking on change by indulging in newness—which can be most evidently shown by fashioning one's body in new clothes—articulates then one's adaptability to the tempo or sensibility of modernity. In his book *Futures Past*, Reinhart Koselleck (2004) provides a detailed study of the semantics of historical time and the mutation of historical experience that emerges in the context of the late eighteenth century. Along with social and political changes, in particular brought by the French Revolution, the impact of science, technology and philosophical thinking opened up time as an infinite space of possibilities and modern expectations, in which the past appears increasingly disposable or in the way of planning and *making* history (Koselleck 2004: 191–3). In this context the idea of modernity is discursively tied together with the idea of the past as a burden or baggage to continuously get rid of in order to keep making space for the new (Assmann 2013: 142). This idea of the disposability of the past comes to manifest itself markedly in the context of fashion, as an agent in the institutionalization of change and the learning of modern consumer habits, including the desire for continuous newness.

Fashion's co-production of new and old

With innovations in manufacturing techniques and the industrialization of the textile and clothing producing sectors over the eighteenth and nineteenth centuries, fashion became a key economic force in the development of euro-modernity (Breward 1995, 2003; Lemire 1997, 2005, 2012). The rise of consumer culture deeply impacted people's relationships to objects (Bauman 2007), with the fashion industry accelerating the tempo at which new clothes were produced, purchased and used, leading towards a quicker devaluation and disposal of new clothing, culminating in the rise of fast fashion in the recent decades (Maynard 2013; Fletcher 2014; Norris 2012).

Prior to the industrialization of clothing production a prolonged use or purchase of previously worn clothes formed an essential part of the everyday clothing practices of the majority of people in both urban and rural areas. Textiles and clothing were expensive and often retained their value over generations. When a garment was no longer worn by one person it was passed on or altered into new clothes, enabling multiple uses over time. Garments along with other material possessions were precisely regulated in people's wills, which attest to the high economic value clothes inhabited in previous centuries (see Roche 1994; Lemire 2005, 2012). Clothing and fabrics were considered family property handed down to the next generation. They were seen as an investment that was either used until the last thread or sold and exchanged for other goods. Their economic worth could be instantly evaluated based on the fabric's quality, weight, construction, or finish and determined their exchange value for other goods or their transformation into cash or credit. When clothing was bought, choices were linked with these economic considerations in mind, pointing to the high value of clothes as an "alternative currency" (see Lemire 2005, 2012).

In her study of the second-hand trade in the early urban context of Renaissance Florence, Carole Collier Frick (2005) points out how second-hand clothing dealers can be seen as the first retailers of clothing and accessories who were as such closely intertwined with the early development of the fashion market. By buying and reselling separate pieces of garments, such as sleeves that were detachable from bodices or bodices that could be detached from skirts, they stimulated experimentation and innovation with used clothing pieces and enabled their new wearers to create fresh ensembles from older garments (Frick 2005: 25–6).

However, essential for the development of the trade in the context of early capitalism was the existence of at least a modest surplus of clothes among the population which provided the material resource for the exchange of money and goods and an awareness of fashion and consumer desires (see Lemire 2012). This surplus of goods necessary to effectively fuel a second cycle of consumption increased with the process of industrialization and urbanization and the expansion and acceleration of fashion production, which produced a larger amount and faster turnover of garments. Technological advances in the textile-producing sector, for example, the mechanization of yarn spinning with the spinning jenny in the 1760s and the Jacquard loom in the early 1800s, paved the way for the mechanization of garment fabrication and the industrialized production of ready-made clothing. Even more so the invention of the sewing machine in the 1850s, and its wider use by the mid-1860s (Breward 1995: 152), as well as the speeding up of machine-powered work through steam, gas and later electricity, led to an acceleration in the making of garments, as well as to greater variation and change in stylistic details.

The increasing production and consumption of new clothing in this context, which Beverly Lemire describes as a time marked by "industrial plenty," impacted the trade in second-hand goods (Lemire 2012: 153). Along with the social (and financial) changes brought by the process of industrialization, she describes how the nature of the second-hand trade changed, with a decline of middle-class customers, who previously pawned some of their clothes when in need of money (Lemire 2012: 153; see also Breward 1999: 122–7). Clothing that was no longer wanted or regarded as at the height of fashion by the higher social classes was often passed on as a part of their wages to servants who could capitalize them as income by selling them to second-hand dealers (Lemire 2005; Ginsburg 1980; Roche 1994). The second-hand clothes trade boomed in turn as a source for cheaper clothes and with it, many associated industries that concentrated on the cleaning and remaking of used garments. Beverly Lemire notes in her historical study of the second-hand trade in England between 1600 and 1850 that the trade had always been organized according to hierarchies or fine distinctions made between old clothes or rags and second-hand clothes that were still wearable and of good quality (Lemire 2005). However, it is with the increasing accessibility of new clothes by larger parts of the population that the wearing of older garments and those purchased via second-hand markets became stigmatized as a sign of poverty, and the purchase of used clothing seen as a lower valued substitute for commodities in the first fashion market. Madeleine Ginsburg refers to these changing social and cultural perceptions of the use of second-hand clothes that undermined this development in the nineteenth century when new clothing consumption increased among the middle classes along with the social changes paralleling the development of industrialization and capitalism (Ginsburg 1980).

With its many technological advances in the nineteenth century, combined with the low-cost "sweated labor" of immigrant and female domestic workers that enabled the accelerated production of a greater amount and variety of textiles and clothing, the fashion industry comes to thrive on the strategy of producing "newness" and the desire for "new" goods—by effectively rendering its recently new produced goods old and therefore undesirable. If the time regime of modernity can be more widely understood as a machine for the production of the new as well as of the old (Assmann 2013: 24), than this co-production of the old and new—or past and present, history and modernity—happens perhaps nowhere more evidently and effectively than in fashion. This is pointedly highlighted in Christopher Breward's comment on fashion's transience that "draws it into the role of cultural clock" (Breward 1995: 185). If colored as a time-keeping apparatus, fashion ticks in the economic and industrialized rhythm of production, distribution, promotion, and proposal of the new, which produces the obsolescence of its own immediacy.

Fashion media take on a powerful role in the necessary story-telling of newness and nowness: "[h]ighly conscious and exploitative of the economic connotations of the passing of time" fashion media construct explanations of *Zeitgeist* (Breward 1995: 184). Drawing attention to the new and now, these *Zeit* narratives of fashion then work against the memory—or at least the memory of ever liking—the fashion of the immediate past. Fashion journals in their enticing combination of image and text inhabited from early on a key role in educating consumers in the desire for the new. Even within the context of Germany, that by 1785—when Friedrich Justus Bertuch launched the *Journal des Luxus und der Moden*—had not yet seen the scope of industrialization like some of the neighboring countries and where, as Daniel Purdy notes, the promoted new fashion luxuries were hardly available for consumption, the fashion journal "dramatically increased the moments in people's lifetimes when they might feel compelled to buy new clothes" thus altering the temporal rhythm of consumer habits (Purdy 2010: 241).

In her study on the promotion of newness, based on an analysis of fashion print media, Aurelie van de Peer highlights how the temporality of fashion is not a given, but an outcome of sophisticated chronometric operations. Among one of them is the organization of fashion change by the season, which she argues can be traced back to attempts occurring in early fashion periodicals, specifically referring to the example of *The Mercure Galant* published between 1672 and 1724 (van de Peer 2014: 328). Drawing on Jennifer Jones' research on fashion in the *Ancien Regime*, she notes that fashion seasons first came to be instituted by King Louis XIV and Jean Colbert as part of the expansion of French mercantilism in the seventeenth century. While these early proclamations of fashion seasons did not actually coincide with the seasons of natural cycles (Jones 2007: 33), van de Peer notes that this temporal anchorage was still very powerful in naturalizing fashion and its change by establishing an analogy with "the universal seasons of nature," and through that also grant "the fickle changes of fashion a 'rationality' of sorts" (van de Peer 2014: 329). Over the course of the nineteenth and twentieth century the fashion system has built a powerful temporal regime that organizes today the debuting of new fall-winter or summer-spring clothes, subdivided in varied market segments, in fashion weeks around the world a season before they arrive in stores. Magazines and fashion media continue the temporal ritual each March and each September by launching especially page and advertising-rich issues showcasing the new "must haves" of the season eagerly awaited by consumers, thus exemplifying how time or "temporality is a mode of implantation through which institutional forces come to seem like somatic facts" (Freeman 2007: 160, cited in West-Pavlov 2013: 5).

Fashion revivals

While Georg Simmel emphasizes in his writing that fashion's first and foremost concern is change, highlighting it as transitory and ephemeral, he also recognizes the particular appeal the past can hold in the present:

> As soon as an earlier fashion has partially been forgotten there is no reason why it should not be allowed to return to favor and why the charm of difference,

which constitutes its very essence, should not be permitted to exercise an influence similar to that which it exerted conversely some time before. (Simmel 2004: 307)

The "charm of difference" Simmel ascribes to fashion revivals in the early twentieth century, is what makes old clothes attractive to new wearers. Simmel's original German text speaks about the "feeling" of the charm of difference. He uses in the German text the word "Reiz," which refers also to a physiological stimulus or sensation, implying a deeper-going sensual or emotional affect caused by the contrast of the past fashion revived in the present (Simmel 1986: 204). His description recalls the affective feelings associated with nostalgia (see Jenss 2013), as a specific mode and mood to engage with or relate to the past. While the word nostalgia emerges in the seventeenth century as a diagnosis of homesickness observed among soldiers who spent significant time away from home (Davis 1979; Boym 2001), the meaning of nostalgia expands in the context of the nineteenth century. As Nancy Martha West has shown in her study on Kodak, the evocation of nostalgic feelings becomes here closely integrated with the development and learning of new socio-technological practices, in particular photography, and is also used to market new commodities (see West 2000). While the word nostalgia starts to lose its military and medical connotation, it is directly interwoven with modernity and the expansion of consumer culture, including fashion (see Jenss 2013).

As Elizabeth Wilson puts it, "modernity repeatedly clothes itself in recon-structions of the past" (2005b: 10). An example for this can be found in the fashion of the light, white chemise dresses à la grecque emerging around the time of the Great French Revolution. This style of clothing was inspired by ideas of "naturalness," promoted in Jean Jacques Rousseau's 1762 book *Emile*, and by the widespread idealization of classical antiquity. The interest in the past was sparked by major archaeological excavations, including at Pompeii and Herculaneum in the first half of the eighteenth century, and the subsequent circulation of antiquarian and art historical publications, prints and costume books that made visual representations of antique artifacts available to wider audiences (see Taylor 2004: 15–16; Ribeiro 1995; Molfino 1986). In addition, it is the establishment of major national museums, such as the opening of the Louvre in Paris in 1793, that is part of the spurring and also institutionalizing of the wider interest in history and the visual and material culture of the past. Following a reorganization of the museum, Napoleon Bonaparte inaugurated the Musée des Antiques on the ground floor of the Petite Galerie on November 9, 1800, commemorating the first anniversary of the *coup d'état* which brought Napoleon to power as First Consul of France (Musée du Louvre 2015). The new gallery showcased many of the antique marble statues that were appropriated through Napoleon's military campaigns and treaties, including Italy's Venus of Medici (Molfino 1986: 31). The circulation of and exposure to antique visual and material culture translated into a wide fashion trend for antique style clothing and coiffure. For Napoleon, the engagement with and appropriation of the visual and material culture of antiquity served, however, as political strategy and legitimization of his empire building. Modernity came here quite literally clothed in "reconstructions of the past," where the recourse to an older antiquity helped to break with the more recent past, the *Ancien Regime* preceding the French Revolution.

For Jean Baudrillard, fashion and the museum are both inventions of modernity that he sees as complicit for their accumulation or recycling of the past: "Together they are the opposite of all previous cultures, made of inequivalent signs and incompatible styles" (Baudrillard 1993: 89). It seems, for him, "that modernity sets up a linear time of technical progress, production and history, and simultaneously, a cyclical time of fashion" (Baudrillard 1993: 89). Yet, as noted earlier on the co-production of the new and old, this is only an apparent contradiction, "since in fact modernity is never radical rupture. Tradition is no longer the pre-eminence of the old over the new: it is unaware of either—modernity itself invents them both at once … it is always and at the same time 'neo-' and '*retro-*', modern and anachronistic" (Baudrillard 1993: 89–90).

The building of museums (indicated in the Louvre's renaming to Musée Napoleon in 1803) was not propelled by an interest in history per se. Instead, it was fueled by the need for historically reassuring images of identity, concomitant with the process of modernity and the formation of the nation state in nineteenth-century Europe (von Plessen 1992, cited in Kaschuba 1999: 229). Fashion and dress were closely interwoven with these cultural and political developments. Eric Hobsbawm speaks of the "invention of tradition" that served to bolster the building of nation states (Hobsbawm 1997). This invention of tradition was for example apparent in the use of civil uniforms and liveries that were modeled on eighteenth-century aristocratic fashion styles, turning European courts and parades during the nineteenth and early twentieth centuries into historical spectacles (see Hobsbawm 1997; Hackspiel-Mikosch 2002).

In her book *Fashion Revivals*, Barbara Burman-Baines (1981) has shown that the use of former fashion styles is not a new phenomenon, dating sartorial revivals back to the sixteenth century (Burman-Baines 1981: 103). Yet it is with the growing interest in history and the collection and wider access to artifacts from the past through the institutionalization of museum collecting, and the visual representation of historical artifacts in prints, books and journals, that the use of past forms of fashion came to spread as a wider cultural trend during the nineteenth century. Especially in the context of art and literature, many of the artists associated with Romanticism, such as Sir Walter Scott or Lord Byron in England and Théophile Gautier in France, turned the use of past styles into a mode for self-fashioning. The costume historian Farid Chenoune describes the eclectic style of these artists as "based on Van Dyck doublets, short archer's pants, hats in style of the philosopher Buridan or painter Rubens, Charles VI haircuts, François I beads, Henry IV ruffles" (1995: 53). Théophile Gautier said of the young Romantics' style mix in *Les Jeunes France* (1833) that it looked "as though they had taken things at random, eyes closed, from second-hand clothes merchants through the ages, in order to compose, as best they could, a complete wardrobe" (Gautier, cited in Chenoune 1995: 53). As Chenoune notes, these historical borrowings were already associated with rather defined ideas of originality, individuality and anti-conformity (Chenoune 1995: 56), which would come to be further associated with the use of second-hand clothes as an alternative fashion choice to new mass-produced clothes in the twentieth century.

Fast fashion: Accelerating production and consumption

Economist Werner Sombart comments on the temporal dynamics of fashion in the early twentieth century: "We can term 'fashion' every change in taste that leads to a reorganization of demand during the lifetime of a generation" (Sombart 2004: 311). He writes, "the wild *tempo of changes in fashion* is also a characteristic trait of the fashion of our age," arguing that fashion in past centuries changed only notably "at most by years," changes now take place "four to five times within one and the same season" (Sombart 2004: 313). The acceleration of production processes that enabled for Sombart a speeding up to a "wild tempo," has a century later only intensified. Zygmunt Bauman sees consumer culture in the twenty-first century marked by an instantaneity and "feverish" rhythm of time that is driven by an ever-rising volume and intensity of desires, which imply in turn the prompt use and speedy replacement of objects (Bauman 2007: 31).

The rise of fast fashion over the last few decades has been centrally bound up with this process, turning clothes into instant commodities, with new clothes entering high street chains every couple of weeks, speeding up conventional seasonal offerings. "Fast speed has become a defining characteristic of today's textile and clothing industry; where sales are tracked with electronic tills and just-in-time manufacturing that has now made it possible to turn a sample or design sketch into a finished product in as little as two to three weeks" (Fletcher 2014: 189, see also Moon 2014). The clothes that are designated fast fashion are not only quickly produced and distributed. Due to their low price, enabled through low-cost labor and materials, they tend to be worn for a shorter length of time—sometimes just once or even never—before they are discarded. For consumers their value lies particularly in the experience and instant—though temporary—gratification of the purchase, so that the clothes cannot only be understood as goods to be worn, but are equally important as items to be bought often and to be quickly replaced. This relationship to clothing as a highly ephemeral good has been particularly fostered through the rise of online shopping. Fresh arrivals of fashion can be instantly spotted in the "new" section on a company's website or they are directly promoted to customers via social media, and once purchased with a few taps on a screen, can reach consumers via expedited shipping in less than 24 hours. By offering continually "rapid access to the latest styles" that sell out fast, chains such as Hennes & Mauritz and Zara—despite their vast production scale (with Zara for example producing 30,000 designs a year; see Soula 2011: 62, quoted in Rocamora 2013: 67)—generate a sense of limitedness of fashion that encourages consumers to shop frequently and to buy immediately so as not to miss out on opportunities (Maynard 2013: 548). While the frequency implied in fast fashion reduces the time these new clothes are worn, it expands the time and mental occupation invested in the ongoing activity and experience shopping for them.

Fast fashion is an epitome of the "promotion of discontinuity" (Fletcher 2014: 191) and the acceleration of commercial cycles. It is interwoven with an experience of temporality that goes along with the velocity of time-space compressing digital media. With the speed and global scale at which information circulates through digitization emerges what Bauman calls a pointillist perception of time, which he sees reflected in today's "nowist" or hurried culture. He points out that a single copy of the Sunday edition of the *New York Times* contains today more information or "news" than a person in the eighteenth or nineteenth century would have consumed in a lifetime, and highlights the impossibility of actually absorbing or dealing with this amount of information (Bauman 2007: 39). The accelerated production and accumulation of information generates a heightened sense of velocity, an experience in which the idea of continuity or progression diminishes, in Bauman's words, towards a very punctuated experience of time, a time that is broken up or "pulverized" into something like eternal instants (Bauman 2007: 32).

For Bauman, "in the 'nowist' life of the denizens of the consumerist era, the motive to hurry is partly the urge to *acquire* and *collect*. But the most pressing need that makes haste truly imperative is nevertheless the necessity to *discard* and *replace*" (Bauman 2007: 36). Despite the actual speeding up of production processes, and the evident increase in clothing waste (see Norris 2012), in the everyday practices of dressing and engaging with clothing the temporalities of fashion are, however, not universal (see Woodward 2007). And it is most notably in the context of the rise of fast fashion that the consumption of old clothes has seen a growing popularity across a wider range of consumers, who value old clothes as an alternative to new mass-produced clothes. Consumer culture clearly thrives on the rapid turnover of commodities, and whenever new purchases are made, "some consumer products are travelling to the dump" (Bauman 2007: 36–7). Yet a large proportion of the clothes that are disposed of to make space in the wardrobe for new acquisitions still have the potential for "many lives"

(Hansen 2003). Fueling second and third cycles of consumption, they do not end in the dump, but often travel widely through time and space, getting new uses and acquiring new values in a highly diversified, global market for used clothing (see Gregson and Crewe 2003; Hansen 2003; Norris 2012). While media and consumer culture in their production and narration of the new can be understood to generate a culture of ephemerality and forgetting, it is equally due to its ongoing surplus production of objects and images a site for the accumulation or piling up of modernity's disposals, and as such, a site or resource for the experience of multiple temporalities. Or in other words: "Time is rich in material culture, and vice versa" (Shove, Trentmann and Wilk 2009: 5). The vast "heterogeneity of materials and the temporalities of fashion cycles and disposal strategies" (Norris 2012: 129) that constitute today's consumer culture have created a vast supply of goods for which a wide range of markets started to emerge in the latter half of the twentieth century.

Notes on shifting terminologies: Retro and vintage

The word vintage entered the international fashion vocabulary in the late 1990s, when it started to be used more widely as an alternative to the word retro. The latter has been used in the context of fashion at least since the 1970s as a word describing a certain style of second-hand clothing that was valued for its marked anachronism, or sartorial-temporal difference, in the context of the contemporary fashion of the time (McRobbie 1994). This use of second-hand clothing from previous decades as an alternative to new mass-produced fashion evolved initially as a kind of anti-fashion in the context of post-war youth and consumer culture (see McRobbie 1994; Samuel 2012: 98), leading to a shift in the evaluation of the consumption of used or old clothes, and eventually to a kind of "mainstreaming" of retro and vintage as a wider fashion trend over the course of the 1990s and 2000s (see Palmer 2005; Cicolini 2005; Cassidy and Bennett 2012).

Both retro and vintage are terms used today quite interchangeably in the sense that both have come to refer to old as well as to new things or styles, produced to be old-looking, such as "new vintage" or retro style (Jenss 2007 and 2010; Aronowsky Cronberg 2009; Baker 2013). In his discussion of "retrochic" in the 1990s, Raphael Samuel points to some national differences noting that the term retro has been more widely used in Britain, while the word retro coexisted in the United States alongside the older term vintage or "vintage chic" (Samuel 2012: 85). The Dictionary of Fashion and Fashion Designers, published in Britain by Thames & Hudson, first included a definition for the word vintage in its 2008 edition, while earlier editions of the publication only included the term retro (see O'Hara 1986; O'Hara Callan 1998; O'Hara Callan and Glover 2008). The 1986 publication defines retro as a "word used in France in the second half of the twentieth century to describe clothing from another era, usually pre-World War II, which are enjoying a revival" (O'Hara 1986: 213). The 1998 and 2008 definitions, however, drop the reference to France and broaden the definition to:

> Word used to describe clothing from a previous era, usually at least twenty years earlier. Many designers feature retro garments in their collections, these clothes, though revisionist in attitude, are remade to work with current looks. During the 1990s flares and crochet, two significant styles of 1960s fashion, reappeared in collections, but in more sophisticated, mainstream form. (O'Hara Callan 1998: 200; O'Hara Callan and Glover 2008: 215)

The change in definition indicates how retro has become a more widely and flexibly used term, that may refer to old clothes as well as to designer remakes of earlier fashion styles, that became fashionable in the 1990s. Yet this definition does set an emphasis on retro as a revising or updating of past forms, a strategy that also helped in the 1990s to rebrand some of the older fashion labels, for example the Gucci brand with the work of the designer Tom Ford (Jenss 2001; see also Brown 2001). Where the term retro remains in this definition open to be used for old things as well as for new retro-designs, the term vintage in the 2008 dictionary edition is more specifically confined to:

> second-hand clothing with a sense of history that is worn in an ironic or nostalgic way. Vintage clothes became increasingly popular in the late 20th century as contemporary fashion developed a less prescriptive, more individualistic approach and favoured a customized referential look. (O'Hara Callan and Glover 2008: 268)

This entry encompasses several meanings attached to the appeal of old clothes, ranging from irony, as a kind of distance to the past to feelings of nostalgia, as well as the association of second-hand—or vintage—clothes with individuality and uniqueness. It situates the popularity of vintage in the late twentieth century, in line with many academic studies, media reports and other entries on second-hand and vintage in recently published fashion encyclopedias (see Palmer 2005; Cicolini 2005; Mackinney-Valentin 2010; Jenss 2010). However, the way this definition limits the term vintage to real historic or second-hand clothes reflects how the term came to be used initially when old clothes turned into fashionable goods more widely in the 1960s (see Samuel 2012: 89). "Vintage Chic" was the name of one of the first boutiques, opened in New York in 1965, offering old clothes as a distinct or alternative fashion style (see Samuel 2012: 89). This store was owned by Harriet Love, who later also published a guidebook on buying, collecting and wearing "antique clothing in high style" (Love 1982). By that time the consumption of second-hand clothing had expanded beyond consumers who relied on it predominantly out of economic necessity, and established itself as a form of "alternative consumerism" among youth and style leaders who were not wealthy, but, as Samuel puts it, were still "drawn from the culturally privileged" (Samuel 2012: 98). The emerging popularity of retro and vintage in the 1960s and 1970s (when clothes were no longer a scarce resource as in the more immediate post-war context), went along with the promotion of flea markets in city centers and the establishment of carefully curated second-hand boutiques catering to middle-class consumers in European and American cities (see Fischer 1980; McRobbie 1994; Gregson and Crewe 2003; Samuel 2012). Yet, it was with the rise of the internet, e-commerce and the global circulation of street-style blogs from the late 1990s onwards that vintage started to thrive as a wide-ranging trend and aesthetic phenomenon, and that the word vintage became more widely used and understood beyond the Anglo-American context.

In Germany for example, the term vintage only entered media reports in the early twenty-first century (see Allstädt 2002) and it is—beyond these reports—particularly due to the use of vintage as a search category and promotional term on eBay, which launched its German website in 1999, that many people heard of the term for the first time. This was also evident in the interviews and field research I conducted in the early 2000s, when the term started to come up in the context of clothing as well as in music. The predominant term in Germany was "second-hand," which was also common to use for stores. Using the English term, instead of the German word *Altkleider* (old clothes), connotes a sense of difference and modernity compared to terms such as used or old clothes. The term retro had become widely popularized in Germany in the 1990s, but it was mainly associated with a wider commercial copying of previous decades' styles and new clothes made to resemble the look of second-hand clothing (for example sportswear brands Puma or Adidas redesigns of old school sneakers and tracksuit jackets).

In this sense, while the term vintage itself and also the objects or practice it refers to have been in long existence, vintage appeared not only as a new word, but moreover as a "new thing." Vintage especially evoked a feeling of "newness" or difference in comparison to retro, a word that had come to carry for some people a more negative connotation. This is in part due to the etymology of retro (from Latin: back or backwards) and the theoretical and media discourse circulating around retro when it is used as a label to describe a wider social or cultural tendency "to look back." Not rarely, this meaning of retro has been framed in quite pathological terms as a "retromania" and "addiction" (Reynolds 2011), as a "retro-mood" (Horx 1995), an "obsession" with or "cannibalistic pillaging" of the past (Jameson 1984), as a symptom (or simulation) of nostalgia, and compensation of an experience of loss or lack, driven by consumer culture (Baudrillard 1993; Keightley and Pickering 2012: 139–64).

In addition to a view on retro as a form of backwardness or cultural regress, retro style is further associated with "retrotyping," a stereotypical versioning of the past and a misrepresentation of history (Keightley and Pickering 2012: 150). This understanding goes back to the way retro emerged in the discourse of French film criticism. The use of the phrase *la mode retro* evolved in France around films of the early 1970s that were critiqued for representing and popularizing the past—specifically the time of the Nazi Occupation during the Second World War—in a stylized and apolitical, revisionist manner (Guffey 2006: 14; Austin 1996: 28). The term came further to be used by "French writers commenting on postmodernist fashion for artists, designers and film-makers to revive and recycle past styles, often very recent ones" (Childs 1999: 455). Jean Baudrillard was one of the writers who theorized the idea of retro in the context of fashion and postmodernity in his book *Symbolic Exchange and Death* (1993), published first in French in 1976. For him, fashion is "always retro … an immediate and total recycling" that is based on the "spectral death and resurrection of forms" (Baudrillard 1993: 88). He conceptualizes fashion as per se "inactual" or out of date, as it is based on "returning" rather than "becoming" structures (Baudrillard 1993: 88). While not directly focused on fashion, Fredric Jameson theorized retro in a similar way in his 1984 article "Postmodernity, Or the Logic of Late Capitalism." For him the referencing of the past in architecture or visual culture, such as film, is a form of historicism or "nostalgia mode" that effaces any "real" history. Postmodern culture, while enticed by a stylistic engagement with the forms of the past, renders the past at the same time meaningless. He sees the aesthetic evocation of the past as a form of empty parody or pastiche that only creates a distance between past and present, leading eventually to the loss of history (Jameson 1984). For Baudrillard and Jameson retro is a symptom of postmodernity, which they conceptualize as driven by the loss of meaning, and a random thrifting through the world of free floating, mediated signs, which have lost any point of reference. As noted in the introduction, these perspectives have been critiqued, especially for their universalizing tendency, in which the perspectives of consumers for example, or the variety of uses of the past, are not taken into account.

While retro has been increasingly linked to motives of irony (Guffey 2006), and also with a subversive play with history (Silverman 1994), due to its etymology in wine culture the term vintage connotes meanings that are other than retro more closely related to ideas of heritage, originality and a sense of superior quality associated with objects that are understood to materialize time, or to get better with time. This makes the term and also the meaning dimensions of vintage in the context of dress somewhat different from the term retro. An excursion on the meaning of vintage in the context of wine culture will further help to understand this, and how the use of terminology aids in the creation of specific values, linking age with the idea of rarity.

Vintage in wine culture: Naturalizing age as superior value

The connotations of the word vintage in relation to temporal identification, introduced in the beginning of this chapter, can be traced back to the roots of the word in wine making. The English word vintage is derived from the Old French word *vendange* rooted in the Latin word *vindemia*, which in combining the noun *vinum* (wine) and the verb *demere* (to remove) refers to the harvest of the grapes. In line with the meaning of the French word, the *Oxford English Dictionary* (2014) defines the Anglicized verb vintage as the gathering or collecting of vine grapes. Vintage as a noun refers to the "produce or yield of the vine, either as grapes or wine; the crop or yield of a vineyard or district in a single season." As such, the term vintage carries a particular meaning dimension of time or temporality: one that is tied to the temporal cycles of nature, weather seasons and vegetation periods, but also to the cultivation of nature for trade and consumption, thereby adding an economic dimension to the term vintage, alluding to time (and natural resources) as a form of value and capital.

In the context of wine culture, the relation between time as a marker of quality and value became more pronounced in the eighteenth century when vintage started to refer more specifically "to the age or year of a particular wine, usually connoting one of good or outstanding quality" and further became used as a label for "a wine made from the grape-crop of a certain district in a good year and kept separate on account of its quality" (*Oxford English Dictionary* 2014). Here the meaning dimension of the term vintage begins to encompass time as well as place, which become key factors in the identification and classification of wine, determining its quality and value as a commodity. The term vintage thus carries connotations of an identifiable origin and, attached to that, cultural ideas of authenticity and heritage.

The specificity of place and time, that is the combination of the soil and climate conditions which impact the growth period and yield, are of key significance to the quality of wines. On a label, vintage may only be used for a wine that is made from the yield of one season. A label for a vintage wine shows the year, region and grape. Determining or understanding a wine's quality then requires a certain knowledge, or in the sense of Pierre Bourdieu (1998), cultural capital among the consumer: for example, the knowledge if a specific year, or vintage, was a good or bad year in the region the wine was made, which is impacted by the weather conditions over the course of the vegetation period in a particular growth region.

The identification of time and place of origin, or year and region, has become central to the determining of the value of wine as a cultural good and commodity. It sets a wine apart from mass-market wines, which can be made from grapes of diverse origins, which are processed according to uniform standards to produce a wine that may consistently taste the same each year. In this sense the quality, or rather the classification of wine, depends not just on pure natural forces, like a region's soil and the weather conditions, but it is inseparable from the making and commodification of place.

A place like a wine region can be understood with Henri Lefebvre's (1991) theories on the production of space, as bound up with the production of hierarchies and a mobilization of differences. Considering the roots of the term vintage in wine culture, it is helpful to look a bit further into the value production in this market, in particular through the spatial and ecological concept of *terroir*. In the context of agricultural products such as wine, *terroir* functions similar to the concept of heritage—a valuing of a native or place-bound past—that is "often presented as harmonious, coherent, respectful, original, natural, threatened, a setting in which people, space and time are organically connected" (Filipuci 2004: 79, cited in Demossier 2011: 687). Yet, as the anthropologist Marion Demossier points out in a discussion of the politics of *terroir*, it is also a process "in which a wide range of actors have become involved in the social construction of the present, which in turn, provides a platform for self-identification" (Demossier 2011: 687). In her study on the Burgundy wine region she highlights the paradoxes and interplay of global and local forces that are part of globalization by showing how the label of *terroir* is used by elite wine makers to endow their region, and their products, with the symbolic values of authenticity, distinctiveness and permanence rooted in place—to the effect of placing themselves within the global market. Demossier shows how through a "rhetoric that emphasizes *terroir* not only as a natural and ecological concept, but also as a historicized and heritagized construction of place, the wine-growers create a suggestive and powerful image that can be passed on, narrated to, or consumed by a discerning group of consumers" (Demossier 2011: 695). This is not a new practice, as Robert Ulin (1995) illuminates in an article on the creation of *Grand Crus* wines in the Bordeaux region, with which French wine makers responded in the mid-nineteenth century to the rising competition from wine markets in Spain and Portugal. Similarly to the concept of *terroir*—that helps to market these wines based on an idea of a permanence of place and a deeply rooted heritage to distinguish and compete in today's global market—the *Grand Crus* or "elite Bordeaux wines, were produced, in contrast to the mass or common wines that saturated European markets" (Ulin 1995: 521–2). In addition to place, it was a development in which a commodification of time became of central importance, as the wines classified as *Grand Crus* (great growth or first growth) were made from old vine stocks, often fifty years in age or in some cases even a hundred years old (Ulin 1995: 521–2). These older vine stocks are a naturally limited resource for wine, producing smaller yields of grapes, which in turn are understood to improve a wine's quality that is further improved through the process (and the involved craft) of aging. This longer, more specialized and labor-intensive process of wine making is a practice historically afforded only by the wealthiest growers, who came to legally assure and protect the distinct status of their *Grand Crus* through the 1855 classification of Bordeaux wines that included only four chateaus as first growths (Ulin 1995: 522).

The 1855 Bordeaux classification is directly tied to constructions of French national identity, as it was instituted in the context of the organization of the *Exposition Universelle*, France's first international exhibition held in Paris in 1855, which acted as an opportunity—under the reign of Napoleon III—to curate and showcase French culture. Presenting the newly classified "age-old" French elite wines in this landmark industry and art exhibition was quite literally a method to fashion the taste of a nation—by naturalizing distinctiveness or superiority not only through place and heritage, but also by naturalizing time or age as of a superior value. In his study of Bordeaux, Ulin discusses how the value attributed to aged wines and older stocks was connected to the aristocratic roots of the land on which the vines grew. He notes how "aristocratic roots" stand metaphorically for both age and depth, which, tied to vine growing culture, came to be "represented in terms of a time that ostensibly passes naturally and therefore can be accounted for and measured objectively" (Ulin 1998: 524). While the "aristocratic roots" of the wine growing soil, or of those who inhabited the chateaus, are rather dubious as Ulin notes, it was effectively a nostalgia for an aristocratic past, about half a century after the French Revolution, that created "a symbolic place for the elite wines at the center of French civilization" (Ulin 1998: 524).

Drawing on Eric Hobsbawm's (1997) concept of the invention of tradition, Ulin's research highlights how "naturalized time as part of winegrowing discourse reinforces the privilege of elite wines and winegrowers through eclipsing the cultural mediation of time and hence the social constitution of the natural" (Ulin 1995: 524). There is an interesting correlation between this occurring commodification of time and conception of "age" as something "naturally" superior in the context of mid-nineteenth-century wine making in France and the naturalization of fashion time as newness and its temporal organization in seasonal change with the rise of the fashion system as discussed earlier in this chapter. Both give examples for the way concepts of time or temporality are bound up with the expansion (and sophisticated chronometric operations) of consumer culture, in which equally the "new" as well as the "old" will find its uses.

Vintage style

The excursion into the field of wine culture alludes to the value and meaning dimensions when the term vintage is transferred to fashion and clothing. It is a term that is not only related to the cultivation of nature, but with that, also to one of the key markets that effectively used and commodified time (and place) for purposes of (self-) identification and distinction—constructing an aura of rarity, authenticity and a "naturally" given exclusiveness through (and around) time and age.

Even when the roots of the term vintage in the context of wine culture (and its historic connection to the production of place, time, nation and also to nature and growth) may be forgotten in contemporary uses of the term, it is useful to consider this etymological heritage of vintage in the context of clothing practices over the recent decades. Vintage carries a connotation not only of time and age, but also of place, tying in with ideas of the place-bound concept of heritage (see Macdonald 2013), which becomes also increasingly important in the context of the globalization of fashion, and specific ideas (such as standardization and homogenization) that have come to be associated with the fast transnational production and distribution of fashion. As a term, vintage started to spread out in the 1990s, initially to refer to and distinguish the "real old" from the just "old looking." Yet, as noted in the section on terminological shifts, similarly to the term retro, its use broadened in the context of fashion to encompass eventually old as well as new clothes, that is "new vintage" clothes made today, which can equally open up in their look or style a sensation of time and memory (see Aronowsky Cronberg 2009).

While today both words, retro and vintage, are often used interchangeably, and can certainly mean the same thing, etymologically they have both different senses attached to them. Retro is foremost a form of abbreviation, for example for retrospection, for looking back, yet it also can refer to back, or backward. This term may be understood to imply temporality in a different sense than the word vintage. Where retro indicates a temporal direction, vintage is an old-fashioned word for "year" and its association with age or aging (and with wine as a concrete material object or consumable), can perhaps be understood to refer to a kind of development or accumulation of time, that is time as mass or matter, which gives the term a more material dimension than the word retro (especially in its visual dimension as retrospection, or looking back) might imply. The use of the term vintage, referring to a thing or consumable that gets better with time, has in this sense some similarity with the word patina: that is material traces of time or age, that are also of high symbolic value and have become markers of distinction as a legitimization through age and history (McCracken 1988: 21)—even when these traces of age did not accumulate but could be carefully manufactured to "add beauty," like the "time-darkened tones" used in eighteenth century painting to resemble the look of varnished paintings (Lowenthal 1985: 159–60). However, even if time and age materially develop in things, as this chapter has shown, the value associated with vintage is not just simply inherent in them—not least because the term vintage refers now to new as well as old things.

While clothes as they acquire age, or "grow old," gain specific qualities, and are valued for their material difference or their materializing of time, as will be shown here in later chapters, the meaning or value production of "vintage" is bound up with fashion markets—both the ones trading in newness, and those trading in the old. The rise of old clothes to the rank of vintage is tied to a classificatory system of used clothes not just in a temporal sense, but also with regard to the diversification of use and reuse markets on a global scale (see Gregson and Crewe 2003; Norris 2012). From a perspective of sorting, what gets evaluated—or branded—as vintage usually just forms a very small percentage of the million tons of garments that provide the raw materials for the global used clothing trade (see Hawley 2006). As Maria Mackinney-Valentin points out on vintage in the *Berg Encyclopedia of World Dress and Fashion*: "Vintage could be regarded as a fashion system in its own right with a hierarchy covering haute couture, ready-to-wear, and retail with an extra level in the form of thrift stores, flea markets, and e-commerce, as well as vintage fashion fairs" (Mackinney-Valentin 2010). It is most notably in a context of mass-production and the surplus of new clothes, as the next chapter will further show, focusing on post-war consumer culture and the rise of the youth market in the 1960s, that *some* of the clothes others no longer want become reclassified and rise from rags to exclusive goods. Appreciated for their age and associated uniqueness they are suitable material for constructions of key values and historical ideas or desires on which fashion thrives: difference and individuality.

3 ICONS OF MODERNITY: SIXTIES FASHION AND YOUTH CULTURE

A s Fred Davis notes, "time is *not a ding an sich* [a thing as such] but rather something we are constantly arranging, defining, structuring, modulating" (Davis 1984: 16). Decade labels are one of the things we use to do this. When we speak about the "the sixties" we are not just using a numerical shorthand to refer to the succession of ten years, but instead this reference to time describes a wider imaginary and often mythic construction of time, or *zeitgeist* narratives, we come to produce around and associate with a past decade, usually in retrospect, and by way of the identification of temporal contrast.

The sixties are a decade that has come to shine brightly as "golden years" (Hobsbawm 1994: 257) especially in the backdrop of the preceding decade of the fifties and in light of the following decade of the seventies. The "distinctive stamp" or "characteristic symbolic texture" of a decade begins to emerge in close temporal proximity to it, influenced by the "period immediately preceding its dawn" (Davis 1984: 17). For the sixties, this kind of time-making is closely tied to the emergence of youth culture as a social and cultural category, so that one of the powerful time narratives circulating around this decade, at least in the Anglo-American context, is that of the "youthquake" (see Steele 1997: 49).

As noted by Davis, in cultural memory, the decade of the sixties tends to be recalled in temporal contrast to the fifties. Such a contrast has already been written up in sartorial terms in Colin MacInnes' novel *Absolute Beginners*, with an early description of mod style. In Britain the mods came to be associated with sartorial innovativeness and modernity and eventually they came to be closely linked with ideas of urban London style and national identity and renewal in the 1960s. Just prior to the start of that decade, in 1959, MacInnes provides a portrait of the figure of the modernist by way of sartorial comparison to the figure of the trad—or teddy boy:

the Dean being a sharp modern jazz creation, and the Kid just a skiffle survival, with horrible leanings to the trad. thing … If you know the contemporary

FIGURE 1 "Flying High" (Jill Kennington) 1966. Photo: John Cowan.

scene, you could tell them apart at once, just like you could a soldier or sailor, with their separate uniforms. Take first the Misery Kid and his trad. drag. Long brushless hair, white stiff-starched collar (rather grubby), striped shirt, tie of all one colour (red today, but it could have been royal-blue or navy), short jacket but an old one (somebody's riding tweed, most likely), very, very tight, tight trousers with wide stripe, no sox, short boots. Now observe the Dean in the modernist number's version. College-boy smooth crop hair with burned-in parting, neat white Italian rounded-collared shirt, short Roman jacket very tailored (two little side vents, three buttons), no-turn-up narrow trousers with 17-inch bottoms absolute maximum, pointed-toe shoes, and a white mac lying folded by his side, compared with Misery's sausage-rolled umbrella. (MacInnes 1959: 65–6)

While the Dean as a sharp modern jazz "creation," is defined as innovative and progressive, the Misery Kid is clearly described as *passé*—a "trad.[itional] thing" and skiffle "survival." MacInnes' portrayal of youth culture at the end of the 1950s, that inscribes an opposing sartorial-temporal orientation in line with the dichotomous narrative of modernity (see Koselleck 2004), played a significant role in the identification of the emerging youth culture of modernists: "an emblem of that supposedly classless class of youth as consumer and pioneer of style and 'cool'" (Vulliamy 2007). While a fictional account, MacInnes' book impacted youth, teaching them how to dress, move and be *modern*.

The main impulse of mod style was musical as the "mod" abbreviation itself stems from modern jazz. Musicians such as Miles Davis and the Modern Jazz Quartet wore Brooks Brothers clothes, which epitomized the British-influenced Ivy League style popularized at American elite universities. Influenced by nineteenth- and twentieth-century British upper-class clothing, Ivy style is until today associated with a sense of understatement, simplicity and quality. The style was defined through "natural-shouldered, narrow-lapelled suits and sports coats with button-down, pin or tab-collared shirts and slim neckwear" (Boyer 2012: 140). Modern jazz musicians were important international inter-mediaries popularizing the style among young Londoners spearheading a new scene around Soho's jazz clubs (see Lentz 2002: 2; Hewitt 2000: 33; Tulloch 1992: 86). Menswear retailer John Simons, who started to import Ivy League style to London in the 1950s, recalls how: "jazz culture was an Ivy League culture. Chet Baker and all those people wore Ivy League from the early '50s. They were your idols so you wanted to wear what they wore" (John Simons, cited in Hewitt 2000: 36).

While constructing a different look, the stylish suit that the mods copied from modern jazz musicians worked in parts similarly like the 1940s zoot suit as a kind of "mask" through which youths could portray themselves as adults and "urban sophisticates" (see Daniels 1997, in Alford 2004: 225). Yet America was not the only sartorial influence: what made mod style so distinctly "modern" was the transnational cross-pollination through which it evolved. Dick Hebdige (1979) emphasizes how British mods embraced and emulated the style of Jamaican immigrants in London, itself a product of transnational, sartorial circuits. As Carol Tulloch points out, fashion in Jamaica was since the early twentieth century heavily influenced by America, with a large Jamaican community in Harlem, that would send packages home with the latest modern clothing styles (Tulloch, in Hewitt 2000: 33).

Further influences came through movies that popularized international fashion styles alongside geographical or cultural imaginaries of France or Italy. The movie *Roman Holiday*, shot in 1953, shows an early prototype of mod style, with Gregory Peck and Audrey Hepburn cruising on a Vespa through Rome. Italian fashion had a substantial impact on the fitted look that became so characteristic of mod style. The "Italian look," credited to Brioni of Rome, consisted of a short, fitted mohair jacket with narrow lapels, and tight trousers that barely reached ankle-length. Nik Cohn describes how British designer Cecil Gee transformed Brioni's line into the famous "bum freezer," tailoring the jackets so tight and short that one "came to look like a man in his kid brother's clothes" (1971: 44). The style emerged in a fusion of diverse influences in which media images of international fashion played as much a role as the concrete material dynamics that are part of the social encounter in urban life. Beyond the impact of Jamaican youth, Cohn also points to the impact of immigrant youth from Italy, from whom the mods adopted new styles of casual wear, such as fitted V-neck or turtleneck sweaters, worn with slacks or jeans imported from America, as well as new ways of combining clothes: for example, wearing turtlenecks or polo shirts with suits (Cohn 1971: 48).

The mods' look was further distinguished through short and neat hairstyles with distinct side parting, popularized most notably by John F. Kennedy, which

FIGURE 2 Shoppers outside the Lord John shop in Carnaby Street, London 1965. Photo: Peter King/Fox Photos/Getty Images.

was later modified through back combing and even teasing to elongate the head and emphasize a lean appearance. The mods' snappy look was coupled with the projection of an overtly cool attitude, based on the belief that their perfectly styled self elevated them a notch above everyone else (see Barnes 1991). To a certain extent the mods may be regarded as the "absolute beginners," as they were part of the first generation that did not live through the war—or that experienced directly the effects of post-war rationing and need. On the contrary, attracted by the city lights of the emerging boutiques, record stores, coffee bars and discotheques that came to form the ground for a "Swinging London," they embraced a lifestyle associated with speed, extravagance and consumerism.

Two steps ahead

One of the first media reports on mods, under the headline "Faces without Shadows" and published in *Town Magazine* in September 1962, provides insight into the consumer practices of these youths (see partial reprint in Rawlings 2000: 42–7). The article revolves around the fifteen-year-old Mark Feld (later, Marc Bolan of the band T-Rex) and his twenty-year-old friends Peter Sugar and Michael Simmonds living in the London neighborhood Stoke Newington. They describe themselves as "faces," pulling off a style that requires: "youth, a sharp eye for dressing, and a general lack of mercy towards the rest of the world" (cited in Rawlings 2000: 42). Feld is still at school, while Sugar and Simmonds work as hairdressers. All three of them live with their parents and spend all their money on clothes and clubbing. The author of the article speaks of shelves and cupboards "bulging with suits and shirts often designed by themselves in bright, strange and violent colours" (cited in Rawlings 2000: 42). Even Mark Feld, son of a lorry driver and a supermarket sales assistant who does not earn his own income yet, boast with what in those days would have been regarded a rather comprehensive collection of fashionable clothing: he owns ten suits, eight sport jackets, fifteen pairs of trousers, thirty to fifty shirts, twenty jumpers, three leather jackets, two suede jackets, five or six pairs of shoes and thirty ties (cited in Rawlings 2000: 43). Clothing is to them "the most important thing in the world" and the means to a very particular end:

> "You've got to be different from the other kids," says Feld. I mean you got to be two steps ahead. The stuff that half the haddocks you see around are wearing I was wearing two years ago. A kid in my class came up to me in his new suit, an Italian box it was, he says. "Just look at the length of your jacket," he says "You're not with it," he says. "I was wearing that style two years ago," I said. (cited in Rawlings 2000: 44)

"Difference" is here achieved through time—through frequent change of stylistic details linked to intricate forms of consumption. Their wardrobe includes items that are custom-made by local tailors or purchased from up-and-coming names in youth fashion: "'All the faces go to Bilgorri. And John Stevens. He's very good on trousers. Hardly any place in London makes good trousers. They're all baggy here.' He tugs at the seat of his own trousers. Barely an inch comes away" (cited in Rawlings 2000: 44). But their clothes are not only tailor-made. Mods take full advantage of the new range of mass-produced fashion, combining their custom-made clothes with items from Woolworths or C&A. Minor modifications allow mass-produced shirts to look just as good as "a four guinea job from John Michael" (cited in Rawlings, 2000: 46). Details such as the height of a jacket's side vents, the number, type and positioning of buttons, the angle of pockets, the width and length of the trouser turn into minute details of subtle distinction (Barnes 1991: 8).

This passionate relationship to clothing and the obsession with details connect the mods with the dandy, to whom Mark Feld refers in the article as a role model: "I read a good book the other day ... The Life of Beau Brummel. He was just like us really. You know came up from nothing. Then he got to meet all the blokes, and he had a lot of clothes" (cited in Rawlings 2000: 46). George Brian (Beau) Brummel is the archetypical English dandy, whose ideas on clothing set a standard that continues to define the stereotypical image of classic English style: "neatness, simplicity and, at all times, correctness" (Cohn 1971: 5). Brummel molded his style around the tenet of understated elegance and developed a refined sartorial lexicon through a miniaturization of the signs that connote distinction (Sennett 1998: 214). The dandy aimed to embody a certain nonchalance and to project the image of a "well dressed man who while taking infinite pains about his appearance, affected indifference to it" (Ribeiro 2002: 21). The mods took this maxim to heart, whereby the dandy's nonchalance, in light of the American lifestyle promoted by pop culture and Hollywood films, was given a modern name: "the mod way of life ... consisted of total devotion to looking and being *cool* at all times" (Barnes 1991: 6–7). In *Sartor Resartus* Thomas Carlyle describes the dandy as "a Clothes-wearing Man, a Man whose trade, office, and existence consists in the wearing of Clothes. Every faculty of his soul, spirit, purse and person is heroically consecrated to this one object, the wearing of Clothes wisely and well: so that as others dress to live, he lives to dress" (Carlyle 2004: 166). The mods also made clothes their *raison d'être*. Like the dandy, they were all about "sartorial art for art's sake" (Green 1998: 41). Like the dandy, they sought to be original, calculating the exact effect of each piece of clothing. Yet there is one significant difference: the dandy, personified by Brummel, was an idler who did not work in order to cover the considerable cost of clothes, and their cleaning. But even if the mods' dandyism is almost the antithesis to the dandy archetype, they nevertheless remain, per George Melly, "true dandies, interested in works of art—themselves" (1989: 168–9). With the social, cultural and economic changes of the post-war years emerged new possibilities of self-portrayal for the less well-off: "Macmillan's affluence had helped create working-class dandies—dedicated followers of fashion" (Melly 1989: 168–9), but these were in no way exclusively men.

Mod women

The style of the mods has played a significant role in the development of subcultural theory in British cultural studies in the 1970s (see Clark 2000; Hebdige 2000). Yet as McRobbie and Garber (2000) have pointed out at the time, in the theory building around youth subcultural style formation, and the reading of style as (working-class) resistance to hegemonic social structures, a consideration of the position of women or girls among youth subcultures has been widely absent. In their important essay "Girls in Subcultures," which appeared together with Clark's and Hebdige's essays on subcultural style in *Resistance through Rituals* (Hall and Jefferson 2000), first published in 1975, they explain this marginalization of girls in subcultural studies with the hegemonic position of male sociologists at the time, as well as with the interests of media in the more sensational and thus newsworthy violent aspects of subcultures, "from which women have tended to be excluded," which in turn have formed a basis for sociological works (McRobbie and Garber 2000: 212). Yet their own text offers insights into the way girls participated in the mod youth culture, highlighting particularly the role of fashion and consumption as an entry to the mod scene.

Colin MacInnes provides in *Absolute Beginners* a description of the early modern jazz girl, who sports a style of "short hemlines, seamless stockings, pointed-toed high-heeled stiletto shoes, crepe nylon rattling petticoat, short blazer jacket, hair done up into the elfin style. Face pale—corpse colour with dash of mauve, plenty of mascara" (MacInnes 1959). Over the course of the 1960s, this style transforms, with mod girls expanding their wardrobe through the incorporation of men's clothing styles such as dress shirts and, most notably, low-waist trousers with front zipper, which were combined with flat shoes (Barnes 1991: 16). In addition, mod girls sported either short haircuts, which closely resembled men's cuts, or long, straight hair. Their make-up set the emphasis on the eye, accentuated with eyeliner, dark eye shadow, layers of mascara and pale face powder, which came to be a characteristic look of the 1960s.

Yet while blurring the boundaries of menswear and womenswear was part of the mod style, Angela McRobbie and Jenny Garber point out that this sartorial crossing in no way represented any liberation for girls from "the constraints of the feminine image" (McRobbie and Garber 2000: 215). Male acceptance, though given in terms of a potential mating partner rather than in recognition as full-fledged member of the scene, was still more readily granted to girls in line with a traditionally "female" look:

> As far as the girls went I'd divide them into two categories. There was a group of girls I'd call no-hopers and they would effect what I'd call a loosely masculine style. They'd have short hair, long suede coats, Hush Puppies, ski pants, probably a crewneck jumper. Go on with them fine but didn't think of them as girls. Then there was another group who were much more stylish. You would get the white lipstick, really severe haircut and they would wear polka dots, white stockings, big plastic jewellery and a very short skirt with big wide belt on it, like a pelmet skirt. They'd wear shoes with hourglass heels and a lot of them were totally unavailable. They really were, in their own way, very stylish and part of the scene. (Ian Hebditch, cited in Hewitt 2000: 61)

Even though mod subculture reproduced the hegemonic gender order, McRobbie and Garber nevertheless see it as "a 'softer' working-class subculture ... in which girls did much more openly and directly participate" (2000: 214). Clothing was important to this, providing girls with a kind of entry ticket to the scene. Not only did boys and girls look increasingly similar on account of the new "unisex" fashions of jeans, shirts, turtleneck jumpers or t-shirts, but mod youth culture was shaped by the traditionally "female" connoted realm of fashion and consumption. "Participation had much to do with clothes, appearance and the stylised look— like her male counterpart the Mod girl demonstrated the same fussiness for detail in clothes, the same over-attention to appearance" (McRobbie and Garber 2000: 217).

Participation in mod culture could also more easily be integrated with domestic life, to which girls were far more bound than boys. There was room for the "new teenage consumer culture *within* the 'culture of the bedroom'—experimenting with make-up, listening to records, reading the mags, sizing up the boyfriends, chatting, jiving" (McRobbie and Garber 2000: 213).

Based on interviews with former mods of the 1960s, Nicola Smallbone found that contrary to the image of the young and independent girl propagated by the media and by fashion designers such as Mary Quant in the 1960s (see Radner 2001), the lives of working-class girls remained steeped in very traditional values and notions of their social role. Girls were much more involved with family life and grew up under the impression that fulfillment would not stem from their profession, but from marriage, children and the satisfaction of their husband's needs. For a "good girl," family came first (Smallbone 1996: 62): "the very culture of being a girl was far more ingrained than any other and overrode the more extreme notions of being a Mod" (Smallbone 1996: 70). Over time and in their leisure, girls' participation in mod style—even if "only" in the name of fashion—allowed them to define themselves according to a youth cultural style

FIGURE 3 A "Mod" girl is measured for a suit in a Carnaby Street tailors, London 1964. Photo: Keystone Features/Getty Images.

and thereby to position themselves with reference to other youths. Yet this does not mean that they were less "mod" than boys. For Smallbone, there existed just as many mod girls as mod boys, though the former were more limited in their participation by social and familial structures: to ride a scooter—the epitome of mod in the 1960s—was largely deemed unacceptable for girls. Parents assumed that girls did not necessarily need a driver's license and therefore only rarely granted their daughters such a privilege (Smallbone 1996: 50). Already for this reason alone, that is limited mobility and dependence on boys to give them a ride, girls found themselves in a less privileged position to participate in this new youth culture.

Yet, as Smallbone concludes: "Mod women had indeed their own feminine culture within the subculture ..." (1996: 70). Clothing, shopping, listening to music at home or dancing in mod clubs formed a space in which they could forge their own self-portrayal. And the question of belonging to a distinct youth cultural scene, and the ideology of difference, was of equal relevance to boys and girls: "You'd see London Mods and try and match them if you could. No one wanted to be ordinary, you were either a Mod or a Rocker" (Ray, cited in Smallbone 1996: 56). And this question was closely linked to class positioning or aspiration, as Smallbone's interviewed mother recalls: "I was working class but the idea was middle class, the style. It made us feel better, above the rest. We probably thought we were the bees knees" (cited in Smallbone 1996: 53).

Dressing up

Phil Cohen was among the first to analyze the mods' style practices from a socio-logical perspective, conceiving it as a problem-solving strategy working-class kids developed as a way of coping with the economic and cultural changes in the early 1960s:

> [T]he original mod style could be interpreted as an attempt to realise, but in an *imaginary relation* the conditions of existence of the socially mobile white collar worker. While their *argot* and ritual forms stressed many of the traditional values of their parent culture, their dress and music reflected the hedonistic image of the affluent consumer. (Cohen 1972, cited in Clarke, Hall, Jefferson and Roberts 2000: 32)

In this understanding, the mods' clothes were a means to tackle the class structure of post-war Britain. Even if class positioning could not as easily be transgressed in reality, it could at least be visually blurred, whereby the relevance of social background could be downplayed. The focus of their life did not consist of work, education and family, but revolved instead around fashion, music and consumerism. Afternoons were spent in espresso bars and nights and weekends were danced away in clubs. The stamina for a weekend of dancing and shopping often came by way of amphetamines: "their pattern of leisure was exceptionally frenetic; a 'furious consumption programme' which seemed to be the grotesque parody of the aspirations of the Mods' parents" (Radcliffe, cited in Laing 1969: 151). Drawing on Claude Levi-Strauss' concept of bricolage, Dick Hebdige described the mods' approach to fashion and style as intricately subversive: while in step with conventional fashion, they seemed "to consciously invert the values associated with smart dress, to deliberately challenge the assumptions, to falsify the expectations derived from such sources" (Hebdige 2000: 88). Yet, in the view of subcultural theory, their style practice nevertheless remained a merely "magical solution:"

> Sub-cultural strategies cannot match, meet or answer the structuring dimen-sions emerging in this period for the class as a whole ... Thus, in the expropriation and fetishisation of consumption and style itself, the 'Mods' cover for the gap between the never-ending-weekend and Monday's resumption of boring, dead-end work. (Clarke, Hall, Jefferson and Roberts 2000: 47–8)

However, the adoption of less striking clothing when compared to teds and rockers, the ownership of a dozen suits and ties (beyond the Sunday best), perfect haircuts and polished shoes, suggests a certain compliance with middle-class values, made possible by the products of a new consumer culture, in which symbols of *bourgeois* distinction (e.g. the suit) became mass-produced wares (see Kaelble 1997: 175). Even if few of the youths may have had the money or the energy to go out every night or to buy the newest records and clothes on a weekly basis, as their media portrayal suggested, 1960s mods stand for the development of a specific consumer mentality:

> The mods converted themselves into objects, they "chose" (in order) to make themselves into mods, attempting to impose systematic control over a narrow domain which was "theirs", and within which they saw their "real" selves invested—the domain of leisure and appearance, of dress and posture. (Hebdige 1988: 111)

David Laing describes the mods as "consumers for whom the object of consumption was to produce active changes in themselves, to produce themselves as Mods, to 'recover the integral person'" (Laing 1969: 151). From sociological studies and also from many of the interviews with former mods, (see Smallbone 1996; Lentz 2002) it seems that mods largely came from working-class and lower middle-class families. However, the emphasis on class as sole interpretational framework has received much criticism in subculture scholarship, as "there is a tendency to imply, without detail or evidence, that subcultures somehow originated through large numbers of disparate individuals all simultaneously and spontaneously reacting in the same way to ascribed social conditions" (Hodkinson 2002: 11). As historian Arthur Marwick points out: "Youth subculture is not exclusively working class: across classes there is '*potential* idealism,' 'healthy skepticism,' condemnation both of squares and 'the Establishment,' as well as shared enthusiasm for certain kinds of music and certain kinds of fashion" (1998: 64). The interpretational focus on class alone undermines the relevance of other subject positions, which equally shape relationships to dress and fashion, for example gender, as McRobbie and Garber have shown, race or ethnicity. Quite a number of early mods were children of Jewish immigrant families, of whom many formed a part of London's clothing industry, working in or owning tailoring and retail businesses. Terry Rawlings sees in this connection a root of the mods' fetishization of fashion (2000: 49).

Consumer pioneers

The mods are seen as symptomatic of the expanding consumer society in the 1960s, which generated an increasing multiplicity of options for self-fashioning, evolving at an accelerating speed. Yet no matter what background, a decisive prerequisite for the participation in it were certain financial means. "Mod was a product of safety," writes Cohn (1971: 81). Youth either received money from their parents or they drew a decent salary from their jobs. "When they worked they were wealthy; even when they didn't, they collected unemployment benefit" (Cohn 1971: 81). While "wealthy" may be an exaggeration, compared to previous generations teenagers in the 1960s did have considerable financial resources they were able to invest in leisure activities. In contrast to the earlier youth culture of teds, the young people that were part of the mod culture in the 1960s were part of the first generation that had no immediate experience of war or its aftermath. Their childhood and youth were spent under conditions that, for a larger part of the population in Britain, were defined by a growing prosperity and an improved social security—a result of the economic boom in the development of an "affluent society" (Wilson 2005a: 82).

While the everyday lives of most children and youths were until well into the twentieth century devoted to work from an early age on, the time following the

FIGURE 4 A young couple coming out of Mates boutique in Carnaby Street, London 1966. Photo: Ray Roberts/Getty Images.

Second World War brought a large-scale, institutionalized fostering of youth (see Osgerby 2000). In England, the Education Act 1944 was instrumental to these developments, ensuring a wide-ranging reform of the British educational system. School became mandatory for all children, and the minimum age for school leavers was raised to fifteen (Osgerby 2000: 9). The baby boom of the post-war years led the number of teenagers to grow from 3 million in 1951 to over 4 million in 1966, at which point teenagers made up 10 per cent of the British population (Osgerby 2000: 21, n.3). The improved standard of living in the post-war years saw children "growing up faster," as a result of which they were not only in terms of quantity, but also in qualitative terms, perceived as a "distinct younger generation" (Osgerby 2000: 9). Compared to former generations, these youth enjoyed not only more free time, but also a much larger disposable income. Between 1951 and 1961 the unemployment rate shrank to a minimum and the average weekly wage doubled at least for men (Marwick 2003: 88). With the emergence of new professional fields through a shift from the heavy industries to the service sector and consumer goods industry, young people especially could find jobs that barely required any training. It seems that many mods rather sought a quick source of income than a long-term job. Most of them dropped out of school aged fifteen, making their money in retail and in the service industry (Marwick 2003: 20–1, Hebdige 2000: 91).

Mark Abrams' 1959 study on teenage consumers solidifies the image of a "newly affluent body of youngsters patronizing a commercial youth market of remarkable scale" (cited in Osgerby 2000: 11). The marketing specialist calcu-lated that the average income of youths had increased by 50 per cent since 1945, whereby their disposable income, largely spent on specific goods (e.g. 44 per cent on records and record players, 39 per cent on bicycles and motorbikes), had increased by 100 per cent (Abrams 1959: 9–10). While Abrams' study should be approached with caution for its homogenizing tendencies (ignoring regional differences and focusing only on 15–25-year-olds from a predominantly working-class background), it provides insights into the new consumer demographic of teenagers. Particularly male teens enjoyed "a degree of relative prosperity on entering the world of work—an affluence which underpinned an exponential expansion of Britain's commercial youth market" (Osgerby 2000: 12).

The cohort of the first mods—who were teenagers from the end of the 1950s to the mid-1960s—can then to a certain extent be described as consumer pioneers. They were the first to face an expansively developing culture and leisure industry in 1960s Britain and who organized their lives explicitly around consumption (see Luger 1991: 210). With rapid changes in fashion and a continuous demand for the new, the mods represented a brand of consumer that set a pace for the new shops and the fashion industry's increase in production—important factors for the economic boom of the time that contribute to the view on the decade as "golden years" (Hobsbawm 1994: 324ff.). In the 1960s consumption had reached a point where youths aged between 15 and 19 contributed 50 per cent of the fashion industry's turnover (Ewing 1974, cited in Wilson 2005a: 82).

Swinging London

"It is the Mods ... who gave the dress trade the impetus to break through the fast-moving, breathtaking, uprooting revolution in which we have played a part since the opening of Bazaar," recalls Mary Quant (1965: 76–7). The Goldsmiths College-educated designer is, together with her partner Alexander Plunkett Green, considered one of the pioneers of the youth fashion market in Britain. In 1955 she opened her first boutique on London's Kings Road, targeting the new, young consumer segment. As the name "Bazaar" implies, her shop was supposed to encourage browsing and rummaging. The store window was constantly redecorated in imaginative ways to attract the attention of its young clientele (see Ashmore 2006). To shop there was not only to acquire goods, but to be part of an event—a pastime—and to make clothing and shopping part of self-fashioning and identification (see Fogg 2003: 8). Boutiques like Quant's created new and attractive employment opportunities for young people. Sales assistants were important intermediaries showing off the newest styles, thereby acquiring the status of role models, making up for the relatively low salaries. This is also where girls especially had the chance to play an active role in mod culture—not only as consumers, but as workers (McRobbie and Garber 2000: 117).

In Quant's eyes, fashion ceased to be a conveyor of social status or class, assuming that her shop would be frequented by "dukes' daughters" and "dockers' daughters" alike (Quant 1965: 75). Instead of social class, age was to form a new category of social distinction. A slim, youthful body, androgynous and childlike in appearance, became the ideal body image of the mid-1960s. This was also a body dressed in the "uniform of the sixties:" the miniskirt (Seeling 1999: 399; see also Figure 1). Quant's mini fashion, already developed in sketches in the 1950s, was first presented in *Vogue* in 1963. The slender line created by the geometric shape of the clothes stands in stark opposition to women's fashion of the 1950s, which relied on supportive bras, corset belts and petticoats, creating a more voluptuous, hourglass figure. Combined with flat shoes or low heel boots, the mini shifted the focus to the legs. The development of tights, replacing stockings, enabled shorter lengths of skirts, allowing for a (relative) freedom of body movement (Hofmann 2009). In her design for modern clothes, Quant found her inspiration by looking back to fashions of the 1920s, which equally promoted an ideal of young and sporty bodies, conveying a changed representation of femininity. Her clothing was intended to give women a new freedom of movement that would let them be "young, free and dynamic" (Whiteley 1987: 96). Here she borrowed equally from menswear and children's fashion, with fitted suit jackets or skirts that were

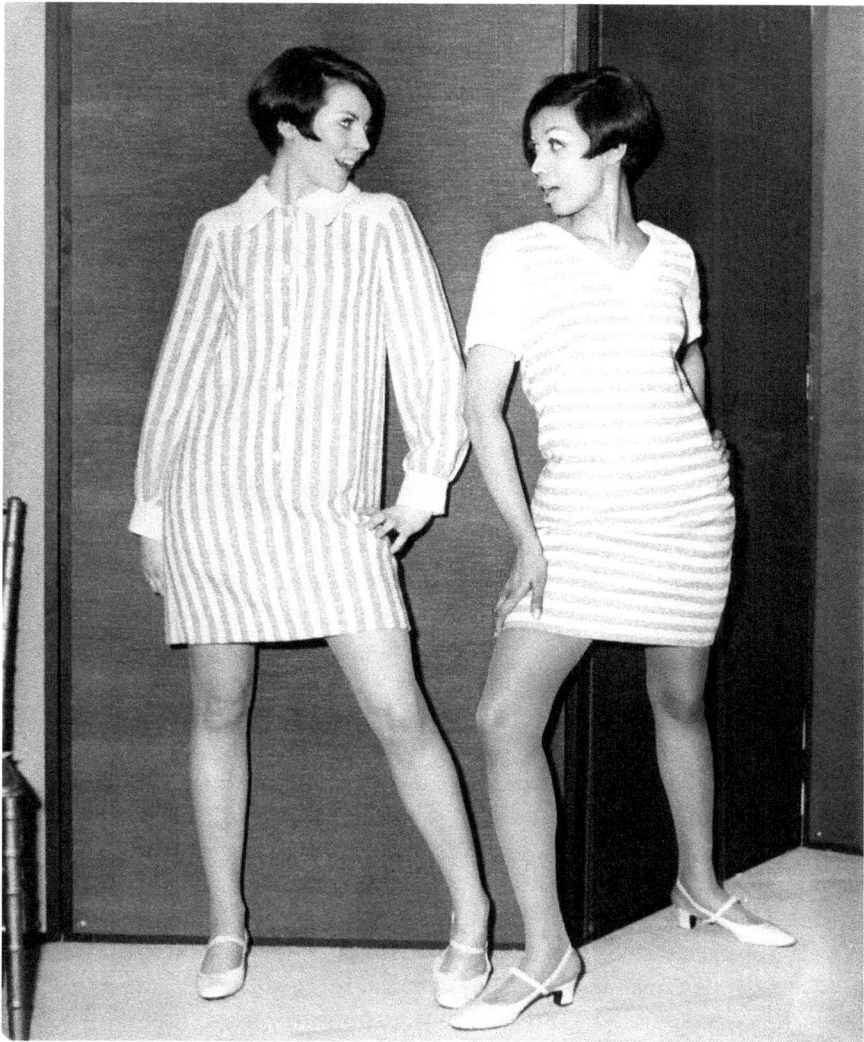

FIGURE 5 Models Jackie Moodie (left) and Faith Ibrahim wearing striped minidresses by Charlotte Warren-Davis at Avantgarde, at the Seekers showrooms in Sloane Street, London 1966. The dresses are from the Autumn and Winter collection 1966. Photo: Keystone/Hulton Archive/Getty Images.

equipped with suspenders. Yet the stress on youthfulness and the tendency towards unisex clothing, or androgyny, also conveyed an infantilization of the female body, as exemplified by Twiggy—model and face of the year 1966.

The miniskirt, which evolved on the level of street fashion as well as designer fashions in London and Paris, has undoubtedly become a sartorial symbol of the sixties (see Figures 1 and 5). Many women who wore it at the time do not necessarily have only positive memories of the miniskirt, but as Viola Hofmann's study of the mini shows, perceived wearing it as uncomfortable and in misfit with their own body image (see Hofmann 2009: 48). Yet it is the clothing item that has become most intricately associated with the social and cultural changes occurring in this decade, particularly with the women's movement: it is seen as epitomizing the "attitudes of an era" (Cawthorne 1999: 108, cited in Hofmann 2009: 35). The mini stands for the idea of a new freedom of movement and for a general sense of euphoria—a narrative that effectively helped to promote the rise of consumer and pop culture, in particular in the British capital branded as "Swinging London."

If Mary Quant is associated with the revolutionizing of 1960s women's wear, the most recognized fashion retailer on the side of menswear is John Stephen, mentioned by Mark Feld in 1962 as a go-to place for mods. Stephen, who had previously worked for menswear pioneer Bill Green's Vince Man's Shop, opened his first store His Clothes on a side street off Carnaby street in 1957 (Cohn 1971: 64–5). As Alistair O'Neill points out, John Stephen has earned a special place in British subcultural history for "offering an accelerated range of choice to young men eager for difference, and for constructing spaces conducive to both shopping and social interaction" (O'Neill 2000: 489). He targeted the younger consumer, just as Mary Quant did: "Because he was young himself, he perceived that basic changes could only come through teenagers. Adults were too scared ever to take a lead; kids had no such inhibitions and Stephen set out to get them" (Cohn 1971: 65). He oriented himself on the colorful range of clothes offered by his previous employer Bill Green, who catered to celebrities and artists, but made sure to undersell him and to produce at a quicker pace in order to keep up with the needs of young consumers. According to Nik Cohn, all "the traditional standards—wear, finish, craftsmanship—were made secondary to the instant, and he changed styles monthly, weekly, even daily" (Cohn 1971: 65–6). As with many of the new boutiques, his success—and speed—relied on the close connection between retail and garment manufacturing in London at the time, enabling the fast paced production of fashion styles (Breward 2006: 19). Stephen was so successful that he was able to expand rapidly: By 1961, he owned four shops on Carnaby Street alone (Cohn 1971: 66). By 1963, he owned eighteen boutiques in and around London— the *Daily Mirror* branded him "King of Carnaby Street" and the *Observer* referred to him as the "Million Pound Mod" (Cohn 1971: 69).

With his Carnaby Street boutiques, Stephen made men's shopping a social event and experience. Young people could leisurely stroll down the street, their music blaring from the shops, luring them inside with colorful, unusual window displays and clothes hanging in the entrance, blown about by the wind (Cohn 1971: 66). Carnaby Street became a magnet for fashion-conscious youths. Though John Stephen's shops remained dominant in the street, a number of other boutiques soon followed suit, such as Paul's Male Boutique or Lord John (Cohn

1971: 70, see also Figure 2). In the period from 1962 to 1966, Carnaby Street, which had once been lined almost entirely by tobacconists, reached its zenith. It evolved into an energy-laden fashion center that soon started attracting attention on a national and international scale (Breward 2006: 19).

Many photos show celebrity mods, such as members of The Small Faces, shopping on Carnaby Street. The band even played a gig in front of Stephen's shop—in exchange for a more generous credit for clothes (see Rawlings 2000: 124). Film and music stars shared the street with thousands of youths. According to Nik Cohn, the street was packed on Saturday afternoons: "everyone shopped there: everyone, as they say, who was anyone" (Cohn 1971: 70). The street represented all that was new and lively and that made it widely attractive beyond the city's boundaries. The shopping destination for extravagant young men with a sense of "difference" slowly but surely developed into a tourist attraction, and it became a symbol of a newly affluent England. By 1966, Carnaby Street had become fundamental to the image of a "Swinging London." American journalists famously branded the British capital "The Swinging City" on a vibrant cover of New York's *Time Magazine* on April 15, 1966. The magazine portrayed London as the city of the decade (see Breward 2006: 8), radically changed into a lively, colorful and creative metropolis that had overcome the effects of the preceding three decades, marked by war, poverty and economic depression. It thus helped generate an image of time, and place, that would come to persist and circulate in cultural memory and add to the color of the clothing associated with it.

Pop

In his comprehensive study on 1960s Britain, historian Arthur Marwick points out that most cultural movements and counter-movements that lay at the center of this period were from the outset linked to entrepreneurial structures such as boutiques, record stores, cafes and discotheques (Marwick 1998: 13). The many complex relations and links between youth and subcultures, the fashion industry and the music industry show that youth cultures never stand entirely opposed to so-called "mainstream culture," but rather that they evolve together. This is particularly so in the case of mod youth culture, which, while it was driven to be "different," created a style that fully identified with the "modernity" of new fashion, consumer and pop culture, rather than claiming to stand outside it.

The persisting image or idea of Swinging London, to which youth consumer culture was such an integral part, is perhaps, nonetheless, still grounded in a kind of disassociation from commerce and an idealization of originality and creativity. According to Caroline Evans, the "association of British fashion with youth culture is one of the sources of a widely held belief that it is more creative but less commercial than fashion in any other country" (Evans 2010: 214). The boom of the youth market in London, that forms an economic backdrop to the image of Swinging London, was made possible through a closely tied network of the art scene, art and design students, retail, music and fashion publishing (Evans 2010: 215). In the 1960s, art played an important role for this merging of the creative and commercial spheres, while still trying to uphold a distance between both.

"'Art' was one aspect of a new cultural spectrum shaped by youth, technological and ethical change and the impact of American culture and 'permissiveness'" (Curtis 2004: 74). Not only were artists involved in fashion, and consumer culture and fashion integrated into art, but the daily praxis of fashion became artistic praxis, in the sense of Warhol's "everyone is an artist." In 1967, novelist Angela Carter remarked on fashion in mid-1960s London: "Fashion today (real fashion, what real people wear) is a question of style ... the presentation of the self as a three-dimensional art object, to be wondered at and handled. And this involves a new attitude to the self which is thus adorned" (Carter 1982: 85–90, cited in Evans 2004: 133).

The popular image of "the sixties" is dominated by the primary colorfulness and the boldness, rich contrasts, seriality and gloss of pop. Pop is not only onomatopoeic, but also an abbreviation of "popular," "population" and "populace." Andy Warhol and The Velvet Underground provide concrete examples for the alliance between pop art and pop music, as does the legendary album cover by Peter Blake for the Beatles' 1967 album *Sgt. Pepper's Lonely Hearts Club Band*, which, in its use of historical phantasy uniforms on the cover, played an important role in triggering an interest in outmoded fashion styles (see Figure 8) and vintage clothes and retro in the 1960s (Baker 2013: 59).

According to Osterwold, pop art became "the central stylistic concept of the Pop scene and a synonym for the cultural movement of the period in general" (1992: 71). It became a dominant artistic current of the 1960s and, in hindsight, it may be seen as the decade's most long-lasting aesthetic impulse: "The subject matter, forms and media of Pop Art reveal the essential characteristics of a cultural atmosphere and way of life we associate with the sixties" (Osterwold 1992: 6). Its motifs were immediately sourced from advertising as well as the objects and media of mass consumer culture, elevating and stylizing them to modern icons, such as Andy Warhol's portraits of Hollywood stars, dollar bills or soup cans. Writing in 1967, Richard Hamilton, artist and professor of industrial design at the Royal College of Art, defined pop art as "popular, transient, expendable, low-cost, mass-produced, young, witty, sexy, gimmicky, glamorous, and Big Business" (Hamilton 1982: 28, cited in Stephens and Stout 2004: 11).

Given the context of the 1960s, fashion provided an ideal partner for pop art and the ideas underpinning it, many of them based on the machine-based serial manifestations of modern consumer and media culture. And, conversely, pop art's portrayal of the world of commodities complemented fashion. A good example is the use of Jasper Johns' target motif, adopted by the British pop artist Peter Blake

FIGURE 6 The Who live on stage with Pete Townshend wearing Union Jack jacket and doing "windmill" arm, 1966. Photo: Chris Morphet/Redferns.

in 1961. By the mid-1960s the military target motif, displayed in different color combinations, though principally held in the national colors of the Royal Air Force, became a trademark for pop art fashion and an emblem of mod culture and "Swinging London." By that time, mod and pop were almost synonymous with each other: "Mod became a blanket term for both male and female Pop fashions" (Whiteley 1987: 101).

The band The Who, with their 1965 pop/mod anthem "My Generation," defined themselves as a total pop art experience: "pop-art clothes, pop-art music and pop-art behaviour ... We live pop-art" (Whiteley 1987: 126). (Pete Townsend would smash his guitar during shows, thereby referencing Gustav Metzger's lectures at Ealing College on auto-destructive art.) The band popularized pop art insignia such as the target and the Union Jack (inspired by Johns' US flag), and turned them into sartorial objects: the Union Jack was transformed into a Union

Jacket (see Figure 6), becoming the icon of British pop culture *par excellence*, one that remains eminently citable.

This refashioning of the national symbol into a component of youth fashion was an ironic take and an attack on the "emblems of British respectability" (see Buruma 2000: 15), yet at the same time, they came to symbolize a renewed image of British identity in the context of the 1960s.

Barry Curtis deems the art of the 1960s to be a living component of a widespread "iconography of innovation" (Curtis 2004), which finds its embodiment in fashion by virtue of the impact of striking designs and the colors, shapes and materials of space age, op and pop art design (see also Breward 2006: 14). "Pop relied on making a large initial impact; its inevitable corollary was small sustaining power. Bright colour, fashionable patterns, bold designs, eccentric, even anti-ergonomic shapes—were all used to capture attention and announce the owner's up-to-dateness" (Whiteley 1987: 6). The kind of star-like self-performance is in step with the "society of the spectacle" spellbound by "intangible as well as tangible things" (Debord 2000: 17). As Guy Debord put it in 1967: "The spectacle cannot be understood as a mere visual deception produced by mass media technologies. It is a worldview that has actually been materialised, a view of a world that has become objective" (2000: 7).

The visual culture of pop is part of the creation of a time image that is both clear and opaque, in which extraordinary and visually stunning forms overshadow the ordinary, so that the former are the ones that tend to crystallize as signs of the times: "The unmodulated brightness of primary colors in Pop Art … the intentional tackiness of plastic shoes and vinyl couture … the mini skirts … the glittering metal segments and plastic buttons … Space age outfits—all of these rather garish visual details retrospectively illustrate the Sixties" (Friedl 2001: 61).

The transformation of modernists

Farid Chenoune has referred to the period between 1961 and 1963 as a "golden age for mods" (1995: 253), when the style was largely restricted to local youth groups in and around London. Per George Melly, the style began to transform by 1963:

> [T]he main thing about the first mods was that they were true purists. Clothes were their only interest, but at the same time, in that they were forerunners of a general trend, they carried with them their own destruction. As the "mod" thing spread it lost its purity. (Melly 1989: 169)

Speaking in hindsight, the once mod Johnny Moke states: "From then on, 1964/65 it wasn't Modernism anymore, it was something different. Attitudes changed

FIGURE 7 Mods on scooters wearing parka coats in the entrance to the Scene Club in London *c.*1964. Photo: David Redfern/Redferns.

within and without, it wasn't being modern. It was more towards being a member of a gang and that's not what we were all about" (as cited in Rawlings 2000: 74). As Green notes, once mod was widely adopted, the style underwent a shift in meaning and established itself as a kind of "uniform," whereas "for the pioneer Mod it was alteration. Clothes not as some kind of tribal totem, but clothes as clothes" (Green 1998: 41). Yet this precise dating of the style is likely only accurate for the city, or more specifically, London. In other British cities, changes in fashion could take up to ten years to percolate: "even Liverpool in the sixties, when the Beatles were emerging and the city had become the center of world teenage myth, used clothes that had already passed out of fashion in London" (Cohn 1970: 3).

The expansion of the style occurred already with the mobility of mods on their scooters (see Figure 7), which allowed them to make group-daytrips to the seaside resorts in South England. Here the interaction between locals and tourists conveyed important information about fashion and youth cultural developments, where London youths were taken to be leaders in style. Yet, the mods' weekend meet-ups at the seaside were also what led to a change of the mod youth culture, when reports of violent clashes between mods and rockers in English resorts made the news in 1964. In his 1973 book *Folk Devils and Moral Panics: The Creation of*

Mods and Rockers, Stanley Cohen provides a critical study of the "seaside riots" phenomenon and recounts how the press stirred up the rivalry between the two groups. The press' negative reporting and labeling of mods led to a tarnishing of their public image and to polarization within youth cultures of mods vs. rockers, which turned into a self-fulfilling prophecy. However, many of those involved in the clashes were just regular kids who, attracted by the media image, came to join the ranks of mods—or of their "rivals." What developed in conjunction with those media reports, nonetheless, was a persisting image of mods that is likely more engrained in popular memory than the mods' careful attention to clothing details: youths in Army parkas on chrome laden scooters who invade seaside resorts on weekends to stage punch-ups with rockers.

Beyond the news reportage, the television music program *Ready Steady Go!* was another form of media for the distribution of mod culture. Dick Hebdige argues that the program both popularized and "defused" mod culture (1974: 1). The show, presented by Keith Fordyce and Cathy McGowan, first aired on British television in 1963 and was typically broadcast on Fridays under the slogan "the weekend starts here"—just hours before young people would make their way out to the dance clubs. Many of the bands that played in London clubs made their first TV appearance on this show. *Ready Steady Go!* staged a party in which youths from the London mod scene could be seen in the newest clothes and performing the latest dance routines, thus accelerating the popularity of their styles (see Barnes 1991: 123; Lentz 2002: 28).

While at the beginning of the 1960s mod style was according to Dick Hebdige restricted to "working class teenagers who lived mainly in London and the new towns of the South and who could be readily identified by characteristic hairstyles, clothing etc." (Hebdige 2000: 87), by 1964 it had become so popular that "mod" was synonymous with the young and dynamic fashion of Carnaby Street, the myth of "Swinging London" and the pop culture associated with it (Hebdige 2000: 87; Whiteley 1987: 101).

The expansion of mod style, however, led also to new youth cultural styles. In 1965 John Simons opened the Ivy Shop in Richmond, which specialized in importing American clothes. The vocabulary of modern clothing of the time consisted of an array of clothes that are now considered classics: American button-down shirts, polo shirts, Levi's jeans and Sta-Prest trousers, loafers, brogues, Harrington jackets and bomber jackets. The brand John Simons remains a retailer for such clothes until today. Ben Sherman is another important brand that launched in the 1960s, starting out with the production of Brooks Brothers style shirts in Brighton (Hewitt 2000: 99–100). Sherman provided the clothes that would become part of the youth cultural style labeled "skinhead" by the *Daily Mirror* in 1969 (Hewitt 2000: 80). The fashion and music markets were also increasingly influenced by American trends that made their way to England on the back of hippie culture. Elements of mod style lived on in hippie, psychedelic, skinhead and rude boy youth culture and were picked up by the Northern Soul movement in the north of England. In addition, many youth who got involved in mod culture during the 1960s maintained their style over a long time, even until today (see Feldman 2009; Weight 2013). Yet, during the later 1960s the style started to disappear from public attention, until its re-emergence in the following decade.

Youth recollecting the past

As fashion scholar Alistair O'Neill notes, "It is generally agreed that around 1965, as with other areas of pop culture, the demand for ever-evolving newness forced a distraction from innovation and invention towards a plundering and interpretation of historical styles" (O'Neill 2000: 497). It is this time context in which Elizabeth Guffey locates the beginning of a culture of revival (Guffey 2006). Through an appropriation of style elements from the Regency era, the earlier historic references to dandyism became strengthened by 1966 and fused with hippie and psychedelic elements. The multiple sartorial references to the past brought about an eclectic historical mixing of frilly shirts, velvet suits, Victorian haircuts, "oriental" gowns, and pop-arty patterns and fancy dress uniforms. The resources for this style were provided by the new second-hand boutiques that were part of the boom of London's new fashion scene. Among them was the store Granny Takes a Trip, promoted in a 1967 city guide to sell "Naughty Nineties" clothes such as ostrich feathered hats, granny shoes and Army redcoats (Hallaz 1967: 119, cited in Samuel 2012: 89). Christopher Breward sees the store as the "most politicized" of the new London fashion outlets: by selling old clothes it "seemed to undermine and critique the shiny consumerist rhetoric put in place by Quant while covertly pursuing its own version of remunerative supply" (Breward 2004: 61). He cites former store owner Nigel Weymouth who recalls going down to Kensington Church Street Market and Portobello Road to collect old clothes, coming up with the idea of opening a shop, which would become a space in which the old takes on a new value—and a new ephemerality: "We started off exclusively with old clothes: rather nice beaded dresses, blazers, all that sort of camp nonsense. That was fun ... The whole point was just to keep it change, change, change" (cited in Green 1999: 80–1, cited in Breward 2004: 62).

Another store was I was Lord Kitchener's Valet on both Portobello Road and Carnaby Street. The name was inspired by the clothing from the Victorian and Edwardian eras in which the store specialized, including military uniforms and liveries, which due to their mass-production survived in great number into the post-war time. Robert Orbach, former director of the store, notes in an interview in 2006 that the store's name "conjured up images of Edwardian smoking jackets, top hats and canes ... pure nostalgia" (Victoria and Albert Museum 2006). In the

FIGURE 8 Outside of the boutique I was Lord Kitchener's Valet in London's Portobello Road 1967. Photo: Hulton Archive/Getty Images.

mid-1960s, as Orbach goes on, "it was only fifty or so years from Victorian times, when we had an empire. We used to buy fur coats by the bale ... we had to throw quite a lot away" (Victoria and Albert Museum 2006). While paired with a sense of irony, for Ian Buruma the retro style fashioned by many British pop bands, popularizing the look in the 1960s, was a melancholic re-enactment of an "aristocratic" form of hedonism. For him these performances seemed as if:

> [A] generation of working-class children had raided a vast stately home and dressed up in the master's old clothes. When British pop stars struck it rich, many of them bought stately homes and lived like stoned lords and ladies. This gave them a sense of style ... It was theatrical, nostalgic, ironic, exciting, and intensely commercial. (Buruma 2000: 15–16)

The sartorial recourse to the national fashion history was paired with influences from abroad. The Beatles' 1967 *Sgt. Pepper's Lonely Hearts Club Band* album, and the style of the band that borrowed by that time heavily from the clothing styles of other cultures and countries, such as kaftans from North Africa or embroidered tunics from India, were an important catalyst for the spreading of a more eclectic fashion style in the late 1960s (Victoria and Albert Museum 2006). Sonia Ashmore cautions to see the use of "ethnic dress" not only as a designer or street-style led phenomenon, but as a practice emerging through "less predictable routes and cultural milieus" in the context of decolonization (Ashmore 2006: 201). The style is in part linked to a move towards multiculturalism and resistance, for example in the context of the American hippie movement that made a stand against political and social conditions, including sexism and racism, and protested with the slogan "make love not war" against the Vietnam War. They also defied mass-consumerism (see Welters 2008: 19–20), and strove for a peaceful, spiritual and more nature-loving existence, with empathy for Native Americans and also the rural movement (Ashmore 2006: 213). However, "ethnic dress" in the context of the 1960s also comes to serve, as noted in one fashion magazine, as a "tranquil alternative to Western fashion" (*Nova*, March 1971, cited in Ashmore 2006: 204). Conceived as "ethnic" dress, it is not seen as "fashion:" that is, not tied to continuous newness or the pressures of "seasonal correctness" (Ashmore 2010: 110). "Othered," or denied "coevalness" (Fabian 2002; van de Peer 2014: 332) as standing outside "Western" fashion time, these clothes become "timeless" and thus suited to counter-cultural desires to resist consumer culture's promotion of newness.

Both of these practices, historical and geographical fashion revivals, have long histories (see Burman-Baines 1981), yet it can be argued that it is especially in the context of the 1960s expansion of youth and consumer culture that newness in fashion becomes in a way recoded to include not only the newly produced but also the old, but newly bought. It is the development of the early second-hand boutiques that specifically target the young "affluent" consumer, not least those who have a choice between wearing old and new clothes, and, in the words of Anne Hollander, the "great costume party of the sixties" (1979), that form a ground for the rise of old clothes to vintage—as fashionable memory modes.

Sixties staying on

Historians date the end of the "long sixties" in the year 1973 (Hobsbawm 1994) or 1974 (Marwick 1998). Many historical events and developments have impacted a wider temporal shift throughout the 1960s, in particular the civil rights movement and the student movement, as well as the rise of youth and consumer culture. The oil crisis in 1973, and the worldwide recession it fomented, is identified as one crucial event that has made the end of the sixties—and an associated enthusiasm for modernity—most notably felt. Yet the products of the decade's consumer culture and its overproduction of fast changing, fashionable commodities stayed on, and the leftovers formed resources for the following generation of youth. The expansion of the youth market, including subcultural niche markets evolving for example with hippies setting up stalls at flea markets, integrated the use of second-hand clothes as an alternative fashion (see McRobbie 1994). As much as youth in the previous two decades, such as the New Edwardians in the late 1940s and 1950s (Breward 2002), or the mods and hippies in the 1960s utilized previous forms of fashion, so did youth in the 1970s unpack the clothing delivered by the past. Style commentator Peter York pinpoints the summer of 1976 as the beginning of the mod revival (York 1980: 201), developing on the back of punk culture. For Joe Foster of the band TV Personalities it was:

> that pop art thing, an affectation almost, dressing up to annoy other art students. They'd all show up with fake dreadlocks and you turn up looking like Brian Jones, it really pisses them off. We couldn't afford to do the full thing on student grants, but it was good enough. (Foster, cited in Lentz 2002: 63)

Many of the punk rock bands that were formed at the time—from Blondie to The Ramones, Generation X or The Buzzcocks—made references to former music and fashion styles. Even the Sex Pistols, at their early concerts, played their own cover versions of The Small Faces and The Who (Lentz 2002: 61). From 1977 and 1978 onwards, a number of new mod bands emerged from the punk scene, such as The Chords (York 1980: 201), The Jam, TV Personalities and the Purple Hearts, who sported an all-round 1960s style and played on the arrogant attitude associated with early mod (Rawlings 2000: 171).

In contrast to the "golden years," however, the youth of the 1970s found themselves in a different social and political climate, with the sense of optimism associated with the 1960s gone and the economic boom replaced by a rising unemployment rate. The punk's much-cited phrase "no future" is a pledge to abandon the belief in social progress, and any well-meaning programs of socio-pedagogical reform for youths (Baacke 1999: 75). In this period, in which no politician would have dared to claim that you "never had it so good," as Conservative Prime Minister Harold Macmillan did in 1957, the new generation of mods no longer wore tailor-made clothes, they were simply unaffordable to them by that point (Rawlings 2000: 160). Before fashion companies began to imitate the style of the sixties, most 1970s mods bought their clothes second-hand or from surplus stock. With their old shops and second-hand stores, streets like Brick Lane or Petticoat Lane, which bore little resemblance to the spectacle of 1960s Carnaby Street, became the "high streets" of the new mod generation:

The shops looked and smelled condemned, the front windows were filthy and forever declaring a closing down sale … Old stock, battered boxes of button down shirts in perishing cellophane wrappers and covered in dust, windcheaters, crew necks and turtle necks. There wasn't much of it but it was there, dirty and unforgotten and unwanted. (Rawlings 2000: 159)

From a 1970s perspective, recourse to clothing from the 1960s was likely seen as a kind of affront to the prevailing fashion taste. In its narrow fit and rather minimal style, it was stylistically distinct from the emerging disco fashion with flares and wide lapels. If one follows fashion historian James Laver and his "cycle of taste," fashion becomes "ridiculous" ten years after its introduction, reaching the level of hideousness fifteen years after its heyday (Laver 1937: 255). Clothing items such as jackets whose lapels "did not touch the shoulders" (Rawlings 2000: 159), but were narrow and complemented with a slim tie, had a differentiating effect due to their "obsoleteness," perhaps especially from a perspective of the generation, remembering wearing the style not only when it was "in" the first time, but also when it got outmoded and discarded by them. Notwithstanding, the style once again developed into a wider phenomenon, culminating in a mod revival that started to peak towards the end of the decade. In 1979 Peter York notes:

There *is* a Mod revival going on, and kids are turning over to the style—an easy uniform of parkas and Fred Perrys and Hush Puppies that freezes five years of subtle change into one big Brighton Beach frame. It has been working through for a year and *Quadrophenia* has brought more. (York 1980: 203)

York lists several reasons that led to the revival of mod style at that time. The perhaps most obvious is that youths liked the style and that it represented for them a fit with their own identity, but he also notes the impact of the generation of those who never ceased being mods, that is, those who continued to belong to scooter clubs or who formed part of the skinhead or Northern Soul scenes. As a result, new mods mingled with their elders (York 1980: 204).

Furthermore, as York notes, record labels such as Polydor cannot be under-estimated. With several of the mod bands like The Who, The Jam and The Chords on their books, they specifically marketed to youths on the back of the movie *Quadrophenia*, released in 1979. The movie, based on The Who's 1973 album, is set in the year 1964 in the context of the Brighton "seaside riots" between mods and rockers. It is an intriguing story about youth cultural identity struggles that came embedded in a hybrid soundtrack of 1960s soul and R&B music and compositions of The Who.

While York points to the role of music, it is not least important the role of images that sparks interest in the past. The 1960s have produced a particular rich material culture tied up with the rise of media and consumer culture that makes the appearance of the past easily accessible and forms, beyond the direct inter-generational transmission of memory, part of an expanding cultural memory—not only of the further away past, as Jan Assmann (1995) defines cultural memory, but also of the very recent, mediated past (see Erll 2010; Zierold 2010: 401).

> Television shows, even puppet TV shows, as well as 1960s movies such as Blow Up and, of course, all the old James Bond films, were continually raided by the "new" stylists in search of ideas. Paul Weller, for example, joined this rush in the early 1980s and uncovered old pieces of 1960s "mod" clothing. (McRobbie 1994: 147)

Paul Weller, at the time lead singer and guitarist of The Jam, attributes his interest in mod style directly to music, and the corresponding imagery, which served for him also as a rejection of the musical vanguard of the time: "I first became interested in the early '60s Mods in late 1974 … I think it was probably through seeing a photograph of a group … The most important aspect was the music of the '70s: I hated all of it …" (Weller 1981: 33). The "uncovering" or recollecting relies on the images, objects and memories with which "the sixties" can come to move beyond their historical context, or their "happening" in time and place, and be "worn" by following generations in other times and places: a theme I will turn to in the next three chapters focusing on the practices, experiences and perspectives of sixties and vintage enthusiasts in Germany in the early twenty-first century.

4 STYLE NARRATIVES: SIXTIES IN THE TWENTY-FIRST CENTURY

Sixties discoveries: Music and style

> For me, music is really important and it all goes together. That's sort of how you start identifying with it. And you do get—you feel something in the music and I think that's how it all happened. (m. 24)

Music has been described by many of the sixties enthusiasts I interviewed to be at the core of, if not initiating, their interest in the sixties, indicating the significant role music plays in the development of style. Music affects our body, moving inside from the outside. Dieter Baacke describes it as a phenomenon that "storms our senses"—one that penetrates and moves the body, it drives our corporeality and expression, it gets us to dance, to tap with our feet, or to calm down and relax. Musical experience can be understood as a deeply existential experience of being in the world, or in the words of Baacke as a "*gestaltdurchdringende Existenzerfahrung*" (Baacke 1997: 13). This means that music is not a partial segment of culture, but an all-encompassing spectrum of life experience. It is rhythmic, affective and socially symbolic, providing frameworks for identification or orientation (Baacke 1997: 14).

Music encompasses a wide field of aesthetic experience, including experiences that transcend beyond the "here and now" of the moment of listening, for example through memory, imagination, dreaming and fantasy (Baacke 1997: 10). For memory, music plays a very significant role, because in its affect on body and mind it is an experience that transgresses time and place. The making of music is inherently bound up with time or temporality, produced through sounds arranged in a rhythmical combination. In our sensory perception of it, music fills our "real" and "virtual" time spaces. It arouses our imagination and conjures up certain worlds of imagery. Musical experience is increasingly visual; it is not just a world of sound, but a visual manifestation. Baacke describes it as the amalgamation of a comprehensive work of art, a *Gesamtkunstwerk* (Baacke 1997: 13). This is particularly so with regard to modern music, that is recorded in audio and visual media. According to Lawrence Grossberg, "rock has always been more than just a soundtrack, more than just 'the noise' … It has involved images, and the memory of a song is always partly visual as well" (Grossberg 1993: 188). Through audio and visual records, the sound and look of the past circulate widely beyond the time context when they were produced, enabling listeners and viewers to enter into a sensuous exchange with the past. This is how listening to music can be seen as a kind of time travel that can transport us into a directly perceptible remembered or imagined world of the past in the present. Music endows this world with a vivid soundtrack or soundscape, so that the past feels present in an affective audio-visual dimension.

FIGURE 9 Record cover of The Manchesters, Diplomat Records *c.*1965. © 2015, Inspired Studios, Inc. All rights reserved.

With music as a form of cultural memory, the images with which it is often associated are those of the musical performers, or the "stars" of the time, where memory can even be sparked by small traces of the past, including haircuts (see Figure 9).

They can be seen on record covers, in stage performances, in films, on YouTube or on television, where music is enacted and "dressed up" (see Miller 2011). As Grossberg notes, fans "have learned to dance from television; they have learned how to dress and act; they have learned new organizations of desire and emotion, and sometimes they have found new objects and narratives of those desires and emotions" (Grossberg 1993: 189). How tightly the experience of music is interwoven with practices of dressing is further emphasized by fashion scholar Patrizia Calefato: "Fashion and music are two intimately connected forms of worldliness, two social practices that go hand in hand, sustaining one another in the forms of mass-communication and drawing on a common sensibility which translates into taste" (Calefato 2004: 117). This power of music, its imagery and translation to dress, is apparent in a sixties-styler's account of his first record that he inherited from his parent, showing how the past is here not only transmitted through mediated memory, but also through direct inter-generational exchange. The record got him hooked on the sixties, and influenced his clothing practices— yet the interest in the sixties was further reinforced in relation to other youth in the 1980s:

It all started with music. I got a record player early on and a pile of singles. As a kid I listened to Schlager [German popular folk music], but at one point, I remember a Beatles single. My mum took it away. I bought one myself with my first pocket money. It was "I am a Loser" and from then on I couldn't stop listening to the Beatles. That's when I wanted to dress like them, to grow my hair long. I somehow managed to scrape together some cash for a suit, had the lapel cut off, and Chelsea boots. And then my Dad gave me a shoebox full of singles that he wanted rid of. The first one I took out was "My Generation." That's when it all went bonkers. Then I wanted a guitar, wanted to make music, everything depended on it. Then I saw the guys from Düsseldorf riding around on scooters, something I already liked as a small child, and then I saved some cash for a scooter and then, all of a sudden, I was part of it. (m. 30)

Music forms a substantial part of the socialization of young people and as such it is an important framework of social orientation, one through which youth cultural affiliations and popcultural (Fiske 1997) or subcultural (Thornton 1995) capital is acquired. Birgit Richard describes music as the most important element of style: it is the aesthetic and cultural core of many youth and subcultures (Richard 1995: 102). This is already evident in the way that many youth cultures acquired their name via music, such as swing kids or the mods, linked to modern jazz, as well as later emerging genres such as punk, hip-hop or techno (Hitzler, Bucher and Niederbacher 2001: 35). The importance of music in the context of youth cultural styles thereby has a wider historical dimension, where the many styles that have developed and diversified since the post-war time function today as a form of youth cultural heritage. While heritage is usually understood as a more place (and nation) bound concept, it can function in the context of youth cultural or subcultural identities in a similar way, as an anchor or a form of legitimization through "roots" in the past that become important in contemporary processes of identity formation (see Macdonald 2013: 109–36). Where mod style may be seen as a "very British style" (Weight 2013), it is a transnational phenomenon that circulates widely beyond 1960s London or Britain (see Feldman 2009), in particular via music, and its imagery. Before turning to the practices of clothing among sixties stylers in the early twenty-first century in Germany, one location of this transnational style, it is important to consider the history of mod in that country.

Mod in West Germany

In 1960s Germany, mod did not garner the same kind of attention it received in England, where, in its association with "Swinging London" and newspaper reports on "seaside riots" between mods and rockers, mod became a media sensation as well as a national icon for the rise of post-war prosperity (see Weight 2013). Yet the modern look of clothing preferred by the British mods existed in other countries as well, and even inspired the look of the British mods in the first place. In his historical study of menswear Farid Chenoune refers for example to the style of the *minets* in France, a group of youth who embraced fashion consumption with an equal enthusiasm as British mods, but who came from a more wealthy family background (Chenoune 1995: 263). Similarly Hiroshi Narumi (2010) describes style practices similar to mods in 1960s Japan.

Dieter Baacke, one of the first sociologists to study youth cultural styles and identities in Germany, includes in his early book *Beat* (1972) a very brief definition of mods: noting that mods are from a predominantly lower middle-class background and like to meet at parties, they can be recognized by their particularly fashionable "twen clothing," which is "symbolic" to them (1972: 22). He includes this short description in a list of other youth cultures he sees prevalent in 1960s Germany, such as rockers, hippies and deadbeats (*Gammler*), which gives an indication of the impact international styles had on German youth.

In America, shortly before the surge of hippie culture, "mod" was marketed in conjunction with the rise of "Beatlemania," which from 1964 onwards impacted youth culture on an international level. The music was closely tied to the marketing of London-based designers and triggered a boom of youthful "Britishness" (Steele

1997: 55–60). The fan culture for the Beatles existed alongside the mod movement and both were frequently seen as one and the same phenomenon. However, the Beatles and the Mersey beat scene, a Liverpool and Merseyside phenomenon, were never fully embraced by the early British mod scene, in part due to its wide commercial success and, possibly, due to its largely female fan base. The music of the Beatles was also not directly targeted to a mod audience as was the music of The Who or The Small Faces, bands that were celebrated by the mods. The distance between beat and mod is also evident in the 1964 movie *A Hard Day's Night*, when Ringo Starr is asked whether he is a mod or a rocker, to which he responds that he is a "mocker," thus ironically rejecting the identification with either of the two styles that have hit the news in that same year (Steele 1997: 56).

In Germany, as in America, the music of the Beatles had a great impact on youth, especially considering that the band had a strong relationship to the country fostered by several longer concert bookings at nightclubs in Hamburg prior to their wide international success in 1964 (see Feldman 2009: 60). In addition, Stuart Sutcliff, part of the early Beatles, had a German fiancée, Astrid Kirchherr, who helped to shape the Beatles' look during the time of their early concerts in Hamburg (Feldman 2009: 71). Due to its location, and its important shipping harbor and long trading history, the northern German city of Hamburg had always been in a closer spatial and cultural proximity to the British Isles. The influence of Britain on the northern parts of West Germany was reinforced in the time following Germany's defeat in the Second World War when British armed forces were stationed in the northwestern parts of the country. When Berlin was separated from the rest of the country during the Cold War, and West Germany was without a major capital, Hamburg was one of the cities that played a key role in cultural exchange. It was a city that held a certain cosmopolitan flair due to its history as a center for international trade, as well as its thriving cultural scene and nightlife brimming with well-established nightclubs and music venues, such as the Indra Musikclub in St. Pauli, where the Beatles played in 1960 and the "beat entered the continent" (www.indramusikclub.com).

In addition to many British bands playing live gigs in the Hamburg clubs, it was the impact of foreign radio stations, specifically the British Forces Broadcasting Service, that played a major role in popularizing the sound of British music acts in Germany. As Christine Feldman notes in her transnational history of the mod youth culture, the British bands and pop culture of the early 1960s played a crucial role in the formation of post-war German youth culture (Feldman 2009: 65). The path for this had already been carved out a few decades earlier, as the example of German swing kids shows, who countered the conformity imposed by the national-socialist regime by wearing English style clothing and listening to "foreign" music (see Savage 2007: 379–80). Another example is the impact of American popular culture through Hollywood movies and Rock 'n' Roll music, popularized in Germany through the music of Elvis, Bill Haley and The Comets, and the movie *Rock Around the Clock*. Yet as Feldman's study, and her interviews with former youth of the 1960s, show, it is the narrative of modernity and youth as new beginnings, tied to the British sound and style of the 1960s, which made it such an ideal fit for the urge among youth in Germany to differentiate themselves from their own country's national-socialist past, and from the parental generation that had served in or lived through it (Feldman 2009: 64–5).

The country's history under National Socialism continues to deeply impact the memory and sense of identity of Germans until today, yet, particularly during the decades immediately following the totalitarian regime, Feldman argues that many youth were especially eager to embrace "all things foreign" (Feldman 2009: 65) to disassociate themselves from the history of fascism passed on to them. British beat and pop music, as well as the associated fashion style sported by respective bands and promoted in German youth magazines, provided an important means for this. While some scholars have seen German youths for their adoption of British and American styles as just "passive recipients" (Müller-Bachmann 2002: 59) of foreign youth innovations, such a perspective undermines that the style of the mods was in itself made up of a variety of cultural influences. In order to be "modern," British youths looked equally beyond their own national boundaries for sources of identification, generating a hybrid style that fused elements from American modern jazz musicians or from Jamaican and Italian immigrant youth to fashion themselves as modern, forward thinking and cosmopolitan. For German youth, adopting a style that was seen as part of an international, modern youth movement opened up a way to establish, at least to a certain extent, a sense of an alternative or more modern, transnational identity. This tendency is also evident in the context of youth and post-adolescents who took on the style of the sixties and British mods in later decades of the twentieth century and early twenty-first century following the revival of the mod style in the 1970s and 1980s. Yet, this desire was particularly heightened among post-war youth growing up in West Germany where a positive perception of Britain or America, two of the country's allies, was also part of a wider post-war educational policy to foster democracy—a political mission entangled with pop and consumer culture.

Mod revival in Germany

While in 1960s Germany the term beat was in more frequent use than the term mod, the latter entered media reports with the mod revival beginning in 1970s England. Similar to the popularity British beat music gained in the 1960s, the revival of the British mod and sixties style was tied to music and the circulation of pop images through media, as well as to the impact British and American youth cultural styles exerted more widely on youth in Western, industrialized nations. This effect is also reflected in the international expansion of the punk and skinhead movement during the 1970s and 1980s (Müller-Bachmann 2002: 59).

The mod revival that had started in England in the 1970s reached Germany with a delay of approximately three to five years. Beyond music groups such as The Jam, the film *Quadrophenia* (1979) formed an important catalyst for the revival of mod style and its dissemination beyond Britain. For German youths this movie was an important cinematic document that referred back to the heyday of mod youth culture in 1964. The movie took the seaside clashes in Brighton as a backdrop—a time and place that was not part of the (youth) cultural memory in Germany. The story of *Quadrophenia* is intriguing with its focus on teenage identity struggles and issues of belonging and youth cultural affiliations, resonating also with German youth in the 1980s. However, those that became part of the mod scene in Germany were quick to critique the movie for its style and "unfaithful" representation of mod and sixties fashion. The movie was compared to a historical drama like *Ben Hur*, only that in *Quadrophenia* all were dressed the same in jeans, rather than showing the actors in authentic mod and sixties gear (Niemczyk 1984: 34). Yet, there is no doubt that the film, and its accompanying record—a double-sleeve, image-heavy album brandishing a musical mix of 1960s tracks and The Who's 1973 compositions—played a key role in popularizing 1960s mod style, as well as scooter riding, among youth in Germany.

The German music magazine *Spex* ran its first longer report on "Mods in Germany" in its January 1984 issue (Niemczyk 1984: 31ff.). The article focuses on mods in Düsseldorf and Hamburg, who had garnered much attention and were forming into an identifiable youth culture within their local music scenes. "Judging by their clothes, they must be MODS, Quadrophenia and the like, with parkas, suits and pigskin shoes ... But wait, MODS in Germany—do they even exist?" (Niemczyk 1984: 31). The author of the article sees a need for elaboration, since the history of mods is not understood to be common knowledge (Niemczyk 1984: 55). With his article, based on Richard Barnes' 1979 illustrated book on mods (Barnes 1991), he outlines the origins and development of this youth cultural style. He also makes a guess on numbers, noting how mods compared to skins and punks are a smaller movement, estimating their number in Germany to be around a thousand followers or greater (Niemczyk 1984: 33).

The author lists Frankfurt, Leverkusen, Wilhelmshaven, Munich, Bamberg and Nuremberg as centers of the mod scene, developing independently from each other in different regions in Germany from the late 1970s onwards. Yet he notes that in all of these cities there are different types and interpretations of mod style. One of his interviewees is adamant that in "Cologne there are quite a few that also wear clothes like us, but they're not mods, they only look like it, they listen to totally different music" (Niemczyk 1984: 33). The cities with the largest concentration of mods and mod events, however, are Düsseldorf and Hamburg, both important cultural centers in Germany with vibrant art and music scenes.

The major German mod bands that are mentioned in the *Spex* article are *Stunde X* and *Die Profis*, both from Düsseldorf, in addition to the band *Dextrin* from Leverkusen.

Two months after the reporting on "Mods in Germany" (Niemczyk 1984), Hamburg's city magazine *Tango* publishes the article "Dandies of the Eighties: Mods," describing the revival of the sixties as a new cultural import (Kraft 1984: 20–3). Seeking an underlying ideology, the author enquires on the meaning of the style and comes to the conclusion that at its core it is driven by a love for the sixties: "for Soul and Beat music, for Pop Art and parties" (Kraft 1984: 22). Yet he also makes a point about the contradiction mod style as a revival is riddled with: "How is a revival of the mod phenomenon possible when it essentially stands for modernity? How can one lay claim to being hip when one is guided by the past?" (Kraft 1984: 22). Jens Kraft finally defines mod as an "elitist fashion scene, whose members spend their pastime by working through the 1960s" (Kraft 1984: 22). That said, he makes a case for the ongoing nature of this "working through," considering the wealth of material from the 1960s that has yet to be discovered and processed. In his opinion, a stagnation of the style will only occur once mods close their catalogue of inspirations (Kraft 1984: 22). However, as further generations of youths and (post-) adolescents come to discover the style anew, and see the past through their own eyes, they may kick off their own selection from the fashion and music of the past decade and relocate it in a new time and place. The meanings British sociologists saw at the core of 1960s mod style, such as the visual blurring of class boundaries (Hebdige 1974 and 2000; Clarke 2000), come to be replaced with new meanings, depending on the present-day wearer and context. Essentially, however, the revival of mod style in the 1980s brought about the crystallization around a certain elitism associated with the style, which is, along with the enthusiasm for the sound and style of the sixties, a focus on "rarity" and "authenticity:" the discovery of rare and original vinyl records of the 1960s and the use of vintage clothing or second-hand items—that are perceived as unique through the passing of time and their individual appropriation to one's own sense of style. With this, the mod revival style ties in with the narrative surrounding 1960s mod style which was driven by a desire to look individual and different, yet also more broadly with an ethos of "alternative" and "indie-culture" emerging among youth in the later twentieth century (Luvaas 2012: 1–22).

From mod to the transnational sixties scene

An article appearing in the Aachen city magazine *Klenkes* in 1995 ("It's a Mod, Mod World" 1995: 24–6), builds a bridge to the German mod revival in the 1980s, quoting a line from the 1984 *Spex* article: "It would be best if the scene stayed as small as it is." In Germany, mod youth culture never permeated the popular awareness to the same extent that punk did for instance; in comparison it had always been a smaller scene. Whereas Jens Kraft (1984: 22) still estimated the number of mods attending an event in a city like Hamburg to reach 150, similar events by 1995 reached such numbers through the participation of mods from all around Germany and visitors from neighboring countries. As the author of the article points out, by then it would have been more apt to write a piece on "the last international dandies," with the subheading "Mods in Europe." He notes how the mod scene in Germany has become more fragmented into smaller, local scenes, which he sees reflected in other European countries as well ("It's a Mod, Mod World" 1995: 24).

The German sixties fanzine *The Scene*, created in the 1990s and written in the English language, also indicated this international orientation. In an article entitled "Mods Today and Mods Tomorrow," the scene is described as a tight-knit network of people from different parts of Europe, who come together at events in varied countries to share their interest in sixties music and style:

[T]he international mod scene has never been so close (sic!) like nowadays … People are travelling around a lot and especially the "New Untouchables" and lots of their English friends show a much more "open-minded" way towards the continent, while people from the continent start to "invent" the scenes in their neighbourhood … Some years ago it was nearly impossible to find foreign people on rallies in other countries without being invited. Meanwhile You (sic!) can find all sorts of nations on the "big" European events … all the travellers have found a lot of friends here … this is, what [makes] the mod scene of today so interesting and special … In my opinion the mods are the ones who live the European idea and don't waste their time talking about it—we live it!! Can there be a better example to show, that mod is more than a movement but a way of life? ("Mod Today and Mods Tomorrow" n.d.)

Fanzines and flyers have always been an important means of communication, fostering the creation and maintenance of a trans-local network among scenes and subcultures (see Hodkinson 2002: 153–94). The internet has not only vastly intensified but also accelerated such networking (Hodkinson 2002: 175–94). This has been a fundamental reason for a growing internationalization among youth cultures and scenes, including the sixties scene, contributing to their longevity and relative coherence over time, even if they are smaller in size: "What is personal, primary, and small-scale, is not necessarily confined in space, and what spans continents need not be large-scale in any other way" (Hannerz 1996: 26).

Yet the scene's consistency relies also on actual face-to-face exchange and partying at concerts, sixties-nights and international weekenders (see Figures

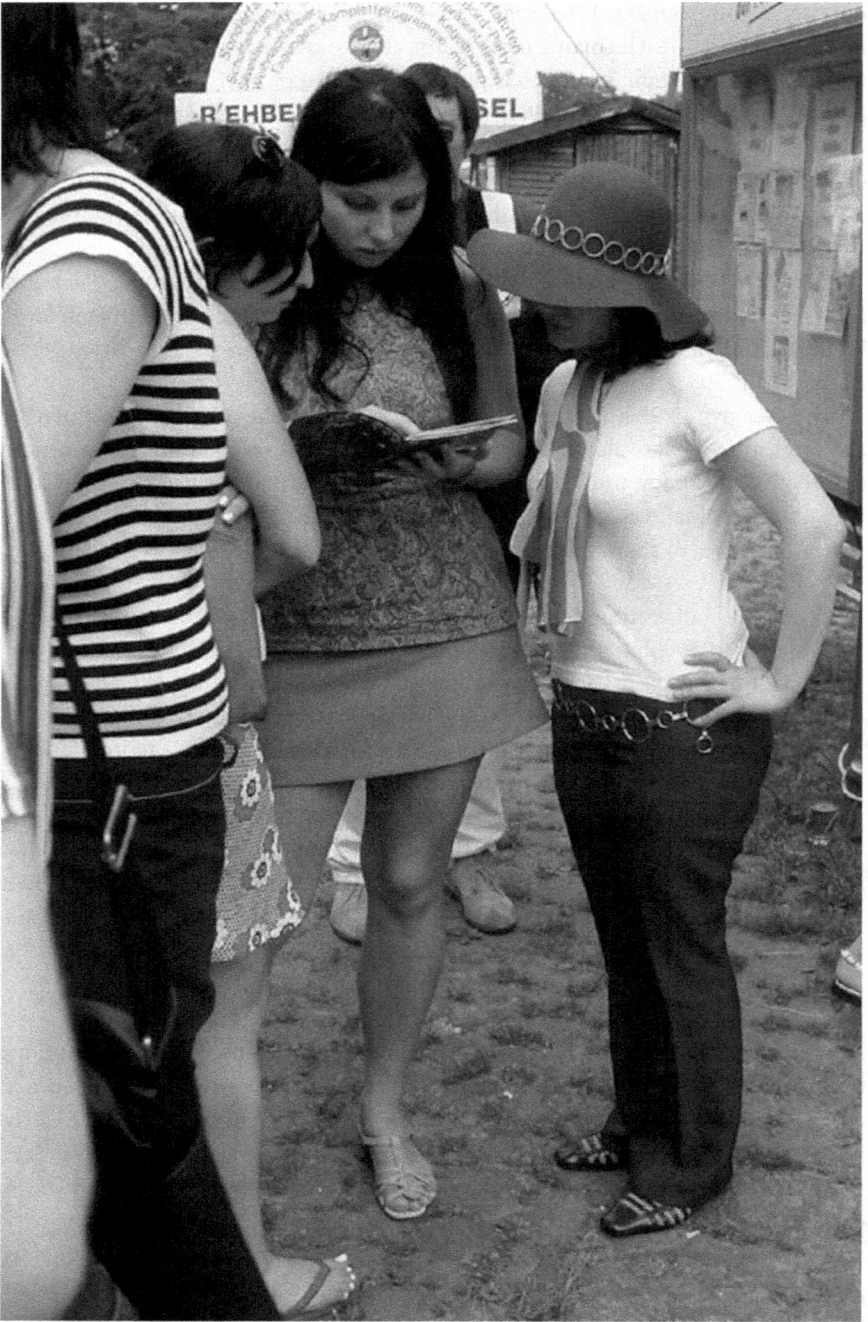

FIGURE 10 "Late sixties" styles worn at a sixties event in Koblenz, Germany.
Photo: author.

10–12). For example, in Germany the annual sixties event organized by Two Men from L.I.N.Z, is a long-standing internationally attended weekender that has celebrated its twentieth anniversary in 2012. Affordable travel across Europe, enabled by low-cost airlines, allows for regular face-to-face exchanges at these national and international sixties fests.

Attendance at those events, for example in England on the Isle of Wight, in London and Brighton, or in Gijón on Spain's Atlantic coast, is often planned as a short holiday getaway. Such trips can also be funded by DJing sets, playing in bands or dealing in clothes and record sales, essentially professionalizing one's interests and contributing to the internal infrastructure of the scene, as is common in other scenes or subcultures (see also Hodkinson 2002).

Andreas Hepp identifies a "politics of choice" that comes with the expansion of the media landscape and the multi-optionality it opens up as a kind of market-place for the supply of "identity narratives" (Hepp, Thomas and Winter 2003: 13). The sixties scene, in its practices bound up with the mediation of style and memory, could be seen as a small "affinity interculture" within a highly differentiated "identity market" (Slobin 1993: 68). Aided by media, it is often quicker and simpler to seek interaction with those who share the same interests "than to interact with one's physically present neighbour" (Hepp, Thomas and Winter 2003: 14). The members of a trans-locally shared scene feel instead united by a shared interest or "theme" (Hitzler 2001), in this case the interest in the music and

FIGURE 11 Two of the mods featured in Dean Chalkley's film *The New Faces* at the Book Club, Shoreditch, London 2010. Photo: PYMCA/UIG via Getty Images.

fashion of the 1960s and the associated practices of collecting rare records, as well as dressing and partying in sixties style (see Figure 11).

This is also how local identities and histories of scenes in different regions or countries can interact within a relatively coherent trans-local or transnational network as a reference framework (see Hodkinson 2002: 27; Kruse 1993: 34). Even if local differences can be made out, there is a common substance to the distinctive trans-local/transnational style through which individual members recognize each other and can easily engage in dialogue, as one interviewee notes in a short documentary by Nina Schermer: "a mod always recognizes a mod" (*Bad Breisig Schwingend* 2008).

From youth culture to youth expanding culture

With regard to demographics, the youths who adopted the mod style in the 1980s were mainly teenagers between the ages of 16 and 18. They assembled their sixties style by purchasing old clothes in second-hand stores, which the author of the *Spex* article describes in 1984 as one of the cheapest ways of participating in an alternative culture (Niemczyk 1984: 33). As he notes at the time, the main point of the style is to communicate youthfulness and difference, echoing the journalist who reported on the early "faces" in London in 1962 (see Rawlings 2000: 42). Those above the age of 18 are advised against attempts to take on the style (Niemczyk 1984: 52), linking mod to youth.

Today, however, most participants in the sixties scene are far beyond their teenage years and have a steady income to afford participation in this now transnational scene, including extensive travel. By the time I started with the interviews and field research in the early 2000s, the age span in the scene was still quite heterogeneous. The youngest of my interviewees was aged fifteen, the oldest thirty-five. Those interviewed estimated the scene's average participant to be aged between twenty-five and thirty-five. Now, about a decade later, many of the interviewees are still active in the scene, and have reached their forties. As one sixties styler notes, the age gap to any new arrivals in the scene is getting larger and larger, so that younger enthusiasts for the sixties might show up at the same concerts, but otherwise develop friendships, and even their own events, with like-minded people closer to their own age (see *Bad Breisig Schwingend* 2008).

The "aging" of the sixties scene is a phenomenon that is visible in other subcultures or scenes as well, which the sociologist Barbara Stauber (2001) sees as the result of a wider societal tendency towards the prolongation of youth, tied to the process of individualization and a breakdown of traditional socialization instances. Longer education periods, later entry into professional careers and later achievement of a level of financial security, along with the delaying of marriage and child-birth, are some of the causes leading to what Stauber calls a "permanency of transition." This term describes how a more clearly defined entry into adulthood has been replaced by a more continual, ongoing process (Stauber 2001: 121). As much as "youth" has come to be seen as a discursive construct (and an idea that has been tightly bound up with the marketing of the teenage consumer in the post-war period) so is "adulthood" or "age" (see Bennett and Hodkinson 2012; Twigg 2013). And accordingly "youth cultural" research is now expanding into the study of "aging" youth cultures (see Bennett and Hodkinson 2012). The fact that many people stay on in youth cultures that are by now several decades old shows that these formations are not that fluid, short-lived or ephemeral as the word "scene" or "youth" suggests. While there is clearly movement in and across scenes, styles are not always as easily and quickly picked up and consumed, as the metaphors of "style surfing" and "supermarket of styles" (Polhemus 1996) imply. The continuity of many youth cultural formations—carried on by the same members over rather long periods of time—shows that the styles, often taken on at a young age, can come to take on long-lasting meaning into adulthood and form a constitutive part for one's sense of social belonging (Bennett and Hodkinson 2012). Even if in advancing age the "partying" is no longer as frequent, due to other commitments such as work and family, or maybe due to a dwindling energy or interest in spending long nights in clubs and bars, the social ties that make up the scene and the friendships and shared memories continue to form a substantial part of the identities and identifications of these "young adults."

Style narratives: Sartorial tempo

A part of my interviews with sixties stylers, commonly at the start, circulated around the moments and times of their getting into the style of the sixties, which varied according to their age. Those who were aged thirty and above by the time of the interviews in the early 2000s discovered the style in the early 1990s during their late teens and early twenties, while some already did so in the late 1980s, at ages fifteen to seventeen. As noted in the beginning of this chapter, the initial discovery of the sixties came through the material and visual circulation of the sixties in music records, images and clothes. But the discovery of the sixties was also dependent on social relationships and exchange, that is in the context of the emergence or existence of mod or sixties scenes, going back to the 1980s mod revival, and their presence in music venues. "*If you don't know someone who's involved and who gives you a bit of an introduction, you'll never connect. If you don't have a person who's connected to them, you won't ever get involved*" (w. 27). Spaces such as clubs, bars and concert venues provide the forum for the alliance of music and style that visually produces scenes. They are the places where youths experience music and forge ties with others. This is how modern jazz and its urban culture of clubs and bars played a pivotal role in the creation of the mods' youth culture in the 1960s. And this continues today, where music remains an important cultural interest and activity, with scenes forming around clubs, bars or music venues. It was usually through friends or acquaintances that those interviewed first attended such events, thus becoming aware of the style and the scene. While they got introduced specifically through the scene's physical presence at specific clubs and events, it could also often happen through its ties to other scenes or, indeed, their overlapping.

> I started out in the scooter scene and ended up in the sixties scene, because I liked it more. The scooter scene got too rowdy. It was all right before. Then techno happened and there was a soul tent and in another tent they played techno. And then the drinking games. Nasty stuff. I got out of there pretty quickly … And then I went to my first sixties party and that was just a lot nicer. In Saarbrücken. That was my first mod weekender. Really nice, that was. Yeah, 1994, end of 1994.
> How did you dress at the time?
> A bit second-hand. My friends got a blouse for me. Not proper sixties yet really. A bit extravagant, but that only really started after the party. My first thought was "Jesus, what's going on here." Bloody mental. (w. 27)

In the mid-1990s, the sixties scene grew significantly in the light of the Britpop phenomenon, again a musical influence coming out of Britain, with bands such as Oasis and Blur, who were heavily influenced by the music from the 1960s. In Cologne and in the Ruhr area, there were numerous Britpop events at which sixties music was also played. This attracted many of the younger sixties stylers to get interested, who found the style "*strange*" and "*fascinating*" at the same time. The sighting of one's "first mods," the initial contact with their aesthetic and style, was disconcerting to some at first, which shows how unusual, or extraordinary, the sixties style appears to outsiders for its perceived "vintage" or out-of-timeliness.

> So we first hung out with the britpoppers, but there were always some mods, because there weren't so many sixties parties. I still remember it exactly: it was at the first Popscene we went to that I thought "but they're all so old." And the way they looked, so bizarre. (w. 19)
> Yeah, I'd already heard about mods, but … (w. 22)
> … we hadn't yet seen any, especially not here in Cologne. I was totally baffled, we went inside and like "wow, what sort of people are those," we were so innocent (laughter). And then we went to more of those parties and, as I

said, those mods were also there and then I was like "right …" and that's how we sort of got to know it. Of course we knew it, the sixties and such, but we didn't know what still goes on nowadays (emphasized). (w. 19)

Those moments of fascination with the strange or "bizarre" were here followed by moments of an intensified engagement with the style. Through the materiality of clothing, this involvement becomes tangible, perceptible and visible in the own appearance making. Often just starting with the adoption of singular clothing items, "a blouse from friends" or smaller stylistic elements. With the practice of wearing and embodiment, as well as research and time investment, and the social exchange with and observation of scene members, this process gradually turns into a process of identification with the aesthetic and style. This process of involvement and identification is material and corporeal; it evolves directly through the use of clothing and the styling of one's body, thus externalizing the involvement visually, and materially, to oneself and to others. Most interviewees described this process as gradual, or paced, not as easy as a change of clothing—but as a change of style. It is a stepwise process of involvement that, as one sixties styler notes, was again shaped by very particular circumstances, including the inter-generational transmission of personal as well as place-bound, or rather transnational, dynamics of memory:

I was about fifteen. My sister, she used to do the rockabilly thing. That's why she also listened to ska and then we ended up going to a concert. And then, at some point, I went to my first mod party. By meeting those people you do get to know those who listen to the same sort of music. It's a bit of a circle. But I only became proper sixties through my apprenticeship. 'Cos my boss, well, I was a hairdressing apprentice and my boss lived in London during the late sixties, early seventies, and worked at a salon there and it was all totally weird. So I was lucky to have a great boss and she did further training in London and we went there together. I worked at the salon even before my apprenticeship and the boss would always tell me loads of stories of the sixties. And I still remember, at some point she painted eyelashes for me, and she thought it was great that I thought it was great and then it became like an exchange.

She passed it on to you?

Yeah that was totally cool. Because then, at some point I also went to London with her, I was given a flight to London for my apprenticeship test. So, proper nice and then we also went to Carnaby Street and then she also showed me where her old salon was. Yeah I remember, we used to watch hairdressing videos from London, they were always totally cool. And then there was this sort of revival, with Beatle haircuts and Nancy Sinatra with "These Boots Are Made for Walkin'" and then those haircuts and I was like "yeah, cool." And then it totally won me over. So I do think she contributed to the fact that I got totally hooked. Especially with London. (w. 29)

As recounted by this sixties styler, the sense of excitement surrounding the sixties aesthetic was transmitted to her through her work, literally passed on from one generation to the next. Interesting here is that this emerges in a work context that is focused on the body, with the styling of hair as well as make-up. Memory of the sixties is here then transmitted through the direct work on the body, the painting of sixties style eyelashes, and thus through an intimate process of bodily transformation. This emerged in lively dialogue with her boss: her sharing stories, reactivating her own memories and showing her places of the time when she lived in "Swinging London," and providing her with examples of how to dress and how to "live it up" during the era. This sparked a material and embodied process of "past presencing" (Macdonald 2013: 16) that extended from the styling of her body to the styling of her apartment:

> It was also the haircuts, because at one point she gave me one of those sixties haircuts. Oh and "in those days" and Mary Quant. She totally like introduced me to it. That was really nice. And I'll never forget how she once painted eyelashes for me. Yeah I'd always bang on about wanting glued-on eyelashes and I'm not up to it. And she then said: "You know, we used to paint eyelashes ourselves. We didn't have the money for that." And she was like swish swosh and I was totally happy. And my apartment then, I already lived alone at seventeen and would copy pictures and hang the copies in the hallway. And the flea markets in those days were still great. There was so much all over the place.
> And so it started—
> At sixteen, seventeen. From my sister I got rockabilly, ska, I always liked that, you know, big sister. But sixties came like through the apprenticeship. Then you got to know the right people and then at some point I was at my first sixties party and then I got hooked. (w. 29)

Another sixties styler emphasized how her interest in the style and music of the 1960s emerged before her first encounter with the scene, by way of material discoveries of sixties objects on flea markets. "*I wasn't made aware of it through the sixties scene, not at all, that came later. That was still quite far off. I just felt inspired by the fashion that I found at the flea market*" (w. 30). Yet she notes that there was a marked intensification of her interest in sixties objects and also in the scene, once she attended events and parties: occasions that presented to her a social setting and stage for her self-performance and immersion in sixties style.

> I already ran around dressed like that because I just liked it. Definitely. It got a lot more intense because of it. Obviously, when you meet like-minded people, that doesn't mean that you get along with all of them, but you share

the same tastes. You obviously get more inspiration and you find more things. (w. 30)

More frequent participation in the scene's events led to an increasing perception and observation of "others." This, in turn, led to an intensification of her own interest in and engagement with the style. Interaction with the scene, being part of scene events and experiencing the style in social space and in action provided her an occasion to situate herself. These processes, either the intensification of an already practiced style, or the transition from a different style, evolve through a course of embodied and stylistic adaptation to the scene's overall look and places—practices directly and materially negotiated through dress and consumption: "*And after that I started going more often ... And that's how it all started. Then I started buying more and more second-hand clothes.*" Dress includes not just clothes, but other forms of body modification and supplements, such as jewellery or scents (Eicher 2010: 3). Joanne Entwistle posits that dress can be understood as a complex "situated bodily practice" (2001: 34): a situation or social context imprints itself on the body in a material way, for example by adapting one's clothing choices to social dress codes or by following certain expectations of what is considered suitable for a certain situation. However, in turn dress as "situated bodily practice" is also itself constitutive to the production of social contexts, or situations: for example as the material for the creation and negotiation of "style"— which Carol Tulloch sees as a form of "self-telling" to expound something about oneself (2010: 276). Style is based on "agency—in the construction of self through the assemblage of garments, accessories, and beauty regimes that may or may not be 'in fashion' at the time of use" (Tulloch 2010: 276). In conceiving style as "story-telling" about oneself, Tulloch introduces the term "style narratives" (2010: 276). This understanding of style helps to highlight the dimension of dress and style as constitutive material and embodied practices for the development of a sense of self, and the telling of oneself to others. Yet, while "the sixties" may not be more widely "in fashion" at the time these sixties stylists discover it, the development of their style still evolves in direct social interaction with others through which choices in dress are influenced and appearance and style molded:

After a year I cut off my hair and up until six months ago it was blond. You know, I'd like it back one day. But it was like in the summer, I remember it exactly, we all like arrived at some point and the whispering started, she's cut her hair. Then I sort of started liking it but then somehow like yeah, of course, you know ... Even though they'd done it all before. And there's also the story of a girl, and it's funny, we got to know her and she looked cool from the start, like short black hair, proper style, the lot. At some point we were told that she had also had long blond hair two months before—chopped off, dyed black. And then like, "oh right, she's also got a regular history." Then all sorts of crazy stories started coming up. Anyone with like short hair and the right clothes was cool. And if you went there with normal clothes, you'd notice. (w. 22)

This example shows the wider social dimension of style as sartorial "story-telling," and the involved editing process that is part of the "becoming collectively with others" through "style-fashion-dress"—practices and concepts which Tulloch and Kaiser hyphenate to emphasize how they are bound up as a tightly interwoven dynamic (Tulloch 2010: 275; Kaiser 2012: 6). In the context of the scene, how one wears the sixties is molded not only in the exchange with others, but additionally through the sixties as a style worn in a previous time, which should be enacted "accurately," with the right hairstyle (here a 1960s bob) and accessories. "Authenticity" and the matching of one's style with the historic model become here an ideal and important measure in the regulation of the individual enacting the sixties as vintage style in the context of this scene.

Relocating the sixties: Temporal order and stylistic hybridity

Even though the film *Quadrophenia* consolidated a certain stereotypical image of mods, the tendency since the 1980s, when German youths began to adopt the mod and sixties style, has always been to incorporate a greater variety of fashion styles (see Figures 10–12).

Scenes, notwithstanding their relative continuity, are not static, but subject to change and transformation, even though this may only ever be partially visible to the outsider. Along with the temporal and spatial, or geographic expansion of the sixties scene, overall style interests have expanded well beyond the British mod cornerstone, which is implied in the term "sixties scene" that was commonly used as a reference point in the interviews. Looking at the varied styles worn by sixties enthusiasts at events, they represent together a stylist mosaic of the decade: from the style of early mods, who donned suits or casual wear such as jeans and turtleneck jumpers, to the style of psychedelics and hippies and on to the 1970s, 1980s and 1990s mod and sixties revivals, influenced by punk, glam rock and britpop. Yet, within the stylistic hybridity, many noted in the interviews that there is nevertheless a tendency to form differentiated categories that are strongly connected to musical preference which was often articulated in temporal terms through a dating according to music as well as fashion history.

What kinds of things are you guys into?

Well, it's best to start with what we aren't into. Although, then again, it overlaps. Maybe you noticed that in Rimini. Lately, it's all been splitting,

FIGURE 12 "Early to mid-sixties" style worn at a sixties event in Koblenz, Germany. Photo: author.

because of the music, in soul and all those psychedelic people. We (emphasized) prefer soul in terms of music, that basically means early sixties and that's then reflected in fashion. Well, that people, the men tend to wear suits, shorter hair—although I don't like it when they're quite so short—but the men definitely wear suits and the women, yeah, definitely dresses, whatever we've got, not necessarily totally floral, it shouldn't be that way for the fantastic early sixties. (w. 22)

One's own positioning is articulated here through "self-dating" one's style and through the demarcation from an "other:" the articulation of who one is *not*, in order to know who one is (Hall 1999: 93). For Stuart Hall, there can be no identity without a dialogical relation to the other. This is because the other is not remote or external, but also within the self. Hall helps to understand identity as an ongoing process, one that is based on a division of self and other (Hall 1999: 93). This is often evident in the way that one's own likes or taste are articulated by describing what is disliked—as a form of self-description through the other. The interviewee does not describe herself with reference to clothes, but by a listing of opposites:

Early sixties means early to mid-1960s?
Yes, until the mid-sixties. But not with petticoats, you know, I'm aware of that, how can I say, those lovely pop art dresses, but nothing floral, that's late sixties already. Then there's the other faction, those psychedelic, psych kids, how they call themselves, and they all run about with hipsters, which we also like, like the trousers, I like that too, but what I hate are those totally colourful floral shirts and those, yuck, I dunno, it's so terrible, then many of the guys have long hair, there are some who have it this long (points to her shoulders). (w. 22)

The order and classification of other sixties event participants, with whom the party is shared, is a matter of appearance. It depends on clothing and certain accessories that show the importance of dress for social orientation. Even within a niche culture, the dynamics of identification and differentiation are here very present and serve as a positioning of oneself. German sociologist Gerhard Schulze describes style as a form of guarantee of personal identifiableness, not only in the eyes of others, but also for oneself (Schulze 2000: 104). Small details in clothing seem to suffice to gain a notion of someone and to classify them aesthetically (2000: 104), and in this case looks and styles are classified based on the relation of music and fashion:

Yes it's really defined by music, but since we, I'm not saying we think psyche-delic stinks, I mean the music, we actually like both and we don't want it this way, to split, I also love hipsters and I also love those brightly colored things, but those flower things. Well, it shouldn't be too over the top. Or what I also hate, a girl in Rimini had one, S., we also know her. Those slouch hats, in pink. You might have seen it. Or W., he was wearing that one night, we always call them shepherds, shepherd's hats. That's also like late sixties and I just don't like it at all. Whatever, regardless of the music or anything, I just don't like stuff like that. Or floral stuff, and bags and chains. (w. 22)

Identification with a specific style implies exclusion in the sense of differentiation. Other styles are portrayed as negative stylistic images. They are referred to in extreme terms: when, for instance, something is "loved," or other elements are "hated." Rather than the floral and ornamental style of hippies and psychedelics, this interviewee likes the pop art styles of the early sixties, which means colorful, but simple shift dresses with large, graphic contrasts, similar to Mondrian's color composition or the op art of Bridget Riley. In this sense, the term "early sixties" is a subjective, fabricated construction. It serves to draw stylistic boundaries within the divisions of fashion history. Yet the dating of fashion history is vague, the categorization of one's own style as early sixties occurs in ideal-typical manner: it does not actually match the fashion of the early 1960s, but rather that of the mid-1960s. This is elucidated with the example of petticoat fashion: early 1960s styles, which were still significantly influenced by 1950s fashion, and are described as such by MacInnes, do not represent here a stylistic reference for sixties stylers.

> I'd say it's very differentiated. Not the early sixties, for example, so none of those little '63 dresses. Late sixties, early seventies. Flares and colorful shirts, yeah, mini skirts, boots. I draw the line at '72. (w. 21)

Many of the styles that are chosen are those which in retrospect are seen as "iconic" of 1960s fashion. This is shown by the association of the preferred style with the era's significant art movements (op and pop art). "*Yes. The early sixties were still totally conservative, in terms of design too. So I definitely tend towards pop and op art. And like space design, for furniture*" (w. 30). Here again, the description of one's own style is preceded by what is disliked. The comparison and negative appraisal of early 1960s design is based on a personal evaluation of design history. This is done in the context of the delimitation and classification of one's own style—with this "identification" being, however, not a particular thing or moment. Instead, with Stuart Hall such positioning can be understood similar to the process of identification, that is identification is bound up with time, never fully stable (Hall 1999: 91). The actual fluidity of this process—and the fluidity of style in one's own "style narrative"— within the temporal repertoire of the sixties, is described in another example:

> One guy, for example, A., it's a great story, a long while back he used to run around in a suit. One of those soul guys, short hair, smarter-looking. Then I met him six months ago and he'd totally changed. He had a beard, almost looked like a hippie; like long hair, until about here (points to her shoulder), was wearing hipsters and one of those kerchiefs like. That's also a sign, kerchief is more late sixties and a tie is more mid-sixties. And now I met him again in Rimini and he looked different again. He'd lost the long hair and the beard and was wearing a suit again, so it always changes like that. (w. 22)

The subject of this story is described to be in a constant transformative process. His mixing-up of this interviewees' own temporal order of sixties fashion and music causes irritation. Identification or recognition, according to Schulze, requires a sense of continuity through repetition (Schulze 2000: 104). At the same time, the above quote shows the dynamic of change within the scene, or among its members, and in keeping with the sixties as a vintage style, how a variety of 1960s styles can be incorporated. As the example in this last interview excerpt shows, styles despite or within the nominator "sixties" are not static. In its relocation or enactment in the present, the sixties vintage style moves in and between times. Yet in its hybridity and fluidity within the scene, it is sharing the sixties style with others, which makes a large part of its appeal to those who participate in or make up the scene.

Sixties events: Vintage style and time warp

"*Of course it's best when you're in a group. Cos then you feel more like time travelling, cos you see the person opposite you*" (w. 22), says one sixties styler pointing to the significance of those who share the sixties style and together contribute to a feeling of an aesthetic experience of the sixties in the now:

> Say, if I'm alone, I don't see myself or I forget what I'm wearing. Sittin' in the tram and lookin' out the window. That's when I totally forget what I'm wearing ... But when I have a few friends in front of me, I look at the situation and think "Ah (enthralled), how smart they all look!" That's when it hits home, that's when you notice and feel it intensely. (w. 22)

"Objects are no longer just objective, but also inter-objective, not just monologic but dialogic as well," writes Celia Lury with reference to Vilem Flusser (2002: 209), who notes that: "Objects of use are ... mediations (media) between myself and other people, not just objects" (Flusser 1999, cited in Lury 2002: 29). This is nothing new in terms of the communicative potential of clothes, but it does highlight the social significance and affect of things as material facilitators in social relations and experiences. Clothes cannot only mediate or grant a feeling of individuality, as often pointed out by sixties stylers, but they are also agents in the sartorial or embodied "story-telling" (of stories that are not fixed but that can be edited and updated) and in the communication and exchange with others. As the material for self-performance, clothes endow the body with a material visibility to the world. As Gabriele Mentges puts it, clothing is not just "filled" by the body, but clothes are enacted and act themselves on the body, and as such they also constitute acts of perception, of seeing and being seen (2005b: 25). With Ann Rose and Peter Stallybrass, Mentges underlines the role of clothing as "material establisher of identity" (Mentges 2005b: 4). To see and be seen plays a big role in the context of sixties events as it is here where "the sixties" come to feel as present through others:

> So when I go to parties, sixties parties, I'm after the time warp. That's exactly what I'm after because I love the aesthetics of it. It totally took my breath away, when I saw that for the first time. I loved the atmosphere, the music, how people carried themselves. (w. 30)

To create this time warp is a spatially complex operation, an event: the product of a collective and interactive performance of the sixties stylers in time and place. The ethnologist Jonas Bjälesjö points to the fact that places are only created through bodily presence and social imaginary: "the place is being made rather than just being there" (Bjälesjö 2002: 22). Places are created through a coming together of actors and they exist in memories, recollections, feelings and imagination. "It is as if a feeling of belonging is generated and transformed into a condensed physical experience" (Bjälesjö 2002: 22). Clothing and embodiment are here essential to a "past presencing" (Macdonald 2013) and spatial rendering of the sixties in the now, as an aesthetic time-space for social and cultural positioning. "To be located, culture has to be *embodied*. Culture is carried into places by bodies," writes Edward Casey (1996: 34), whereas it is usually dressed bodies that are responsible for the embodiment of culture, place and space. For Mentges, clothing is a central agent in embodiment and in the production and organization of space—it makes space dynamic as place through its movement and malleability (Mentges 2005b: 29).

Sixties events organized and happening in specific places over several days, such as international weekenders, provide an opportunity for social interaction, as well as for individual and collective performances that the clothes render "special." "*Those regular clothes that were already around last year, you've always got to try to improve, to be more striking*," states one sixties styler (w. 19). The choice of clothing is therefore one of the most important steps in the lead up to a sixties event. It is particularly important to avoid a replay of the same clothes, as the memory of them—as part of the dynamics of fashion—makes them no longer special. They are in a social sense dead (see Hansen 2003), at least for certain uses:

> Over here it's like, a dress that I've—well, let me put it this way, it's not that important at local parties in Cologne, we're not totally done up, we'll wear a nice dress, but I'll tend to wear it quite frequently—but I would never wear what I wore in Rimini last year for Unkel. First off, there's lots of people who'd remember what I wore—I tend to remember lots of things worn by men and women—but it's happened too often that men come up to me and say: But you've worn that previously or that's on the photo from the Isle of Wight or

something like that. It's something to do with the weekenders. I'd never do it. (w. 22)

Putting together a new set of vintage clothes belongs to the anticipation, preparation and fun of the happening of the sixties event as a unique social and aesthetic experience, which is achieved by creating and maintaining both order and change in dress. The sought after "time-warp" is created through the scene members' continuity or repetitive and collective embodiment of sixties-style. But the uniqueness of the experience of a sixties event also relies on changing clothes, with sixties stylers presenting themselves ideally in new or updated outfits. Hansen's (2003) concept of the social death of clothes, which occurs when garments or ensembles are worn too often, or recognized as being worn at previous occasions, relates to the need to "disguise" time in dress and fashion, discussed here earlier in relation to the early *Vogue* advice on how previously worn clothes can make a new debut (see Chapter 2). Showing up in the same clothes too many times may dilute the experience of a sixties-event as something special or extraordinary. In addition, sixties events are an opportunity to literally show one's personal "investment" in and knowledge of sixties fashion and to present the sartorial "trophies" through which men and women gain recognition. This also explains the ongoing demand for new old clothes. Vintage clothes are here not outside the social and temporal dynamics of fashion, in the sense that the desire for change, and for the new—even if the new is the old—is maintained. Shopping and consumption are integral practices to making and keeping "the sixties," or the engagement and identification with the style/s and aesthetics of the decade, to self and others present.

5 INVESTING (IN) TIME: COLLECTING AND CONSUMING THE PAST

"Sixties Dress Only," a line that was sometimes found printed on flyers for sixties events, describes the kind of clothing sixties enthusiasts prioritize. While none of the interviewed sixties stylers wear 1960s originals exclusively, these tend to rank highest in their wardrobes, which consist of an assemblage of used and old stock 1960s clothes, as well as new and custom-made clothes in 1960s style. Old clothes are appreciated as material witnesses of the past that have distinct aesthetic qualities; and it is their age and materialization of time that make them a rare good. *"I've got a feeling that most of it has been snapped up,"* notes one sixties styler, pointing to one of the stakes of being a consumer of 1960s commodities in the present: *"Finding good originals is rare. Especially when it's clothes"* (w. 29). Male interviewees particularly stressed how difficult it is to find fitting garments. While it is still possible to get a hold of shirts and jackets, trousers and complete, undamaged two-piece suits are harder to come by: *"You can forget about suits. If I do find one that I like—and that in itself is remarkable—then it tends to have ridiculous measurements"* (m. 35). He describes how clothing items have trouser legs or sleeves that are either too long or, as he finds more frequently, too wide and impossible to alter in a way that would make them fit his body. Whereas he finds that women have it easier finding clothes, at least minidresses, whose relatively simple lines can be altered easily.

In the 1970s and 1980s, when young people started to get interested in 1960s clothes, original garments from this decade were by far more accessible to both men and women. The 1960s were at a distance of only ten to fifteen years, a time difference that made them a much less limited resource, considering that the previous fashion generation may have just started to get rid of their old clothes. The situation is comparable to the current increased availability and interest in purchasing fashion from the 1990s and the first decade of the twenty-first century, which enters in greater number into the second consumption cycle. Clothing today is rarely kept over several decades. Instead, the much lower prices for clothing have impacted the use value of clothes, so that they are thrown out much faster to clear the way for the acquisition of new fashion (see Fletcher 2014: 91), a process beginning with the expansion of fashion and consumer culture in the 1960s (see Lister 2006).

And while youths in the 1980s could still find the odd piece of 1960s clothing in the wardrobes of parents or relatives, five decades on it is more unlikely for sixties enthusiasts to inherit their parents' old clothes from that decade—if their parents are of that generation: *"My mum threw away some imitation Courrèges stuff—and she still enjoys talking about it when she wants to tease me,"* recalls a sixties styler (w. 30). To make up for the relative scarcity of material witnesses from the 1960s in flea markets, sixties enthusiasts seek out a wide range of resources for second-hand goods and frequent these spots regularly to increase the chances of good finds. Flea markets are among the common venues in the search for clothes and other items. What they have on offer is usually determined by a mix of professional and private dealers, who sell not only clothes, but a vast variety of leftover goods from previous decades, including books, furniture, tapes, CDs and vinyl records, china, bags, suitcases, carpets, photo albums, lamps, all sorts of tools, cosmetics and much more.

Searching flea markets and vintage stores

In Germany, markets for used goods, including clothes, have a long history, yet their patronage from consumers who do not rely on them out of economic necessity emerges, as in other European countries, more widely in the 1970s. Volker Fischer's 1980 book on the "nostalgia market" in Germany provides a comprehensive overview of the development of the trade, and the shift in value of old things in the context of the 1970s, when there is surplus in goods and also (compared to the post-war time) greater disposable income among the population. During this decade the buying and use of second-hand goods has become more widely disconnected from the meanings associated with second-hand consumption during war and post-war times in Germany, when it was for many a necessity (Fischer 1980: 231). Long before the word vintage came into use in Germany, Fischer discusses the logic of temporality on which the re/circulation of old things in this market thrives, that is, when buying "surviving" things is played out against the frequent consumption of new commodities in an "affluent society." The common German term for flea market is *Trödelmarkt*, and the word for the associated activity of shopping or selling in this market is *trödeln*, which in English means to dawdle, to be slow, to spend time slowly, or to waste time. In this sense it describes a market that has a time concept opposite to the tempo of mass-production or that is commonly associated with the rationality and "efficiency" of industrialized time.

In Germany, flea markets enjoy great popularity. They are part of almost any town, with bigger cities having several or larger established ones that form attractions for visitors. Flea markets are held on specific days of the month at specific locations, sometimes in parks, or in empty parking lots on weekends: outdoor spaces, which transform into popular leisure and consumption sites to track down objects from the past on a Saturday or Sunday morning. Getting there early to sort through the freshly set up selection before anyone else is key, yet to be successful in the hunt for 1960s items requires certain competences, including persistence, a good hand, a sharp eye and, often, simply luck. Whether one will make a find or not is unpredictable, a matter of being at the right place at the right time, which is a reason why the opportunities to make finds are often sought. Also, due to the limitedness of goods, time may not be wasted "dawdling" as the German word *trödeln* might suggest.

> It's quite funny, if you came shopping with me, it would probably be very, very stressful. I check out every stall and breeze through the whole place. I like notice eye catchers right away, I say to myself, hey, that's cool. I don't need to choose. I can see it right away if something is right for me. (w. 30)

Yet, in addition to the issue of sizing, sixties stylers find it difficult to find specifically the kind of clothes that match their taste and imaginary conception of 1960s style, although there is always something to be found: "*at the very least some bric-a-brac, an umbrella or buttons or records*" (w. 30).

While second-hand stores became a very popular alternative to conventional fashion retail in the 1970s, this market is by now much more diversified (see Gregson and Crewe 2003; Norris 2012). Catering to a wide range of clientele, second-hand stores specialize in a great variety of clothing, from children's clothing to contemporary or last season's designer wear or the recirculation of current fast fashion items. Given the comparative scarcity of 1960s fashion, sixties stylers are most interested in stores that explicitly deal in vintage clothing from the era. Here the clothes have been carefully preselected and the customer chooses from a far smaller, curated range than at the bigger flea markets or charity shops. While these clothes tend to be cleaner and instantly wearable, they are at the same time more expensive, since professional dealers are aware of the rarity of well-preserved items, which increases in value with the further passing of time.

> I've really noticed that Cologne has been swept and it's pretty expensive. Definitely true with all the shops I know. Outlaw is about the only shop that's relatively cheap and you've like got to watch out with the stuff, it's often a bit battered.

The furniture?

Yes, furniture, not so much the clothes. Although I bought this nice pair of shoes there yesterday for 18 Euros. That's really cheap. And that's where I got this table from, for 25 Euros, but it was pretty battered just as it is now. (w. 29)

Still, a price tag of €18 is higher compared to prices on flea markets, especially if they are located in more remote neighborhoods where one can still sometimes be lucky and find affordable 1960s relics at a much cheaper rate. The luckiest find mentioned was perhaps an orange Courrèges coat for €3.50. The low price may be simply due to ignorance or lack of business sense of the amateur seller, who simply wants to get rid of their wares. Otherwise, professional dealers who run their own second-hand stores take on a key role in producing and heightening the value of old clothes through space. Here old clothes are arranged like in boutiques or designer stores, which contributes significantly to an object's perceived value. Through their carefully curated selection these places can draw people's attention to certain objects or design periods and play an important role in the shaping of their customers' taste. One sixties styler, who started out with an affinity for the 1970s, switched gear and turned to the 1960s by way of music and the look and feel of record sleeves he found in a vintage store:

At some point I came across a funk record sleeve that had a 1970s wallpaper print. And I thought, that doesn't look so bad. So I started to look more into it. Somehow I didn't find the sixties that interesting before, it felt so demure to me. But then being in this shop I noted how it isn't so demure at all. (m. 24)

He refers to the shop Vertigo in Recklinghausen in the Ruhr area, specializing in 1960s pop design from furniture to clothing items. The shop display is similar to modern design stores, except with old wares, so that it arranges its tables, chairs and accessories the way a living room might have looked in the 1960s. Entering the shop does not feel like entering the usual second-hand or bric-a-brac store. Instead one encounters a unitary time arrangement, in the style of high pop, creating the illusion that one is in fact standing in a 1960s shop that sells new objects. This illusion is only betrayed by the noticeable traces that time and age have left behind on those objects. These effects or feelings of time travel are often increased through a kind of stripped down interior, with walls painted white and objects presented as if they were in a museum setting, an effect Nicky Gregson and Louise Crewe see as characteristic for modern retro shops: "We are clearly being positioned here to look and to admire; to see these goods not just as goods for sale but as design icons, as things that are to be valued for their aesthetic qualities and place in design history" (Gregson and Crewe 2003: 65).

As design items, clothes are positioned here amidst other design objects such as radios, telephones or original wallpaper. It is the presentation of such vestiges of the past that increases or enhances their value. They turn into valuable collector's items, which in turn determines their price that often equals the price of new clothes. Yet, it is the scarcity with which these original clothes become imbued that triggers people's desire to own them, and to spend more money on them.

> Moneywise—the most I've spent on a dress is 30 Euros. It's a white dress. I've lent it to a friend, a white dress with a belt. That was the most expensive and it's not a lot of cash for a dress. And shoes, yeah, 65 Euros. Besides that, coats. I don't tend to spend much money on those either. Except for a one-time 45 Euros and I don't think it's much money, well I'm not ruining myself. Even though I wouldn't care, if I like something—be it new or old—then I get this feeling: yeah I've got to get this, I need to take this with me. It's the same with records. I'm a bit of a chance buyer. I tend to think that I never again have this opportunity, I'll never cross paths with that thing again, I have to have it. (w. 30)

The consumption of 1960s clothes is thus not a much cheaper alternative to the purchase of new mass-produced clothes, let's say a copy of a sixties dress at Zara. Price is here not directly the motivation. Rather, it is in a new time context, in which the clothes, previously discarded and declared worthless by their owners, become invested with new values on account of their aesthetic qualities and their temporality, age and perception as a "carrier of the past" (see Korff and Roth 1990: 19). Nonetheless, while in the 1980s youth started to buy 1960s second-hand clothes as a "cheap way to do something different" (Niemczyk 1984: 33), this changed a decade later, as Madeleine Marsh notes in *Miller's Collecting the 1960s*: "It is not just what we keep that makes objects collectable, but what we discard … 1960s decorative arts are now appearing in antique shops to be purchased by a new generation of trend-setting shoppers" (Marsh 1999: 7).

Collecting and consumption guides like Marsh's, which also exist for the wearing or styling of vintage clothing (see Tolkien 2000; Dubin and Berman 2000; Baxter 2006), contribute, along with increasing reports in fashion magazines since the 1990s and the formation of specialized blogs (for example *collectorsweekly. com*), to the discourse and value production around old clothes (see Palmer 2005). And since 1960s artifacts have found their way into design museums and exhibitions, and have become increasingly interesting for a wide range of collectors—not just sixties stylers—this has clearly impacted their market value. Those interviewed here, however, generally didn't spend vast sums. Instead of investing high amounts of money, they invest a lot of time in the seeking and finding of 1960s objects—and it is this time investment in the practice of sixties shopping, the regularity of the hunt, that in turn increases the chances for frequent great finds at relatively low prices. As one sixties styler says: "*I'm a chance buyer. I obviously can't see that I'll have the chance before*" (w. 30). That is, in second-hand consumption, one cannot expect a certain range of items or fits as in the high street. Rather, because this kind of consumption focuses on a particular style and time period, it is largely made up of moments of the unexpected. It is impossible to know whether or when one will find something. But it is the frequency of shopping and the regular seeking out of opportunities for the hunt that increases the chance of finds. All it takes is to invest the time, and to be on a constant lookout.

Unworn past: New old clothes

Among one of the most exciting finds for sixties enthusiasts is the discovery of old stock, especially when it provides extraordinary finds as was the case of the store Budin, located in a neighborhood of the city of Dortmund: A fashion retail store founded in the 1950s that sold surplus from several decades, because it never held a clearance sale. When the store was inherited by the owners' daughter, she found herself confronted with backrooms filled to the ceiling with unopened box-loads of clothes: from simple t-shirts, to underwear, swimwear, tights, dresses, coats, shirts, jackets, trousers and suits—a remarkable opportunity to acquire a variety of unworn, "brand new" clothes from the 1950s to the 1980s. While I accompanied a sixties styler on her shopping trip to Budin, she told me that employees restock the salesroom with new "old" clothes several times a day.

The store entrance is located to the side of the separated main store, which is selling new clothes, marking the old stock section by way of a rack filled with roughly forty jumpers. They are skinny turtleneck and rib jumpers in bright colors, typical of 1960s and 1970s fashion. They are made of synthetic fibers that show no visible sign of aging. Only the white and off-white jumpers seem a little dusty. Then in the salesroom, there is rack upon rack filled with skirts in the most varied styles—attesting to several decades of fashion change. There are also rolling racks with old-fashioned metal baskets that are filled with bras—delicate material witnesses that in their temporal mix provide intimate insights into several decades of changing fashion silhouettes and beauty ideals and the sartorial structuring of women's body shapes. A wide staircase leads to the upper salesroom. Here is where the real finds are. While the more basic style of clothes, such as shirts and sweaters on the ground floor, still look like they might blend in with current fashion, the first floor has row upon row of racks with the dresses that in their style and finishing look more evidently old and can be dated back to the decades of the 1950s to the 1970s.

Sixties stylers living in nearby cities were quick to latch on to the source, notwithstanding efforts to keep it a secret so it may not sell out as fast and dry up as a source for the supply of original 1960s clothes. Given the exceptionally low prices, some sixties stylers not only significantly expanded their wardrobe, but also bought in bulk to resell the clothes at sixties events, flea markets and over the internet. The exact location was only passed on among those friends who were surprised to see them dressed in ever more new old clothes. Some of those interviewed knew of Budin and they were enthusiastic about the prospect of being able to, as it were, buy the past in bulk. After all, it is a sixties styler's dream to be able to travel back just once for a weekend, so that they may buy all the things they struggle to get their hands on today—from sixties clothes to furniture. Shopping at Budin was described as a unique event, and an entirely new experience of second-hand consumption.

Even if the shop radiated through the aesthetics of the old clothes, and the scent of time and age captured in them a similar atmosphere to a used clothing store, buying the old still "new" and unworn was a novel experience for most.

FIGURE 13 Clothing tag of a 1960s coat by the company Hecoma, sold at Budin store. Photo: author.

Having never enveloped a human body, these clothes showed no traces of wear, yet their age was transmitted powerfully by their smell and by their unique material and haptic qualities, which make them distinct from current clothing. In contrast to a second-hand shop, the clothes at Budin still carried the original manufacturer's labels, including their previous price. The tags themselves were of elaborate graphic quality, much distinct from tags on today's common high street clothes, and acted as a further incentive to buy—even if the clothing item itself may not have been of interest.

This is the case of the graphic design for a tag of the clothing company Hecoma (see Figure 13), conveying typical characteristics of the 1960s aesthetic—lending a face to the clothes and to the time. The tag shows the black and white image of a woman's portrait. The layout has black bars running across the upper and lower edges, and another across the middle of the woman's face, bearing the company name. Yet, the use of these black bars also conjures up images of mattes used in old films. The image composition draws the attention to the eyes and mouth, highlighting the typical features of 1960s make-up art with black eyeliner and pale lipstick. Compared to contemporary clothes tags, these old ones are found to be more aesthetically interesting and are appreciated for their attention to detail. For sixties stylers, they are almost design objects in their own right, valued as certificates of authenticity for the age of the clothes, yet equally a testament of their "newness," a guarantee that they have not been worn. In addition, the original price tags provide important insights into the realities of fashion and consumption in the 1960s, where a high-quality garment such as a simple shift dress had cost DM80. In today's warehouse clearance, €7.50 is not only far below what the garment cost originally, but is also lower than the price of garments in second-hand stores. There was even a discount for bulk buyers, which led many sixties stylers to buy whole loads of clothes. It was especially unusual that the same items were available in various sizes, adding to the feeling that one would shop for these clothes in the store back in the 1960s. While second-hand shops might oftentimes have just one or two items that might appeal to sixties stylers, Budin had row upon row of interesting 1960s clothes, from miniskirts in a great variety of colors, dresses with large-scale geometric patterns, or late sixties dresses with floral motifs, in addition to trousers in all sorts of shapes, blouses, jackets, jumpers, etc.

The urge to buy here was potentiated by the shop assistant who moved between the salesroom and back room to restock new old clothes and who talked about the overwhelming amount of clothes they had to deal with in the storage room, pointing to many treasures that had yet to be unpacked, waiting to be brought to light, until space opened up in the already packed salesroom. This promising fact, the potential to continue to find exciting treasures from the past, was an incentive for sixties stylers to visit the shop frequently, in the hope of finding ever more new old things. Yet this sheer amount of clothes on offer was almost overwhelming—as the person I accompanied to the store, who succumbed to a sixties shopping frenzy, found herself exiting the store after several hours with four bag loads full of clothes. The sheer, seemingly infinite, volume of items from the past on offer brought a different dimension to the contemporary consumption of the 1960s. Buying clothes that are unworn, available in large quantities and in a variety of sizes makes the shopping act almost similar to buying current mass-produced fashion. Nevertheless, there remained an acute awareness, facing the unique quantity of the otherwise limited rare goods, that this resource of the past—and the time to consume it—could soon be exhausted, its time running out, urging so many to buy in bulk. Experiencing this opportunity to buy new old originals was then felt as an encounter of the temporality and limited material availability of the past, requiring hunting and searching for new sources.

Accelerating consumption of the past: eBay expertise and memory making

There can be no denying the impact new technologies had on the consumption of second-hand clothing (see also Palmer 2005) especially since eBay, the leading internet auctioneer, has triggered a mass consumption of second-hand goods beginning in the 1990s (see Hillis, Petit and Eplay 2006). While local resources may become more rare, online shopping expands the availability of 1960s clothes through the time-space compression associated with new media (Harvey 1990).

While internet auctions are no substitute for the spatial and social experience of flea markets and second-hand stores where one can leisurely rummage, touch and feel through the past's material remains, and engage in face-to-face exchange with sellers or other buyers, the internet has become an increasingly important purveyor of sixties items. "Real-time" shopping at flea markets is determined by chance, the sudden unexpected find of a unique item among a thousand generic others. Online shopping, described by Anne Friedberg as the exposure to a permanently accessible shop window (Friedberg 2002), offers a far more targeted and systematic search for specific objects among an apparently endless variety of goods in a worldwide market.

The California-based internet auctioneer eBay was initially founded in 1995 under the name Auction Web, as a forum for the exchange of collectibles. It established itself quickly as one of the most profitable e-commerce sites, enabling the trading in used, and also new, commodities, on a regional, national and worldwide level. Twenty years after its founding, it has fourteen international eBay websites. The German branch of eBay was opened in Berlin in 1999, but sixties stylers do not limit themselves to the search on the German website alone. In fact buying from abroad adds great value to the items: they are not only sixties purchases that are charged with time, but also with place or geographic imaginary.

Overall eBay offers worldwide approximately 800 million items on a daily basis that are systematically searchable. Clothes from the 1960s can be found under "clothes and accessories" and respective subcategories of types of clothing, which can also be searched by color, size, etc. Moreover, and important for sixties stylers, the search can be refined by reference to the decade: 1950s, 1960s, 1980s, etc. A further category under which 1960s clothes are listed is "collectables" with the respective subcategory of clothing and accessories, again divided into decades. The listings for 1960s clothing are here fewer, presumably because clothes are most frequently searched under the clothing category, although it could also be that the collectable category implies more valuable and expensive items.

Using specific terms such as "mod," "sixties" or "Twiggy" help to further systematize the search or, from a seller's perspective, to market the offered items. The story-telling, or in fact branding, of second-hand commodities has become highly important, as in the first market, to make items stand out in a vast marketplace. And the created stories also help to shape the value of old clothes as "vintage" and material witnesses of the past. It is here where digital technology and e-commerce add significantly to the production and circulation of cultural memory, or what Hillis calls a "superfluity of memory" (Hillis 2006). He refers mainly to the branding of personally owned items and the commodification of personal memory or stories. But the view on memory making can equally be expanded to the trade in vintage clothes when items come along with person-alized or invented stories about a previous wearer, to reinforce the temporal imaginary or sartorial, cultural memory that adds to the value of the garment as an authentic witness of time. eBay can here literally be understood as a "memory machine" (Desjardins 2006: 39), which further propels the rising value and meaning of vintage as a good that mediates a feeling of time and a mnemonic and corporeal exchange with the past. But eBay is not only a memory-making machine for its trade in stories, images and objects, but on another level, for its embedding of consumption into a social media network.

Auctions tend to go on for a week and experienced users of eBay tend to favor late bids so as not to inflate prices. Therefore, the auction's final minutes are most crucial and stopwatch-timed by seasoned users who submit winning bids at the last moment. Whereas in the early days of internet auctions, time was of an essence in the sense that items were often chosen according to the time their auction ends to ensure one would be at a place with internet access, mobile devices enable the access to online shopping—and thus the material access to the past—at all times. On the website, eBay automatically creates a member history, publicly tracking purchases and sales, as well as ratings from other users. The latter give some indication as to trustworthiness, shipment speed and the condition in which items reach buyers. However, somebody's consumption history also conveys cues to one's taste and shopping interests, further supporting a memory tied to commodities: if a seller or buyer specializes in 1960s items and, when dealing in clothes, is of the same sex as a prospective buyer or has a similar size or taste, it is not unusual that these become known among each other as regulars or "usual suspects" in the bidding for certain items. This repeated encounter with the same names may spur a more personalized competition over sixties items.

Overall, sixties stylers describe how the instant access to the sixties via online shopping can unleash intense emotions similar to hunting fever. Yet, the hunt does not end once an item has been found, but only intensifies from the moment the desired item is placed under watch during an auction. This process lasts several days, which can create an intimate virtual relationship to the object, an a priori ownership, involving the anticipated wearing and showing off of one's hunting trophy. Given the investment of time and emotions that is involved in this process, the disappointment, should one be outbid at the last second, hits therefore even harder. With this, technology and time-space compression through media brings a whole new dimension to the hunt for objects of 1960s material culture. Emotional investment is potentiated by nail-biting competition and virtual or imaginary ownership. The elements of anticipation and "predatory instinct" heighten the desire to own an item, and oftentimes the willingness to invest a larger amount of money in the end than one might have initially planned (see also Hillis 2006).

Digital technology makes the past eternally accessible and ever more consumable, stirring the thrill of hunting down the past. The allure of winning bids and items—by working with the ticking auction clock down to the second—become here just as important as the item itself. Yet, while the investment of time and emotion increases the value of the item itself, it is anything but stable, since the equally increased availability of the past—the constant discovery of new old items in the digital marketplace—can in turn reduce the amount of time an old item is appreciated, worn and replaced through the purchase of new second-hand items. This makes the circuit of online second-hand consumption quite similar to the practice of first market consumption, which is kept afloat by the constant desire for the new. Yet notwithstanding, the offering of the first fashion market can still be bypassed (see Palmer 2005: 199).

With its digitalization of the flea market, eBay has significantly expanded the access to 1960s fashion. The range of items on offer is far larger, as is the number of potential buyers who no longer require insider knowledge to find suitable sixties items. While some interviewees who started to get into the sixties in the early 1990s would often spend months without finding a single desirable or fitting clothing item, the internet has partly reduced such lack or scarcity. This does not imply that the supply will be infinite, but the wider fashionability of and access to the past through various online markets has certainly multiplied the opportunities for second-hand purchases. After all, eBay is no longer the only major resource to buy sixties items online, but it is joined by a wide range of vintage dealers that have set up shop online with an ever more heterogeneous and specialized or curated selection on sale.

Some of the more seasoned sixties stylers buy clothes now directly with the expectation that they can be easily resold, for example when clothes no longer fit or when they find more desirable items. One sixties styler resells her jewelry and handbags as soon as she finds that they no longer suit her taste or preferences. For example, she sold a black handbag with a short handle because she found one that looked similar yet more beautiful in its details, and had a long enough handle to carry as a more practical shoulder bag. The regular engagement with sixties objects and the buying and selling of second-hand clothes over time lead to rising levels of expertise and the demand for "better," more extravagant or high-quality sixties clothes: "*You just find so much more over the internet. I'm trying to find a scarf for a friend or a Pucci tie for me. Maybe I'll find a handmade suit … we now buy the better stuff. They're collector's items. It's fun*" (m. 30).

The interest in 1960s designer labels resembles an emphasis on distinction, that is similar to the hierarchies in the first market, in which brands connote a sense of difference to no-name mass-fashion. It seems that with increased possibilities come increased expectations towards one's wardrobe, when more distinctive or expensive clothing items replace the more generic. The increased access to unique clothing items, such as 1960s designer wear, or even its replicas, in addition to a much wider selection of clothes that stimulate a higher frequency of clothing purchases, can more quickly decrease the appeal of one's already owned second-hand clothes. This, in turn, may lead to their more rapid disposal, or rather, an accelerated reintroduction into the consumer cycle. Choices for clothing purchases are made much faster and easier in the knowledge that they can straightforwardly be resold. They are not seen as wasted money or a bad buy, but as an investment to be resold at a profit.

Collecting the past

While the increased possibilities for systematic searching and finding do lead to an accelerated use and discarding of clothes, not everyone, however, can part with their clothes—especially if they become part of a collection and, as such, are not viewed as mere commodities (Haubl 2000: 33).

What matters most to me is the search. To search and to find—it's so fun. I don't know, how can I describe it? For example, I also enjoy going out looking for mushrooms. I like to do that in the autumn. I just love finding stuff. And that plays a huge part in it. I'll find blue and yellow shoes and then I want something that matches, so I go on the desperate hunt for yellow trousers, and I'll make sure I find a blue top. It's totally silly, but you're happy when, little by little, you bring the pieces together. You're just happy about it. They're just banalities. It shouldn't be what defines your life, it's just fun really. (w. 30)

The mattering of the search, the seeking and finding described by this sixties styler is part of the collection process that characterizes the approach to the consumption of 1960s material culture. As Rolf Haubl notes, the practice of collecting is a very particular way of owning and using things (Haubl 2000: 31). Collecting is defined by principles of completion and rarity, principles that also can be observed among the consumption practices of sixties stylers where the acquisition of one specific object, for example a pair of shoes, leads to the searching for other objects to form a complete set. This can make the consumption of 1960s fashion quite an arduous process that is colored by an emotional up and down of euphoria and disappointment. Here consumption can be understood to follow almost the principle of hard work, a conscious effort, to match the historic model or the "shape of time" since one defining feature of 1960s fashion was the "total look:" it consisted of the color-coordination of clothing, accessories and even make-up, with the effect of creating a kind of self-imposed micro-uniformity to complete an outfit.

Yet, this kind of matching and coordinating requires the purchase of a great range and number of clothes and accessories in different colors and patterns to make sure that one can still create a variety of matching ensembles (see Figures 14 and 15). *"That's what defined sixties style. It fits like a puzzle. A belt here, a belt there and then at some point you have thirty belts in every possible color and eventually*

FIGURE 14 Detail of matching accessories, green dress worn with red handbag, gloves and boots. Photo: author.

it all fits together" (w. 30). Prior to the 1960s, female appearances were already defined by the color-coordination of gloves, shoes and handbags or the matching arrangement of textures and patterns. Yet, 1960s youth fashion was marked by an attention to such micro details, for example the unitary repetition of the shape of clothing details, prints and jewelry—like coordinating daisy shaped buttons of a jacket with daisy earrings.

> I made my first steps here at the flea market. I bought quite a few dresses at one stall, like where I'd combine them properly, with like silver shoes, I'm into lurex and sparkly things anyway. I thought that was really great, with like a bag and all. I've also got matching jewelry, but that started a bit later. It's not easy to find that sort of stuff instantly. For a while, I bought pendants and the like, I'm into all those plastic rings anyway. But it took me a while to find stuff that matched my expectations. And then all of a sudden, I like bought a ring at every flea market I went to. That's how I eventually ended up with twenty of them. I'd always, that's the way I like it, combine them. So, if I'm wearing something black and white, I'll wear matching rings or shoes or a bag. (w. 29)

In the sixties enthusiasts' recreation of the past style it is important to pay close attention to these details in order to match the sartorial look of the sixties. "*I find these yellow and blue shoes and a colorful belt from somewhere and a matching yellow jumper somewhere else,*" notes one sixties styler, who goes on to describe how she color-coordinates head to toe. And a further interviewee remarks: "*The stuff doesn't look good otherwise. After all, the shoes I got are so colorful that nothing matches unless you color-coordinate*" (w. 29).

But she also points out that it can be quite a challenge to find clothes or accessories in the desired colors, especially when they do not align with seasonal styles and the color palettes offered in contemporary fashion retail, beside the fact that second-hand finds are more defined by chance. That is why, in the face of such difficulties, it is a particularly satisfying feeling to find ideal clothing matches, since the occasion of the rare find is even more joyful. To find exactly what one is looking for triggers the kind of intense emotions that Haubl (2000: 34) considers as such an important aspect of the commitment to the practice of collecting, which is also emphasized by a sixties styler:

> It's like a collector's obsession. My clothes rack is about to fall apart and the one in the hallway just broke because there are too many jackets on it. I just can't get rid of stuff, I've already put away a lot of jackets, but somehow it's like a collector's, well no, not collector's passion—it's just a passion, to own such clothes. You also know that you'll never find anything that's quite the same. (w. 29)

FIGURE 15 Sixties styler's shoe collection. Photo: author.

According to James Clifford, an "excessive, sometimes even rapacious need to *have* is transformed into rule-governed, meaningful desire" (1995: 53). He describes collecting as a strategy for the deployment of a possessive self: collecting as an "assemblage of a material 'world' … involves the accumulation of possessions, the idea that identity is a kind of wealth (of objects, knowledge, memories, experience)" (Clifford 1995: 52). And a wealth in collected trophies and possessions of the 1960s (see Figure 15) brings with it respect and acknowledgment from fellow sixties enthusiasts, who set their own trends:

> You always have a go at what's in—you've just got to have silver boots, or golden boots, something like that. Anything that shines and gets attention is also totally popular in the scene. Silver and golden boots.
>
> Is that recent?
>
> Since last year, I'd say. It always starts with one person who has it and another who checks it out, like "I want that, too, I want that, too, it looks totally cool." And that, yeah, silver and golden boots are really hard to get. I don't have any, I've been looking for them for years. I did have a pair of golden boots, but unfortunately they were too small. So I couldn't buy them and was annoyed. But that's, that's still one of those trophy items. Yeah, 'cos when I get them, I'll be the coolest. That's how it is. If you've got silver boots, you've really got something in your wardrobe. (w. 19)

According to Haubl, a successful hunt for rare collector's items is rewarded with feelings of pride and triumph. If it is a rare piece, and the collector acted more quickly and decisively than anyone else, the item rises to the rank of a trophy (Haubl 2000: 34). For sixties stylers, an item's incorporation into the collection is an intimate affair, since they are mainly clothing items displayed on the own body, revitalizing the object's time in the new context (see Figure 16). The idea of a revitalization of these objects through re-embodiment, or in fact their perception as vital matter, is indicated in the comparison between second-hand consumption and finding and harvesting mushrooms, which in a way equates clothes to "collector's items" consumed by the body. They are cherished material memories of the past, but they are not only put on display on the rack in the hallway, they are also displayed and worn on the body: they are being *used* and *consumed* with each bodily display and revitalization.

Wearing and valuing (certain) material memories

Even if the consumption of old clothes has widely expanded with the fashion-ability of vintage, and old clothes are appreciated and valued for the time they contain or accumulate and materialize, many consumers still feel a level of reluctance towards second-hand clothes. Given that they are pre-owned items, worn by "strangers," who have left their mark in and on these clothes—from the inevitable wear and tear to stains or holes—their reuse is oftentimes perceived as unhygienic. The anxiety of wearing clothes that have previously enveloped another body, one that is moreover unknown, goes back to a deep-seated fear of disease and parasites inherited over generations (Willingmann 2001: 197). Upon their disposal, old clothes are referred to as "rubbish" or "rags" that are declared unwanted and no longer of any value to their previous owner (Botticello 2012). It is for this reason that the reuse of old clothes has long-standing associations with poverty and need (Ginsburg 1980). In the logic of fashion and its idealization of newness, clothes that are disposed of are no longer regarded as current, fresh and fashionable—and therefore become worthless. For sixties stylers, however, it is precisely the clothes' age and the time they carry in or with them that makes them relevant and valuable—especially in comparison to new clothes. This is explained as follows by one sixties styler:

> When I lived at home, my mum would always accuse me of hoarding, of never chucking anything. I can't get rid of anything. And I just think that many of these things, that they fascinate me, that there's a story behind them. They're not all from some kind of factory where they've just been thrown together—but

they have really been on earth now for decades and have experienced what not, I love the thought of that. (w. 29)

Contrary to "soulless" machine-made mass clothing ("from some factory"), objects from the 1960s convey vitality ("earth"). Clothes from the 1960s are, because of their age and cultural biography, seen as matter with memory, thus providing a vibrant link to the past. Since they are original 1960s-made and used clothes, they are witnesses of their time, recalling a period most relevant to sixties stylers. They convey a visual as well as physical experience of and link to the past, forming a kind of material, mobile meeting place with the sixties. In contrast to new clothes, used clothes are perceived as charged with memory and emotions, and found to be more aesthetically pleasing due to traces of time embodied in their materiality. For sixties stylers, these clothes have a special status as surviving artifacts of the sixties, appreciated not only for their aesthetic qualities, but also as carriers of cultural memory.

As material survivals from the 1960s these clothes store and carry time and memory also for those who due to their age did not personally experience the desired era. "In Western traditions, objects serve memory … they constitute our picture of the past," writes Marius Kwint (1999: 2). As products of the 1960s, worn in the past as well as today, they can be seen as inherited objects with a particular material-mnemonic potency, which has also been ascribed to the value of authenticity in museum pieces (see Korff and Roth 1990: 16). The museum object is considered an authentic document and testimony. Yet, since authenticity refers to more than just realness or originality, the museum object conveys a further quality: it is a sensuous and affective dimension that makes the world of objects in a museum so fascinating. The fascination for the authentic is stirred by a sensuous tension between a feeling of material immediacy and historical distance, the simultaneity of the temporally present and the historically other (Korff and Roth 1990: 17).

The clothes inherited from the 1960s are past-in-present: they stir associations and become tools for remembering the past in a new temporal context. Their material, temporal immediacy and at the same time their temporal otherness and unfamiliarity in the present, constitute a particular appeal for the generation who can only encounter and remember the past in retrospect—without their own lived experience. In addition to the material capacities of the clothes, it is the *idea* of memory ("*I love the thought of that*"), which becomes here a value in its own right. As material memories of the 1960s, these objects enable a new generation to get in touch with the past, to feel it with all senses and to wear it intimately with their body and movement (see Figure 16).

The old pieces of clothing are felt to be charged with memory and time, and to convey a material and experiential dimension of temporality—and otherness—that new clothes do not mediate: "*But when I know it's something old, that's nice.*

FIGURE 16 Sixties styler in Columbus chair, wearing 1960s dress and boots.
Photo: author.

They're made differently. And you notice that the fabric or the zips are different or I always find them really lovely. The old labels that are always at the back, they're always really lovely" (w. 29). The adjectives "lovely" and "different" are repeated as a way of highlighting the aesthetics of originals and the look and feel of their material distinctiveness. The time inscribed in these garments and worn with the body opens up a corporeal experience of difference "between times," gained from the garment's fabric and finish. A garment's time is not only apparent in its shape or *gestalt*, but in its entire material construction, attesting to levels of innovation in textile technology (see Vinken 2005: 68–9).

Today, the predominant materials for fashionable garments are cotton, viscose and synthetics equipped with Lycra. These stretch materials, now used in almost all clothing items from suits to denim, enable a figure-hugging garment to fit without sacrificing comfort because these highly flexible materials adapt to the shape and movement of the body. Modern stretch garments, that follow and adapt to the individual shape of the body, produce a very different bodily appearance than clothes of the 1960s that give a different shape and feel to the body in their fitted tailoring. To modern wearers who are used to the comfort of Lycra, 1960s clothes can feel more restrictive or even stiff, also due in part to the thickness of garment fabrics and added lining. Fashion in the 1960s relied heavily on new polyesters, such as Diolen, Diolen Loft, Trevira, Trevira 2000, as well as acrylic materials and woolen blends. These early synthetic materials, also often used in textured fabrics, provide a very different haptic experience to that of natural fibers and define—in addition to the brightness of colors—the "plastic character" of many 1960s clothes (see Figure 13). And it is their synthetic nature and resistance against moths and other forms of decay that also ensures the material survival of these old clothes.

Beyond the garment construction and fit, the materiality of these synthetic clothes imprints itself on the body and feeling of comfort in another way: since these older synthetic materials are oftentimes thicker and heavier they are less breathable and known to have quite a "steamy" effect on the body that heightens perspiration and potentially body odor. The olfactory effect or quality of these used garments is further intensified by the "scents of time" that are already layered into the fibers of these clothes—a mixture of stale perfume, dust, lavender and moth-balls (see Trosse 1999: 20). While these scents get reactivated in the interchange between the wearer and the garment, some fabrics also develop their own distinct smell through the passage of time—that is through the aging of the textile material itself (Trosse 1999: 20–1). While one of the attractive selling arguments was that these synthetic fabrics are "easy care" so that they can be quickly washed and dried, it is nearly impossible to rid them today of the smell of their age or time passed, which instead gets intensely reactivated once the item is worn again. This particular quality of aged garments—their olfactory capturing and transmission of time and the olfactory memory imprint of a former body—is a side effect of the wearing of vintage clothes that is perceived as the most challenging one, especially in light of contemporary expectations of hygiene and cleanliness.

In addition to the olfactory encounter with the passage of time, the garment's age also has a haptic effect, since the feel of fabrics changes over time as well. Hence the time and historical otherness that constitute the unique quality of aged garments is transmitted in all dimensions of a garment—and affects intimately all human senses. Due to the intimate relationship between clothing and the body, the wearing of old clothes generates an instant temporary exchange between the current wearer and the material past, between the body in the present and body history. There is likely no other object in material culture through which this kind of immediacy and at the same time temporal distance between present and past can be felt in a more intimate and immediate way.

Yet, the age and passing of time over the course of several decades, which make these clothes so appealing as material survivals, is also what renders them susceptible to decay. If they are to last and endure further passing of time—and further wear—they require careful treatment and maintenance. The aging process materializes in an increasing fragility of the material and construction of the clothes. The garments are especially vulnerable at the seams, which, once damaged, can make them unsuitable for everyday use:

> Sometimes you'll wash the stuff and notice that the seams are totally brittle and that the trousers are no longer any good … Or shoes. It's a bit of a problem to get original shoes. Then you're glad to find an unworn pair and then you wear them twice and, great, the glue no longer holds. It makes sense when they've been lying about somewhere for decades. Then you take them to the cobbler about five times, cos they mean something to you, well, it gets a bit much sometimes. (m. 35)

Sixties stylers aim to preserve 1960s fashion, though not like in a museum collection with the mission to preserve the past for future generations, protecting it from the decay of time and use. Instead, the clothes serve their personal interests and devotion to the sixties aesthetic. Yet they look after the old clothes, they repair them carefully when needed and tend to wear their favorite pieces sparingly and consciously, to ensure that they last them a long time and many wears. This also means that the clothes are not thrown in the washer and dryer, but they prefer to wash them by hand in the sink, or larger pieces in the bathtub. But even the most careful handling eventually impacts the durability of clothes and their wear accelerates their material decay. The way sixties stylers engage with their garments is reminiscent of clothing practices, which Andrea Hauser describes as typical for pre-industrial societies, that engaged with things in a more intensive way, that is either by caring and maintaining them, or equally by using them extensively until they fall apart. With the expansion of modern mass-production, however, the practice of repairing and maintaining things has been largely replaced by the practice of buying the ever new. This paramount emphasis on newness, combined with a much wider scale of object variety, led to the increasing devaluing and accelerating disposal and replacement of things (Hauser 1994: 22; see also Fletcher 2014). In this light, the careful treatment of 1960s clothes indicates a great respect for them as things that have acquired material qualities and value over time and are found to be not as easily replaceable as new mass-produced clothes. Yet, notwithstanding their care, repair and selected occasional wear, the old clothes are nevertheless used and consumed. And their use and consumption extends as far as the entire alteration of the old clothes—unthinkable in the context of the preservation of clothes in the museum—to adapt them to one's body and taste.

> I once found a dress, it was made of a really thin fabric, it really wouldn't flatter my figure and there was no way of altering it because the fabric was just too thin, so I just cut it off … I thought the print was so lovely—I loved it. I just had to have it, for 1 Euro. I didn't immediately know what I was going to do with it, but I just got it anyway. (w. 30)

Here the buying of second-hand clothes—even if just for the beauty of the print—works like a future investment or original raw material that can be recycled for something else, in this case the making of a new sixties dress from old fabric. This practice also helps to make up for limited financial means.

> Well, I don't spend that much anyway. In a month, I'll spend perhaps about 25 Euros for a lovely dress. See this dress [points to a Pucci-style mini dress hanging decoratively at her wardrobe] was really long, I made it mini and from the leftover I want to make a mini-skirt with belt loops. I always think that makes it worth it. Well, cos I get two out of one. And I tinker with it and think to myself that it was worth it. And they end up like really perfect, just the way I want them. (w. 21)

The interest in real material survivals of the sixties goes along with the aim to remain close to the style of the time. For sixties stylers, 1960s design stands out as an aesthetic that is unique. Colorful, with round, organic shapes, the things mediate for them something of a sense of *joie de vivre* and dynamism associated with the sixties. *"Those things convey something, too. It's not only that you find them beautiful, yeah, you can relate to it, it's a feeling you have, but I also think that those things carry a particular* zeitgeist *and that's why they're interesting"* (m. 30).

As Wolfgang Schepers notes, the political ideas of the 1960s have largely been reduced to the aesthetic (Schepers 1998: 7). Yet the aesthetic provides for sixties stylers still a concrete material connection to the decade, which resonates with them in the context of the present. For Schepers, the remarkable optimism associated with the 1960s and its faith in better times provide a stark contrast to society several decades later (1998: 7), which is for him one reason they are appealing to consumers in retrospect. This is reflected in the accounts of sixties stylers:

> Well it's not just the aesthetic dimension. It's sort of the whole decade. It's not enough to focus only on the clothes. Maybe you express that feeling or visually transmit it to others. But it's just a time in which so much happened, where people still hit the streets and were less disillusioned than nowadays. (w. 29)

Even if, as one sixties styler claims, the difference in time leads to an element of glorification, the clothes allow the wearer to connect to the time. Yet the connection is embedded in the present, where there is an echo of the narrative of the sixties and the youth cultural interest in "difference" that remains as relevant for consumers today: "*There's no need to be dragged along by fashion, you can also dress and behave differently*" (m. 30). Many of those interviewed relate wearing the sixties with the idea "*not to be told what to do, that's important, to differentiate oneself*" (m. 30). For these reasons the time and effort invested in searching, collecting and using 1960s clothes is gladly taken into account, co-constituting along with the aesthetics the value they place on 1960s vintage clothes. After all, to consume and appreciate the authentic, to deal with the original old clothing on a daily basis and to adapt it to daily needs rubs off on one's sense of self. The newly defined value of the old is determined by the value the object has for the current self. It is not only the material qualities or the time context or narrative of the sixties but also the temporal distance that makes these things valuable and distinctive to the sixties styler: "*I prefer unique items and old things have a certain charm, in my opinion. That's what things need to have, it needs to be there*" (m. 24). The aura of the original and the "charm" of the old, to which Georg Simmel (2004) referred in his writing on fashion, make it fitting to distinguish it from the new, which for most sixties stylers is simply uniform and monotonous:

> Yeah, especially at H&M everything looks the same. At least they used to have slim suits for work, classics, basics in inverted commas. Nowadays it's all so uniform. Now stone grey or that army look or whatever. You can't get anything else. That's actually a real shame and that's why they're more interesting (the sixties), cos you say to yourself, well, there's no real variety in contemporary fashion. (m. 35)

In contrast to the mass-produced wares of the fashion industry, old clothes— themselves once mass-produced—become distinct over time, and fit with the desire to be individual. The argument that everything is uniform and that there is no variety in fashion may not hold so easily, not least considering that vintage—as old or old-looking clothes—is firmly integrated in the fashion market. But perhaps the vastness of fashion in the market, and the change of variations propelled by fast fashion, lets it come to appear "all the same." The focus on one particular style, here of the 1960s, provides then a sense of stability, as one sixties styler mentions how her clothes and her style make her feel like a "*tower of strength*" (w. 30). To focus on a particular era can, to some extent, immunize against the rapid change promoted by the fashion industry. But that is not to say that sixties enthusiasts are immune to consumption: "*Yeah, I'm still a consumer. But my consumerism has changed, I don't go to some sort of boutique to get fully kitted out, but I try my luck at flea markets and on the internet. Of course you're still a consumer, cos you're a collector of some stuff you can't get enough of, you always want more or something better, something more outrageous*" (m. 33).

6 VINTAGE STYLE AND MEDIATED MEMORIES: SIXTIES DIY

Originals and copies

In spite of the importance attributed to old, original second-hand clothes, it is not the case that all clothes worn by sixties stylers are actual survivors from the 1960s. A restriction to old clothes would lead to a rather reduced wardrobe, since not all clothes desired are available any longer—or may have ever existed in the past. The rarity of old clothes that fit with the current tastes and contemporary interest in sixties style makes it essential to also buy and wear new clothes. In addition, it is sometimes the lack of fit of old clothes, or their material conditions, including imprints of former wearers, that set limits on the use and appreciation of "material memories:"

> What's sometimes a bit unpleasant, you've got these nice things, but they smell so badly that you think to yourself, just let them hang. There's no way of losing the stench. Well, nowadays you can buy a lot of stuff new, like lots of slightly flared trousers, a sixties flare, not a seventies flare. You can buy really nice stuff new, even shoes and such. It's quite nice actually. (w. 27)

The Swedish fashion chain Hennes & Mauritz was in several interviews referenced as an important resource to make up for the lack of fitting old clothes. The company opened its first stores in Germany in the late 1980s and quickly established itself during the 1990s as a leader in the fashion market, ranking today among the most profitable vertically integrated clothing companies. Its success is based on an affordable product range, made possible through a global production network that provides vast quantities of clothes to the large number of stores worldwide, with many cities having several stores. The largely young clientele is attracted by the wide range of products and styles on offer, and by the speed with which trends are translated in their designs. This includes recycling many of the styles of past decades, copying the style of second-hand or vintage clothes and bringing back elements from the most diverse youth cultural styles, from swing and rock 'n' roll to hippie and psychedelic through to punk rock, new wave, hip-hop, metal, grunge and rave. As a mass producer of fashion they are also a bulk supplier of recent fashion history, frequently offering exact replicas of old clothes.

Those interviewed remain ambivalent about the mass-produced retro or vintage-style clothes. On the one hand the mass-distribution of new, old-looking clothes is perceived to lead to a dilution, assuming that most consumers wear it only because it is "in fashion," which is seen as ephemeral and not part of a deeper commitment to the sixties style: "*I think it's a shame when people wear it cos it's fashionable. I think it's a shame. I'd like it if people said, 'Hey, finally some proper clothes, I love it. I've finally found something.' But I don't believe that's the case. In my opinion, 80* per cent *of people wear it cos it's trendy*" (w. 30). Yet, many also make a point for the need of new vintage or sixties style clothing:

Well, there's two sides to it. It doesn't really bother me when someone wears something from H&M. The trousers I'm wearing are also from H&M.

Oh, really?

No, you wouldn't think so. H&M is actually great. I really think so. What did someone say, "individuality off the rack." But it always amazes me. I find H&M really great. At any other place you might pay a fortune for it. … I'd prefer to find only originals. Of course that'd be great, second-hand clothes tell much more of a story than the new. But I still think that there's nothing wrong with new stuff, especially the basics you might need. A t-shirt or whatever here and there … Well, I'm not so strict about it. Cos, I couldn't wear red trousers otherwise. Otherwise, I don't find trousers in my size from back in the sixties. It's totally unrealistic to think, I'll only wear original trousers, cos I definitely won't find any. (w. 30)

Almost all interviewees found that original trousers that fit are most difficult to find so that many buy them in the first fashion market when they come in a fit that can be integrated into the sixties style along with second-hand clothing. In order to avoid a situation where "*someone is wearing the same stuff*," however, many develop strategies to individualize the new vintage clothes so that they are no longer "*uniform mass-fashion*," but fit instead with their image of sixties style. A scenario in which someone is wearing the same thing or where it could be identified as mass-produced presents itself as a terrifying thought, which could be described with Gabriele Mentges as "an anxiety of uniformity" (Mentges 2005a). It makes such clothes unsuitable for the desire to be individual—it is impossible to say "that's mine" when others wear the same clothes. It is an example of how clothes as a part of one's style, shape more than body and appearance, they provide a substance for the story-telling of oneself, a material reassurance of the "I" to signal, as Virginia Postrel puts it in an equation, "*I like that—I'm like that*" (Postrel 2003: 102).

Contemporary clothes are adapted to look like they are from the past as it is transmitted in images and objects of the time, in order to not disturb the authenticity sixties stylists strive after in their particular use of sixties things. As one sixties styler put it, it is "*exactly the accessories. They make the difference. You can see it straight away if someone is into it or not. Most people don't go the extra mile*" (m. 30). In line with Bourdieu (1984), the consumer and connoisseur of original items can make out the details that set him or her apart, here from consumers of new retro or vintage clothes who do not look like they are going for an "authentic" sixties style. Part of the expertise acquired in collecting the sixties consists of the ability to distinguish between original and copy, with the original having a higher value for its material and temporal qualities. One interviewee notes her preference for originals:

> I develop an affinity for the clothing item as such. Just the thought that the piece of clothing has travelled so far. That's one reason and I can also tell the difference. That bothers me about the new purple shoes that I can't dance with them. Or I notice that they're more bulky. I know I've got a sharp eye for details. I see the difference myself. If I didn't see it, it might be something else. It wouldn't bother me then. (w. 30)

The appreciation for the design features of old vintage clothes, the sensual quality and the feeling of the original's difference is potentiated in the comparison with new reproductions of 1960s designs. This is key to the working of vintage and the production of its superior value, emerging in the context of the mass-production of the new. As Hillel Schwarz (2000) notes in his book on the culture of the copy, copies are necessary for the definition of authenticity, they are the evidence or assurance of the value of originality, as the idea of uniqueness only emerges in the context of reproducibility. That is, the better the copies, the more important the original becomes (Schwarz 2000: 219). "*I just see that I find it more aesthetic ... in terms of the material, the cut, the playful details*" (w. 30). The material qualities of originals are valued more highly than those of 1960s reproductions, and they are experienced as mediating a different feel on the body: "*Some of the thin or delicate fabrics cling too much to the body, you don't feel so comfortable in them and cos it fits weirdly they immediately crinkle*" (w. 30). While the body often determines the shape of many contemporary clothes, it is the tailoring of old 1960s clothes that is felt to determine the shape of the body. Often made of synthetic fibers, fabrics used for clothes in the 1960s (see Pavitt 2008: 33–9) are described as thicker and heavier than those of contemporary clothes, often made of thinner cotton or viscose and usually without any lining. As Petra Leutner notes, the formal and material structure of the minidresses of the 1960s creates a much more "technical body" in appearance. Compared to newer, softer and tight-fitting clothes, those of the 1960s appear "stiff" and tailored according to a geometrical conception of the body where the garment takes on a shape of its own that is independent from the body (Leutner 2004: 296–7). When made with Lyrca, new vintage-style clothes were felt to be more figure-hugging, imprinting themselves as a "second skin" and accentuating the shape of the body more than the garments from the 1960s with a more tailored structure. In addition to the different feel, new vintage-style clothes also tend to be seen to be deficient in their material qualities and details, making them inferior to 1960s originals, as can be seen in the following example:

> I got a jacket from H&M. You really notice how it's thrown together. You can tell from the material. But the cut's quite nice. And there are boring black plastic buttons and it looks, the jacket looks like nothing much at all really. And if you put some buttons on it, nice buttons, it looks quite different. It's somehow the attention to detail. (w. 30)

By substituting one detail for another, the "boring" black plastic buttons for original "nice" buttons from the flea market, the new copy is modified and upgraded in a way that makes it closer to a sixties piece. Adding the old to the new, the latter fuses with the former and becomes a material hybrid between past and present. Accessories and additions to clothing such as buttons and belt loops thus become minute details, adding authenticity to the new, through which they can come closer to a vintage garment that is valued for its temporal difference and uniqueness.

Making and embodying time: Updating the past

In much the same way that the new can be made "dated" to look like a 1960s vintage item, old clothes are altered and adapted according to contemporary needs. This is particularly true with dresses and skirts, which are usually shortened by sixties stylers so as to make them match with their vision of the sixties. This could be seen in the context of Budin, the aforementioned clothing shop with the old stock of unworn 1960s clothes. The dresses and skirts from the 1960s sold here were all "moderate" in length, ending the width of a hand above the knee, reflecting the length of the early mini fashion of the mid-1960s. The women I interviewed who shopped in the store found this length too average, and shortened them to late 1960s and early 1970s standards, when skirt lengths were the shortest (see Hofmann 2009).

Another example of a misfit between old clothes and new bodies is the tailoring used to mold the female body shape in the 1960s. The women felt the bodily difference most notably in the tight armholes, narrow-cut shoulders or the positioning of tucks. A body that is more used to the comfort of stretchable garments feels here the material boundary between past and present body images. The interviewees note how the bust line was set much higher, which they feel they could only adapt to by wearing more rigid underwear with very structured, pointy bras, a look they perceived as uncomfortable and "unnatural."

The extent to which old garments produce a very different body shape and look from today was for example evident in the underwear and swimwear of the 1960s, which was on sale at Budin. Many sixties stylers bulk-bought bikinis and swimsuits in order to sell them at sixties events and online, but were largely unsuccessful at doing so. The heavier and stiffer materials of the bikinis, along with their multipartite tailoring, were not perceived to suit the contemporary wearer. This is especially in comparison to modern swimwear, made of lighter, stretch fabrics. In contrast to this, historical bikini tops with wide straps, fiddly fasteners and inflexible bra cups shape the bust into a torpedo-like form. Tops are combined with swim shorts that fastened at the body with elastic bands at the waist and thighs, creating a balloon-shaped bottom. Here, sixties stylers noted that they preferred comfort over historical accuracy, choosing new vintage-style swimwear, which updates old patterns with new materials. Original 1960s swimwear, at least, was summed up in the following terms: "*You'll drown in that.*" While some in principle would wear the underwear and swimwear of the 1960s, they formed a clear minority among the interviewees, since such clothes were seen as "unwearable."

In the wearing of the sixties style the contemporary body becomes a matter of boundary or threshold between past and present. While the clothes are arranged and worn to produce a look in close fit to the style of the 1960s, they are embodied through a contemporary wearer who is affected by current body ideals and beauty regimes.

Compared to pictures of mod girls of the 1960s, who incorporated male clothing items and leisure wear into their wardrobes and created an androgynous or "boyish" look with short hair styles and minimal make-up (see Barnes 1981), the women in the sixties scene tend to focus on the pop-art and op-art inspired clothes associated with the looks of "Swinging London" as they circulate widely in books about 1960s fashion and design, in films and photography. This more gendered and body revealing look seems to resonate more with the current wearer as noted by one woman, who points out the difference to early mod style, which she finds too conventional for her taste:

You really do notice it with the girls, really good-looking, slim girls, super sexy clothes, yeah not as conventionally dressed as before, more experimental. And

I do think that, yeah sexy, that women should be sexily styled and not like so androgynous. (w. 29)

As another interviewee notes, "*I think that it's not only an influence of the sixties scene, but that people are inevitably influenced by the current context.*" She refers to the way styles worn in the sixties scene tend to be in line with current trends, in which elements of sixties fashion—along with other past decades—have inspired contemporary fashion season and season again, not just in clothes but also with regard to styling and accessories: "*Round cuts are simply fashionable again and I do believe that many people are indirectly influenced … Somehow they're all influenced, which is normal, which is even good. It would be a bit weird if it all remained the same for decades*" (w. 29). The sixties stylers draw then from the whole panoply of material on offer in the first and second-hand clothing markets. The use of new fashion towards the old style enables them to make up for the lack of clothes that do not fit—either their body or their taste. And equally the updating of old clothes is used to adapt the past style to the now. This is done through selection, picking out specific garments from the 1960s, or through temporal layering and the mixing of old and new in one outfit, as well as through the customizing of old clothes and the tailoring of new garments based on old models. The sixties style is then not conserved in time, but infused with and updated in the now.

The "tinkering" with the past through clothes is part of the appeal of vintage and dressing in sixties style. For example one sixties styler talks about the joy she gains from spending time with the modification and altering of sixties clothes. When she can get hold of them at a good price, she buys second-hand clothes even if they do not fit to use them as a resource to make two out of one: by shortening a long dress and using the excess fabric for a short skirt or by making a hot pants outfit from a long cat suit, using the excess trouser legs to make belt loops. "*I don't actually sew anything myself, I just alter it. Tighter, shorter, belt loop, no belt loop. But I've made a pair of trousers and some skirts, but that's really easy*" (w. 21). To experiment with old clothes and modify them to become new, so that they are exactly as she likes them, gives her as much pleasure as the hunt for originals. The significance of the sensuous experience is grounded in this material exchange with old things from the 1960s, where she wonders what the items have "gone through" or who might have worn them. She speaks with great enthusiasm about the work and time she spends customizing and individualizing old clothes: "*Yes. Well it's, when I find something, it's a joy. It makes me happy, euphoric, I'm happy all day long. And I also look forward to the sewing*" (w. 21). She not only enjoys working on the clothes, but also relishes the process of conceptualizing the clothes and the prospect of wearing them and to fashion herself in them. The modification and making of the clothes allows her to design the clothes according to her own ideas, through which she feels independent from the contemporary fashion market. But she feels nevertheless constrained by the decreasing availability of suitable 1960s vintage clothes in the second-hand market.

Home or tailor-made clothes have become increasing practices to substitute for the scarcity. For many of the interviewees, it is just a small step from the modification of old and new clothes to the own design or creation of clothing, but with a notable gender twist: none of the male interviewees even considered the idea of making their own clothes, preferring instead the services of professional tailors. This is due in part to the preconception of sewing considered as a traditional "female activity." But it is also due to the greater difficulty of tailoring menswear suits, trousers and shirts compared to miniskirts and simple shift dresses in the silhouette of the 1960s, which some women described to be able to craft themselves without having advanced sewing skills or training.

> We come up with them ourselves. We don't have original patterns, you can buy them, but it's tough to get hold of and the clothes are usually boring, in the places you find them, you know. That's why we always do it ourselves. There's a shop in London, it sells everything from the 20s to the 70s, well they sell everything, even bric-a-brac. And they have patterns, well I never bought anything there, it's so expensive, but they only have really plain stuff, I can do that myself. (w. 22)

What is interesting to note here is that original patterns are not used, as this sixties styler finds them all too boring. It is more likely that a certain dress is taken as the starting point from which variations in color and material can be made, allowing the sixties to be molded and reproduced according to one's own ideas. To make one's own clothes is an affordable alternative, described especially by younger sixties stylers, in this case two students. Older interviewees with a steady income, however, are getting more used to tailor-made clothes. It has become, as noted in one interview, the "norm" for those wishing to get what can no longer be bought second-hand. This is corroborated by a sixties styler who cannot sew, and who, similar to men who get their suits made, goes to the tailor:

> I also wasn't lucky enough that my mum hung onto lots of stuff. Others are lucky and told me they still find things like that from relatives. And when I started looking for things hesitantly in second-hand shops, there were still a few things left, you could still get lucky, at flea markets and in second-hand shops. But nowadays not so much. Rarely. That's why I've turned to having lots of stuff tailor made. That and combining new things, so lots and lots of tailor made stuff. (w. 29)

With access to historic models of 1960s fashion in photography and design books and online—and buying synthetic fabrics that come close to 1960s materials—she

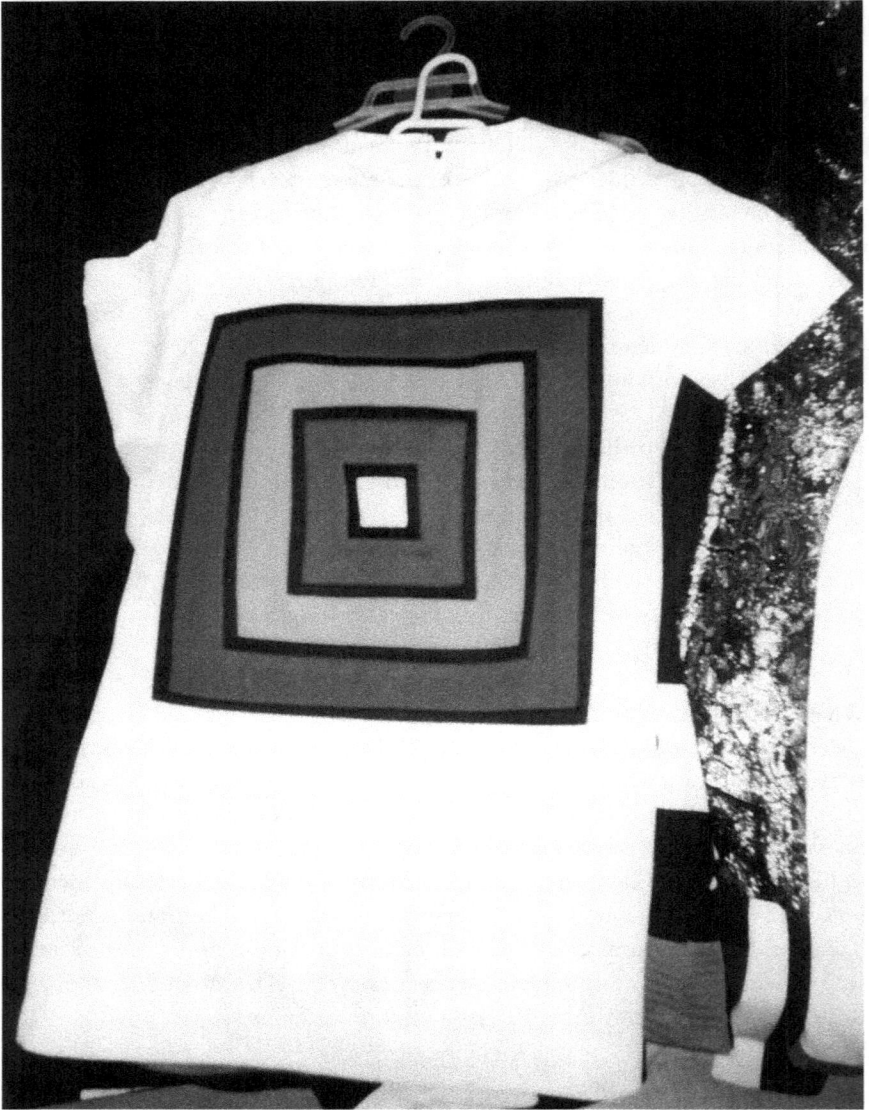

FIGURE 17 Custom-made sixties dress in pop art style. Photo: author.

goes to the tailor and gets bespoke replicas in the style of 1960s designs by Yves Saint Laurent, André Courrèges and Rudi Gernreich. She is particularly fascinated by dresses inspired by art, such as the Mondrian dress, or with color block contrasts and geometric patterns in the design of "archetypal" sixties pieces (see Figure 17), that she adapts to her taste and measurements with personal changes made to details such as sleeves, lengths and color combinations.

Imaging the past

Wearing sixties style is not only based on the consumption of objects, such as old clothes or new, vintage-style clothes, but equally relies on the consumption of images (see Figure 18).

Looks from the 1960s circulate widely and are mediated in a range of sources, from old fashion magazines to contemporary coffee table books on 1960s design—and of course on the internet which provides non-stop access to photos, film and music recordings of the 1960s. Remediated old films, television series and music programs provide rich sources from which to draw in the process of self-fashioning in sixties style. Oftentimes an interest in the narrative content of these sources, particularly with regard to the replay of 1960s television programming, has been described as secondary to the costumes and styles shown in them:

> Where do you get ideas for your clothes? What inspires you?
>> Films. We record a lot of films. (w. 22)
>> Even when they're mediocre. (w. 19)
>> We make sure, right, it's from around the time, there'll be lots of women in nice dresses. (w. 22)
>> Also, what's your favorite film again? Something with … (w. 19)
>> "Himmel voller Erde". (w. 22)

FIGURE 18 Object and image collage in the bedroom of a sixties styler. Photo: author.

Yes, "Himmel voller Erde" or "Wir Hau'n die Pauker" [laughs]. Those great German films. Or, it's going to be on again next week, our favorite film, that great Austrian film "Bel Ami 2000" from the sixties or "Das Go-Go-Girl vom Blow Up." Our film, that no one seems to know, it's really cool, from the sixties. A German film, set in Munich and Vienna, I think. But they're totally ridiculous plots, but there's lots of nice mini-dresses in them. That means that we then stop the film and I then make a sketch of it. (w. 19)

The two interviewees talk about how they trawl through TV-guides for films from the sixties and record them to get a better picture of the era's fashion and to specifically search for clothes that they can recreate. Pausing the film, and putting the look of the sixties on hold, they sketch the dresses and thus create their own record of a personal, interest-based survey of sixties fashion. This gives an example of the very selective, image based engagement with 1960s fashion history, where only images are collected that resonate with their current taste and interest. Such a television viewer may be described as what Francisca Roller (1997) has called a conscious "trash converter" of the cheap programming of privately owned television stations, that fill their programs outside prime time with the rerun of old shows. It is a form of television viewing that Roller sees as characteristic of the expansion of mass media. This includes many cable stations in Germany lowering their content quality since the 1980s and 1990s, where the choice lies for her between a total abstention from television and an entirely new way of watching it (1997: 213). Usually the recycled television shows that are broadcast are of the more recent decades, but movies and TV shows from the 1960s still make their way onto today's screen and are accessible on YouTube or other online film and video services such as netflix. And not only do old series fascinate for their looks, but also those that are made to look old, such as the more recent American television show *Mad Men*, launched in 2007, which also propelled another sixties revival in fashion.

For sixties enthusiasts, *Mad Men*, broadcast on German television with a delay of two years in 2009, is particularly appealing for its careful attention to detail and historical accuracy aiming to recreate the style of the 1960s as authentic as possible. In addition the series is set in a design context, with the story based on Don Draper, head of a rising advertising agency on Madison Avenue. The first season is set in the beginning of the 1960s, still embedded in 1950s style, and progresses forward over several seasons to the late 1960s. The series makes the change of time (and with that also the temporalities of fashion) in 1960s America its theme (see also Murugan 2011; Stoddard 2011). With its attempt for historical accuracy and its initial setting in the early 1960s, the show also moved away from the presentation of styles and images that have been more widely repeated and that are more prominently associated with the "swinging sixties" (see Warner 2014: 94). In countering the popular memory of the "hyperversion" of the mid-to-late sixties, popularized for example a decade earlier in the comedic *Austin Powers* movies (1997–2002), *Mad Men* started out, by comparison, in a more "toned down" early sixties style. It was a style that stood out for its apparent "historical accuracy"—breaking with the circulating popular images of the 1960s through a look that seemed more anachronistic or "dated" and old-fashioned when it first emerged in the context of the latter half of the 2000s. Through this change in visual representation, the series gave the sixties again a newness and "fashionability" that quickly translated into contemporary fashion design—and also did not leave the style preferences of sixties stylers untouched (see for example the style in Dean Chalkley's *The New Faces*, 2010).

Images have played an important role in the rise of retro and vintage fashion. The interest in earlier fashion times and styles is usually not sparked by sartorial objects alone, but by clothes that are mediated and encoded in images. The most important medium for this in the context of the sixties style is the role of photography, which turned in the 1960s into a major tool for the promotion of fashion and clothing, replacing the use of illustration. Photography is a medium with a very particular relationship to time or temporality, for its capturing and "freezing" of a moment, removing it as a fragment from the flux of time (Busch 1995: 362), which enters as image into new time contexts. Susan Sontag has referred to photography as a form of acquisition, both through the production of an image of a subject or moment, and through the viewing. She describes the latter as a "consumer's relation to events, both to events which are part of our experience and to those which are not—a distinction between types of experience that such habit-forming consumership blurs" (Sontag 1973: 155–6). She alludes with this to the experience of time or transience through photography.

Elizabeth Wilson comments on the close relationship between fashion and photography that they both "function as potent visual representation of history; of the past" (Wilson 2013: 94). She further notes how with the rise of mass media technologies, from early amateur snapshots, photography has become a "major bearer of personal memories, just as images in the mass media become the archives of public memory" (Wilson 2013: 94). With Sontag, Wilson refers to the ghostliness of these images, with the persons caught on camera "testifying to the relentless passage of time," wearing the clothes of their time that are now outmoded, which only further contributes to the sense of transience old photographs—and old clothes—convey (Wilson 2013: 97–8).

However, for the viewers of old images, such as sixties stylers, these media or image bound memories often spark interest and the recollection and reanimation of former styles. In contrast to second-hand clothes available as material objects, their mediation in images, such as fashion photography, or the old images broadcasted on television and circulating online, shows the clothes embodied

FIGURE 19 Sixties styler wearing self-made fringe dress modeled on film. Photo: author.

or "animated." The images give an understanding of how the clothes were worn and performed with the body, showing their interplay with other clothes, styling and accessories. This is particularly the case with moving images, in which old films for example convey a sense of the bodily habitus of a time, showing how a body walks or dances in clothes, and what kind of postures a specific form of clothing enacts with the body. So even while they may be constructed images and stories, old photos and films offer a fragmentary, yet somewhat vivid image of the look of a time. Films provide in this sense a kind of record of historical body performances, which serve as source of inspiration and also as guide in the contemporary performance of sixties style. And they can also come to serve as evidence to legitimate the use of certain clothing items.

> But the pink dress with the white fringe, I mean, that's not really sixties. And when I sewed it last year, a friend of mine said on the Isle of Wight, "Well that doesn't look sixties at all." But I'd seen it in the great "Go-Go Girl vom Blow Up Club" film and it was sixties then, even though it also looks twenties, cos it's a bit Charleston-style. But I just loved it. But it's not like we have to get the cut right all the time, it shouldn't look modern, but it ... (w. 22)
>
> Yeah, it should somehow fit. (w. 19)
>
> Yeah, it should somehow fit, but I'll wear it and I won't think of my friend, who said "Oh dear, that doesn't look at all sixties." (w. 22)

Wearing the sixties, as described by the interviewees, not only requires a good knowledge of where to source one's clothes and accessories, but also an understanding of the relevant fashion history. This entails a feeling for the correct clothes, complemented by the right sort of jewelry, shoes and bags, in addition to matching sixties-style make-up and hairstyle (see Figure 20).

Another sixties styler recounts how she gained a knowledge of fashion history and, specifically, of 1960s fashion by watching old films and televisions series. For her, films are "contemporary witnesses" of the 1960s that, lagging by a year, give an accurate picture of the style of the time: "*I've always liked watching sixties films, for as long as I can remember. And I always checked, whenever I watched a film and found it appealing, which year it's from exactly. And that somehow stays with you*" (w. 30).

FIGURE 20 Sixties styler at the Book Club, Shoreditch, London 2010. Photo:
PYMCA/UIG via Getty Images.

Mediated memories

The knowledge of fashion history that guides in the performance of the sixties style is here drawn from the mediation of the 1960s in film and television, that was part of the media socialization of youth. While my interviewees did not live in the 1960s, growing up in the 1970s, 1980s and 1990s, they still experienced the visual impact of the decade. Having no first-hand experience of the 1960s, these visual resources are part of the cultural memory that may come to feel intimate and personal, and they imprint themselves in later aesthetic preferences—even, or sometimes especially, if what is remembered as sixties has nothing to do with any "real" everyday life, but is informed by the highly fictional narratives of the 1960s in popular culture that have become iconic for the time, such as science fiction and Cold War spy movies: "*I already liked them as a child, James Bond and such. But there are also those strange secret agent films and fantasy or science fiction and those Japanese ones*" (m. 24).

Examples for fashion history, however, are drawn not only from the past or the rendering of 1960s fashion in films and photos, but also from the past style performed in the present: through direct interaction with others in the scene, by observing and "dating" the clothes worn at parties and the photos made thereof. Sixties events are bound up with the mediation of memory, for example by photographically capturing party moments and people's outfits. These photos can then be found in the picture galleries of sixties websites or on Facebook. There is a whole array of archived information on clothing—as mediated, sartorial memory—that, with a certain time lag, when the clothes are no longer immediately remembered, are used by other sixties stylers for their own self-fashioning:

> Or we have a look at, that's what I did yesterday, photos of some party that happened a while ago. Then, I look who's on them, and then you see that sort of thing and we make the clothes, not in the same colors, 'cos that's not allowed, others are wearing them. I take the same cut and use other colors. Or I come up with something myself or take it off the internet. (w. 22)
> Exactly, there are so many pictures. (w. 19)

The others are important as sources of inspiration, but also in order to develop a set of scene-specific fashion skills. While the look of others may not be directly copied, their observation and evaluation forms a crucial basis from which to develop one's own style through, so to speak, lessons in embodied fashion history interactively imparted in the social—and sartorial—exchange with others. For example, one sixties styler explains the joy it brings her to observe others and put a date to their clothing: "*If you pay attention to detail, you can just see it. You just develop an eye for it. I've talked to a friend about this a lot. That must be or from which year must that be. It's a lot of fun*" (w. 30).

The example shows again the importance of social and aesthetic interaction with others for the development of style and clothing competences, including the familiarity with, or visual knowledge of, the historical reference framework that forms a context for the dating of the clothes worn by others, and also to make sense of or process their appearance. It further shows the temporal and trans-medial scope and dynamics of fashion as embodied, material and visual culture. Fashion cultures, including niche scenes such as those of sixties enthusiasts, deliver and are made of, as Gabriele Mentges and Gudrun König put it, powerful visual worlds that are in a continuous transfer and interwoven with the circulation and fusion of images across time and space (2010: viii). These image worlds are nothing external to us but, through looking and our socio-technological practices, they are part of the configuration of our being and becoming in the world, part of everyday practices, imagination and of our remembering—even of a time in which we did not live.

It is the mediation of the past in images, in addition to the material-sartorial presence of the past in surviving objects, that enables the fashioning of memory—or what could be called "past presencing"—through modes of clothing and embodiment. Anthropologist Sharon Macdonald introduces the term "past presencing" as an alternative to move beyond a dichotomy of ("real") history versus (potentially "fake") memory, and to encompass with the term also the often "unconscious or embodied relationships with the past" (Macdonald 2013: 16). The term highlights more clearly a "presentist" perspective, a concern with "how the past is related to at specific moments or stretches of time" (2013: 16). The notion of past presencing:

> does not take for granted what will be considered "past" or "present" in practice, neither indeed whether a distinction will operate between these; on the contrary, part of its point is to indicate the elision and indeterminacy that is so often involved, and the disruption of linear notions of past preceding present preceding future. (Macdonald 2013: 16)

The visual and material culture of clothing and fashion, through which bodies become in the words of Kaja Silverman (1994) "culturally visible" in time and place, are one of the modes "by which the past may inhabit the present—and the future—or perhaps that a continuous past may embrace the present and future" (Macdonald 2013: 16). In imagery such as photographs, the appearance of the past can be fixed as a trace of a previous time, thereby providing a launch pad from which cultural actors can seek access to it. Such traces and memories of the sartorial and embodied past can then be *remembered* or *fashioned*—that is made present or enacted—with one's own body and mind.

Ordinary and extraordinary past

"*What fascinates me is the picture I saw of the time. Of course, what remains of the time only exists in fragments*," states one sixties styler (m. 33). As the use of the term "past presencing" implies, the scene's perception of or relationship to the past, the sixties, is embedded in the "present" and driven by their individual and socially shared interests. Conceived as a mode of remembering, that is as engaging from a position of the present with the past—here with the sixties through the material and visual culture of dress, fashion and music—their engagement with or fashioning of the past can be understood, like other "*modes of remembering in culture*" (Erll 2010: 7), as inevitably selective, temporally, individually and socially shaped. If the past is not a given as such, but "must instead continually be re-constructed and re-presented ... memories of past events can vary to a great degree" (Erll 2010: 7). Elizabeth Wilson notes for example the dramatic discrepancy between everyday life in the 1960s and the popularized version of the sixties, which can both equally be encountered in media and imagery, referring to the 1967 documentary *The London Nobody Knows*. The film:

> showed older women, at least, still dressed in the same headscarves and coats, still trawling the street market stalls for second-hand clothes ... There was more to "the swinging sixties" than Twiggy in a miniskirt and young blades tearing around on scooters. (Wilson 2013: 47)

For Wilson, "rather than reinforcing the clichéd images of media memory, [film] can also memorialize the persistence of the old in the midst of the new," constituting for Wilson a reminder that "memories are always false memories" (2013: 47). But maybe they are just that: memories, which may not necessarily be understood as per se "false," but as inevitably fragmented versions or representations of the past. The discrepancy between the varied versions of the sixties as mediated in images was also noted by one interviewee who, used to the highly mediated "pop" version of the sixties, was in turn struck by the "ordinary:"

> What a contrast. How extraordinary the ordinary man looked at the time. I found an old slide-case at the second-hand shop the other day, private slides, they were from the mid- to late sixties. Fantastic. Totally middle-class family really, you can tell by the cars, it's from the mid-sixties or so. There's a massive difference, they look as if it were still the fifties. (m. 33)

Another interviewee refers directly to the edited and fragmentary nature of the image and fashion based remembering of the sixties in the present context: "*All we have are magazines and old films and record sleeves, you can't know how it really was*" (m. 30). In the world of imagery and imaginary, the everyday or ordinary 1960s are not the ones that tend to stick, but instead, those versions of the 1960s have made their mark that circulate—and come to appeal—at a specific time more widely in cultural memory and popular culture—here, in the case of the sixties scene, particularly the ones that are bound up with powerful time narratives, such as "youthquake" and "modernity."

In the context of the 1990s and early 2000s for example, when many of the sixties stylers became interested in the style, a number of books engaged with the popular culture of the 1960s and the British mods, often including oral histories (Badman and Rawlings 1997; Hewitt 1999 and 2000; Rawlings 2000; Lentz 2002; also Polhemus 1994 and 1996; Schepers 1998). The sixties also resonated strongly with new musical acts at the time as, for example, the band Oasis. In the fusion of image, sound, narrative, memory and imaginary, the sixties crystallized once again as an interesting style as well as a historical point in time, which some of the interviewees described as having something that they felt lacking in the present:

> Well, I do get nostalgic at times when I watch old films. From the seventies, too. I think to myself, it was partly, it's hard to say, but the mood was different. I actually find what gets through to me more pleasant.
>   What do you find more pleasant?
>   Well, yes, it's all less cold. More euphoric. Whereas the seventies were already quite grim. The sixties was a decade of great vision, involvement, for so many things. (m. 33)

The sixties stylers struggled to define their own image of the time. The descriptions of what they imagined reflected more broadly the narrative around the 1960s in cultural memory as a progressive, more innovative decade, emerging with the workings of decade labeling: that is, in their temporal contrasting to the 1970s as a less optimistic decade (Davis 1984; Curtis 2004).

> When you read reports or look at photos. You tend to think, wow, back then there were so many new things, revolution, too. Miniskirts, how can it be so remarkable when a woman wears one. Inventions like that. It's not like that anymore. That's what I think, that stuff happened in those days. It was colorful, shimmering. It had lots of aspects, which nowadays, well, it's all been done before. Everything is retro, 60s, 70s, 90s, 50s. (w. 29)

Different forms of media provide access to the looks and narratives of and around past decades. This allows for detail-oriented research—and conscious recollecting: drawing today from a vast amount of material that was unavailable to youths of the 1970s and 1980s not only due to technology, but also due to an insufficient gap in time for information, knowledge, images and imaginary to develop and circulate—representations of the past that become integrated with the experience of contemporary culture, and that can exert an appeal, for their look, for their familiarity, or for a sense of strangeness and difference: "*In my mind, when I see films of the past, I tend to think, my God, it's so strange, funny, and also so different. In terms of the music, the whole youth culture, and of course, the clothes*" (w. 29).

As Norbert Elias points out, in his book on time, history and the past are a product of contemporary perception and interpretation, based on the human ability to experience and to remember (Elias 1997: 46–7). This ability is always shaped by various forms of media (see Erll and Nünning 2010; Keightley 2012). Sabine Trosse (1999), who has researched the representation of retro-trends in fashion editorials in the German magazine *Brigitte*, draws on the work of philosopher Vilem Flusser to connect the eclectic use of the past in fashion with a transforming perception of time and history from a linear mode of perception to a mosaic-like mode of perception, configured through digital media rather than the linearity of text. Seen in this light, retro looks and vintage styles reflect or are riddled by the simultaneity of multiple times and temporalities in the present: not only in media, but also in the richness of time in material culture. Yet, as Alaida Assmann reminds us, the capacity of memory is limited, which makes memory or the act of remembering highly selective (Assmann 2011: 334). While material and visual culture are rich in time, and time is rich in visual and material culture, the "continuous process of forgetting is part of social normality" (Assmann 2011: 334)—so that, particularly, with reference to clothing and fashion, the extraordinary may come to "shimmer," as described by the interviewee above, and persists in memory over the ordinary (see Buckley and Clark 2012). However, equally, the ordinary may also be discovered and become the extraordinary.

No total recall

> It's the design that is most aesthetically appealing to my eye. It was just like yeah, instinctively. It's hard to describe, it's probably similar to music. Either you like it or you don't. And it's what I find most visually appealing. Cos like, sixties fashion is really playful and I pay great attention to detail. I just like those zippers there and those buttons in the same color and I like loops there and it's all really playful and I just like that. (w. 30)

The availability of images and objects from the past enable us to appropriate fragments of the most varied times and to transfer them into current uses and contexts. Framed through the lens of memory, and in light of its limitedness and selectivity, the uses of the past are not random acts, but, as seen on the example of sixties stylists, they are quite conscious choices. While these choices may be linked

FIGURE 21 Apartment of sixties styler, Berlin, Germany. Photo: author.

to narratives attached to the aesthetics, styles and fashions from the past, it is a vibrant exchange between the objects and images of the past and contemporary interests that spark them. The interest in the material and visual culture of the 1960s cannot be pinned down to one exclusive motive, and as the interviewee notes above, reasons why one "likes" and feels affection for specific things or aesthetics are not easily put into words. One aspect that makes things from the past appealing is certainly their perceived difference in the contemporary context, their temporality. For the sixties stylers they are part of an immersion into the aesthetic of the past—through clothes, styling, music, dancing—and usually this also extends to the interior decoration of living spaces (see Figure 21) or car choices.

Yet the aesthetic immersion in and embodiment of the sixties style from head to toe cannot simply be read as a sign for the desire of wanting to return to the past—notwithstanding the wish to do so temporally:

to spend a day in one of those great sixties department stores, where everything can be bought, where they have everything. Or to experience the spirit of those days once. But otherwise, there you wouldn't strike anyone as different anymore, you would be part of the mass, and it would be nothing special. (w. 19)

To wear and perform the fashion of the sixties as vintage, is here part of the self-positioning in the now, in relation to others, including the building and maintaining of social relationships with people who share the same "likes." If understood in its interplay with style, fashion and dress, it is inevitably framed through the dynamics of consumer culture in the now, it is part of the creation of one's aesthetic world and lifestyle—one that seeks to be true to the aesthetics of the past, with the awareness that time is in flux:

> I always enjoy talking to original hippies. We've found a textile shop run by an older guy from India, he sells fabrics, old curtains and things like that. And we like the psychedelic patterns and that's making a bit of a comeback. And he said: "Yeah, but that's not the time, the zeitgeist." That's true, of course. But today, there are so many categories.
> Yeah, it's a different spirit. (w. 21)
> Yeah, the spirit's different, that's right. But I wouldn't necessarily want to live in the sixties. In terms of music first of all. You wouldn't have been able to get hold of the stuff that you can nowadays get on samplers and records. And the parties were definitely not as wild in those days. You weren't as mobile and if, by chance, you didn't live in a great city, like not in London or somewhere like that, you'd never have had as many possibilities. Nah, today's a lot better. Even if it isn't the original zeitgeist, you've got a lot more possibilities. You couldn't have afforded the furniture in those days. Nor the clothes. You've actually got a lot more possibilities to take up the style nowadays. (m. 35)

It is time—or temporal distance—that enables the appreciation of the past style in the present, and it is time through which it becomes appropriate for self-fashioning. With the wider access to the past, enabled greatly through technology, the material and visual culture of the past can be meticulously researched for current performances, where it seems that the aesthetics of the past can be cherry-picked:

> What is worn in today's mod scene is not what was worn in the sixties. They're the clothes of rock stars … I also think that, when I joined the mod scene years ago, everyone was proper sixties, the way it was in the sixties. A bit grey. Everyone had a brown suit or a grey one and that was it. Now it's something that was not worn by many. It was worn in London, the really colorful Carnaby style, but that was admittedly always in the rock or music scene. People on stage wore that sort of thing and now we try and mirror the photos you see of famous people. Oh look, Ron Wood wore that lovely striped jacket, oh yeah, I'd also like a nice striped jacket and also Peggy Moffitt. Alright, they copy them and only have about two or three books and all the outfits appear every year in a different country. It's all copied. Taken from the big names, we still wear the old stuff, but only when we're at home, otherwise it's all become bright and colorful. (m. 33)

FIGURE 22 Sixties styler, Cologne, Germany. Photo: author.

FIGURE 23 Twiggy 1966. © Roger-Viollet/Image Works.

The perception and interpretation of the sixties is not static, but changes based on time. The idea that the "real sixties" were a little gray perhaps stems from the black and white photos of the time in early mod publications (for example Barnes 1991), or is based on the access to family photos of simpler everyday fashion in the 1960s, and black and white film and television series (early seasons of *The Avengers*, *Miss Marple*, etc.). The more "colorful" perception of the sixties is a result of the wider representation and circulation of the style in coffee table books, access to old magazines and photos that can be bought on eBay, and of course, found on the internet.

This sixties styler describes how today's looks are, in contrast to mods and sixties stylists earlier in the 1990s, based on music stars and models of the sixties (see Figures 22 and 23), where, as noted in the previous section, the extraordinary overshadows the ordinary.

> I do think that this "I want to look like Twiggy, I want to look like Brigitte Bardot, Peggy Moffitt"—it's a really classic imitation … It's got to the point where you say, wow, the sixties scene has become a bit of a catwalk. Where women should have great bodies. Which is like today, modern, the dominant zeitgeist, which infiltrates the scene as well. (w. 29)

On the context of art, Stephan Waetzold writes in his book on "authenticity fetishism" in the late 1970s that copies can never be perfect reproductions but are instead originals in their own right. A copy depends on the creator, since the copyist is part of history, a subject in time. He notes that there is always an element of the present in the copied work (Waetzold 1979: 21). This was written before reproduction technologies had become refined through digital media, where it now seems possible to recreate the look of the past exactly as it was in its time. Yet, at least in the context of the body, however, the temporality of a copy of a past look still shines through. Examples are movies like historical dramas, which costume historian Edward Maeder wrote about in *Hollywood and History* (1987): "People in each age create a style that is the acceptable and comfortable aesthetic for their day. Accordingly when we try to re-create historical costumes … our vision is so influenced by contemporary style that we cannot be objective, and the result is always an interpretation" (Maeder 1987: 9). For films with a historical setting, costumes play a key role in creating an image of the past. However, they also show the impossibility of exact reconstruction. Maeder gives the example of the 1963 film *Cleopatra*, starring Elizabeth Taylor, which rather than showing what ancient Egypt looked like, illustrates which aspects of ancient Egypt were considered interesting at the time and what was in hindsight "typical" of fashion in the 1960s: Cleopatra is thus portrayed with a beehive hairstyle, low cleavage and corset, conveying the body image of the early 1960s (Maeder 1987: 50).

For a more recent example of the way body and fashion, as well as vintage styles and retro looks, are embedded in the aesthetics of a time, I want to briefly return to the *Austin Powers* films and the *Mad Men* series. At the time when these visual representations of the sixties came out, they appeared to offer "authentic" versions of the fashion from the past. Clearly with *Austin Powers* as a movie that mocks the 1960s, an ironic take on 1960s secret agent films, it draws in its costuming on many of the "hyperversions" of the past decade, which resonate with the audience, for example the silhouette with boot-cut or flared trousers fashionable in the 1990s. *Mad Men*, several years later, presents in its early seasons a more muted version of the 1960s. Clearly this is due to a different setting of the story and the effort to represent the temporality of everyday fashion in the early 1960s. Yet as Helen Warner notes in her discussion of *Mad Men*, it may "well be that this was a strategic decision to ensure that *Mad Men*, developed a distinct aesthetic, signaling its difference from other screen representations of the 'sixties'" (Warner 2014: 94). Despite all efforts towards accuracy, the show conveys how the past is seen in the present, in the 2000s; this includes the notion to show the 1960s in a new light. In its effort for authenticity, it not only pays minute attention to clothing details, to reveal what the everyday sixties looked like, but also tries to represent the social reality of 1960s America, including its racial and gender inequalities (see for a discussion Stoddard 2011). It thus presents a different version, a different memory, and also a different look and "feel" of the sixties. Yet it is a look that remains distinct of its own time, with a style that, no matter how "regressive" or ambiguously the 1960s were presented in the show, still resonated widely and sparked a wave of new sixties parties in the 2000s. In all their ambiguity, the sixties still came to "look" fresh and appealing to the present, boosting once again sales of sixties style clothing in high streets, and arguably also adding to the rising interest in vintage (see Cassidy and Bennett 2012: 248; Jenss 2013).

In contrast to film productions, the sixties scene need not appeal to a large audience. Notwithstanding this, their styles are equally embedded in the present, visible in the bodily performance and in the choice of looks to be reproduced, moving in their selection between styles of the early to the late sixties, and fusing them with the revivals that are layered in-between then and now. However, despite the association of the sixties style with youth, as one sixties styler commented: "*It's the best style to age in,*" noting how the fashion of the 1960s provides a wide repertoire for all age-groups, including the modern casual styles now considered "classics:" denim jeans, polo shirts and turtlenecks.

7 UN/TIMELY FASHION

Pointing out the timeliness of fashion, Elizabeth Wilson writes: "We choose the clothes we wear every day in order to look right now—today. In that sense fashion is very much about the present. It is about fitting in, while, perhaps remaining distinctive" (2013: 96). Fashion, new or old, is the material we choose from in our everyday clothing practices in order to make an appearance and to articulate a sense of self, including the "when" and "where" we are in time and place (see Kaiser 2012: 6–7). Susan Kaiser describes these sartorial and bodily articulations as moments of temporary closure—"it works for now" (2012: 6). In that sense, as Elizabeth Wilson goes on, "the everyday practice of fashion has nothing to do with the past or with memory. In fact, the wish is to efface the past, to erase any memory of our having been other than what we are or how we wish to appear today" (2013: 96). It is a reminder of Roland Barthes' comment on fashion, as a "refusal to inherit" (1990: 273). And there is no doubt that the desire to rid oneself of the past or of feelings of "datedness" is a profitable emotion that keeps the fashion industry thriving.

As Sherry Turkle notes on the change brought about by industrialization and the clock's production of time as "discrete units" that made possible a new way of thinking: "Capitalism depends on regimenting human time and human bodies" (Turkle 2007: 310). In providing the things we use to dress and situate ourselves in time and place, fashion, too, plays a constitutive role in the way we learn to keep up with time, and with "modernity." Annette Geiger (2011) has commented on the problem of temporariness inherent in fashion's narrative of the "now," arguing that "the disturbing truth has to be that one cannot just be 'up to date,' because it is impossible to experience the present in such a way" (Geiger 2011: 153). As she puts it, the present "has already slipped into the past at the time I start noticing it. The moment I assume notice is always already a memory" (2011: 153). Fashion, here as fashioning body and self, can be understood as a material mode of "making time," perhaps as an effort of making time and present materially graspable, of inscribing oneself into the moment. In this way, the wearing of fashion, as a "moment of temporary closure," could then further be seen as a kind of temporal anchorage, of manifesting a moment. As has been shown the temporality of fashion is not absolute or universal as its narration of newness and ephemerality suggests, rather in everyday life fashion is part of the creating, coexistence and experience of multiple temporalities (see also Shove, Trentmann and Wilk 2009: 3). Despite the proclamation of seasonal change and even weekly promotions of "new arrivals," the space and content of most wardrobes accumulates things from varied times, that are used and re-worn over stretches of time (see Woodward 2007). And as has been noted here before, despite all attempts to work against memory and stimulate forgetting with the proposal of the new, memory is constitutive to the workings of the temporal dynamics of fashion—not least because it is through our ability to remember that we come to recognize and identify what is "new" or "old". In that sense again, fashion is effectively part of "memory"—or "fashioning memory."

The growing interest in old clothes as vintage, as recognizably "old," shows not only the tendency in fashion to refuse the past, but also the desire to recall—though usually with a temporal twist—through a certain distance in time. This distance is perhaps the one needed in order to blur any immediate personal or sartorial remembrance with the dynamics of cultural memory—incorporating other people's memories. Vintage gives old clothes a new name, and connotes with that a meaning that comes to evolve through passing a temporal (and commercial) threshold: from passé to "past"—from outmoded to ripe to be "old-fashioned." Vintage means, at least currently, not the clothes from last season—in the way the term was used by *Vogue* in 1913. While vintage works with memory, it does not do so with the "short-term" memory of just a few seasons; on the contrary.

In his book *Taste and Fashion*, published in 1937, dress historian James Laver included a kind of timetable accounting for the different emotional responses, or attitudes, to old or passing fashions. According to his system a style, once it has been fashionable, looks "dowdy" after three years, "hideous" after a distance of ten years and "ridiculous" after twenty years. The past fashion style becomes "amusing" after thirty years, "quaint" after fifty years, looks "charming" after seventy, and it takes more than hundred years to be "beautiful" (Laver 1937: 255). Certainly perceptions or experiences of past fashion, or the experience of time and taste, cannot be universalized like this. Any perception of fashion or aesthetics varies not at the very least depending on age, on one's memories, one's own (also sartorial) biography, on positions or paths in and through time and place.

However, with regard to the transition of old clothes into vintage, or retro, there still seems to be some timeliness to the ten-to-twenty-year marks, as the needed distance for some fashion styles to come to crystallize as "past." At least this tends to be the time when some styles appear to become *old-fashioned*, to be worn for their temporal difference—and this not rarely first by a new generation. An example for this is the time when "the sixties" started to be first discovered by a new generation who began to take on and identify with the style in the 1970s that cumulated in a mod revival. But as Peter York (1980) noted on the mod revival at the time, there were not only new kids picking up the style, but many of the people who got into mod in the 1960s had also never dropped the style, hinting to the multiple temporalities of fashion and style in everyday life.

Vintage is tied to the idea of old clothes being fashioned "again" rather than still being worn. Vintage is in this sense bound more widely to aging, not only to the aging of objects, but also to the aging of wearers. This is for example the case when old clothes are being redefined as vintage through a new generation, considering Laver's ten-to-twenty-year marks, between hideousness and ridicule. The current revival of the more recent 1990s is a style that seems particularly prominent in the market that caters to a younger consumer group, as for example stores and online retailers Urban Outfitters, Asos and Nasty Gal—stores that thrive on vintage clothes or on a vintage aesthetic. This is the generation of consumers who now come to remember through clothes the time and aesthetics that surrounded them during—and impact their memory of—their childhood years (including the fashion styles worn at the time by pop celebrities, siblings or parents). It is in this case through young wearers (and young bodies) that old clothes are here given a "new look" as vintage. If these same styles were still worn by the generation who inhabited the clothes in the 1990s, they might instead likely be viewed as "dowdy" or out of date (see Twigg 2013: 87).

Fifteen years into the new millennium, people will begin to pick up the early 2000s, adding further to the various and multilayered styles of the other decades that are also in fashion at the same time. In this sense there is no acceleration or shrinking distance to the time older fashion styles are being picked up, compared to the workings of fashion revivals in the earlier decades of the twentieth century, as sometimes assumed. The shrinking distance is more likely an effect of the multiplicity of varied fashion times as already noted by Burman-Baines (1981)— and of the multiple temporalities, and generations or age cohorts, that are part of fashion and consumer culture.

An example of the multiple material temporalities of fashion could also be seen in the clothing and style practices of the sixties scene. Many of the members in this scene stay with the style for many years, and even decades. They remain committed to buying sixties second-hand clothes, no matter if the sixties are "in fashion" or not. As one sixties styler noted, "*It is the aesthetic that I like the very best*," where the complete immersion in the style of the sixties provides not only a sense of assurance and continuity but quite literally a material substance to a feeling of stability and identity. The old is played out against the fast changing new, the "ephemerality" of fashion. Old vintage clothes are here part of making and enacting authenticity, of realness, through things (and by extension people) that are seen as legitimated through the past, and through temporal duration or endurance (see also Jenss 2004). The feeling of authenticity can here emerge through "networks of relationships" in the sense that authenticity is usually "attributed especially to things or relationships that are able to make connec- tions—not only social but also material … and historical, linking past and present" (Macdonald 2013: 130). But even if the style is maintained, it is updated, remembered and reassembled over time, the sixties style is "tinkered" with—including the buying of ever new old clothes, that are part of fashioning the style in a timely manner with the wearer. This is part of the social interaction and social dynamics of clothes and fashion, bound up with the desire (and/or pressure) to look new to self and others, for example by avoiding the continuous wearing of the same clothes. Karen Tranberg Hansen (2003) has described a similar practice in the use of second-hand clothing among women in Zambia, where the change of outfits in the context of social events "showcases rapid turnover," yet through recombination and ensemble building of maintained clothing. Clothing choices are intertwined with the evaluation of how one "wants to be seen, where, when and by whom" (Hansen 2003: 306). For the sixties enthusiasts, describing the need for new clothes for events, despite their vintage, if they are too often seen by others in the same clothes, they might bear the danger of undermining one's timeliness—as if appearing forever stuck in a "moment of temporary closure."

The valuing of authenticity can be traced back to the nineteenth century idealization of originality and authenticity in Romanticism. In the context of the counter movement to industrialization, the idea of authenticity became an antithesis to the "loss of aura" and "loss of meaning" associated with the serial reproducibility of art (Benjamin 2008), and the commodification of culture—leading at the same time, however, to the rise of an "authenticity industry" (Macdonald 2013: 109). The recollecting of the material culture of the sixties is in a similar way tied to an idea of uniqueness associated with old items, due to their temporal distance. They are further items made in a decade that has been viewed as innovative, an era of profound social change—and as a time that had "plenty of future on offer" (Swift 1983: 20, cited in Assmann 2013: 9). Despite their uniqueness now achieved through temporal distance, these items are also reminders of the surplus of a decade in which fashion came to be celebrated as an instant commodity, finding its peak in throwaway paper dresses. As discussed in this book it is in this context that the commodification of old clothes comes to serve as a fashionable alternative to the new, which became part of the rise of the so-called "nostalgia market" (Fischer 1980).

Alaida Assmann pinpoints in her book *Zeitregime* (2013) the decade of the 1960s as the one in which a historic reconfiguration of the perception of time and of the relations among past, present and future emerges. Indicators for this shift in "time regimes" are a declining idealization of the future as a promise of progress, as inherent in the narrative of modernity, and an increasing engagement with the past, in particular through the lens or experiential dynamics of memory. The historical shift in temporal sensibility is also seen as the sign or trigger of what would be called the "memory boom" in the latter half of the twentieth century (see Huyssen 2003). For scholars of post/modernity, it is particularly the time-space compression produced and evoked through the impact of media, technological change, and "new patterns of consumption, work, and global mobility" that has brought a "palpable transformation of temporality in our lives" (Huyssen 2003: 21). One of the most significant effects or indicators of this changing experience of temporality discussed by Andreas Huyssen is the shift from the modern privileging of present and future, to an increased engagement with the past, which comes to serve as a kind of temporal anchorage in the experience of a process and heightened feeling of cultural acceleration to "secure some continuity within time, to provide some extension of lived space within which we can breathe and move" (Huyssen 2003: 24). Huyssen argues adamantly against theories that see the "looking back" and engagement with the past and memory purely as a form of cultural compensation for the loss of social stability, but highlights the role of technology and consumer culture as playing a key role in impacting how time or temporality is experienced and imagined. That is time (and space), while being "fundamental categories of human experience and perception," are not immutable, but "they are very much subject to historical change" (Huyssen 2003: 24).

Fashion or more specifically the popularity of vintage clothes could be seen as a substantial materialization of this change, with fashion impacting the experience of time and the use of old clothes providing a sense of "temporal anchorage" for the need for continuity, to pause, to put time on hold, to make time or to "buy time" (see Miller 2009b; Aronowsky Cronberg 2009). This might be especially so, in a time context driven by a heightened tempo through the integration of new digital media into our lives. Agnes Rocamora (2013) discusses how the acceleration of production and communication processes directly impacts fashion, arguing that in the context of digital media we are facing "new fashion times." Time speeds up—digital technologies bring a new quality to the experience of time, it is the principle of instantaneity and newness that drives contemporary experiences—including relationships to fashion, dress and consumption (2013: 65), with fast fashion being the most evident pendant to the fast communication of fashion on style blogs, Twitter and Instagram. Vintage clothes could then be seen as a counter movement to the speed generated through technology and the fast consumption of commodities, except that they are also interwoven with these processes of acceleration, including the increasing desire for "new" old clothes. Vintage and retro styles are bound up with time-space compression and, as Raphael Samuel notes in *Theatres of Memory*, retro chic or vintage thrive on technology (2012: 83). This is evident in mediated memories stimulating interests in past clothing styles or the increased buying of old clothes online, with eBay's service, as noted here earlier, acting as a kind of memory or time machine. Other examples are the use of social media to create and share memories, for example Throwback Thursdays (#TBT) photos on Instagram, or the use of photoapps to create images in which one looks instantly vintage, generating nostalgia evoking visual aesthetics and affects.

Integrated in consumer culture, such experiences of time and memory have been critiqued, for example by Fredric Jameson, on the example of 1970s retro films. Arjun Appadurai described them in the context of fashion marketing as a technique to produce an "armchair" nostalgia among consumers. This kind of ersatz nostalgia does not generate a connection with one's own lived and memorized experience of the past, he argues, but rather fosters a feeling of desire or longing for an imagined past; one that can be directly translated or channeled into consumer desires: "The workings of ersatz nostalgia create the simulacra of periods that constitute the flow of time, conceived as lost, absent or distant," which feed back into the consumption of commodities, "powered by an implosive, retrospective construction of time, in which repetition is itself an artifact of ersatz nostalgia and imagined precursory moments" (Appadurai 1996: 78–9). Appadurai sees this commercial use of nostalgia as an opposite to a more real nostalgia that is based on the experience of a loss or displacement. This, however, assumes the existence of just one or two modes of nostalgia, whereas historically nostalgia—or nostalgias—has been conceived as well as experienced in more varied ways.

Clearly marketing techniques have perfected the evocation of feelings and emotions to get consumers to buy things. More broadly the tendency to critique nostalgia in the context of media or commodities, however, might relate to what Sharon Macdonald refers to as "commodification anxiety," that she sees as part of the discourse around memory and authenticity, a discourse that tends to oppose "'spheres' or 'assemblage elements' of heritage/memory/identity, etc. on the one hand and commodities/industry/the market on the other" (Macdonald 2013: 110). This is an opposition that, especially in the context of fashion, which is here understood as integral to the processes and practices having to do with bodies, identities, and also memories, is difficult if not unproductive to uphold.

Nostalgia has been commonly seen as a "bad word" (Boym 2001: xiv), or bad feeling. Historically, it is a term that was coined by Johannes Hofer in the seventeenth century as a medical diagnosis for "homesickness" (combining the Greek words *nostos*, meaning "to return home", and *algia* for "pain"). This kind of nostalgia does not fit with the ideas of innovation, progress and mobility promoted by the narrative of modernity. Susan J. Matt, in her history of homesickness in America, shows how such emotions have become strategically controlled—especially over the course of the twentieth century, when homesickness came to be seen increasingly as a sign of weakness and immaturity, a danger to individualism and the idea of modern progress (Matt 2011: 253). At the same time it can be observed, as I discussed elsewhere, that nostalgia became closely interwoven with the development of consumer culture as a site where giving in to cross-temporal or cross-spatial longing is not only acceptable, but also encouraged (see Jenss 2013). Growing up and living in consumer culture, commodities—from food to songs to clothes and scents—are constitutive components of our identities, memories and experiences in and through time and place, including sometimes feelings of nostalgia, which can, however, be experienced in greater varieties than a distinction of real vs. ersatz, or a "progressive" versus "regressive" nostalgia (see Boym 2001) suggests.

As Macdonald highlights through a discussion of anthropological studies, even within one person nostalgia may operate variously and with many nuances (see Macdonald 2013: 93). Vintage clothes or former fashion styles may or may not be part of a nostalgic mood or mode (see Jenss 2013; see on nostalgia as mood and mode Grainge 2002; Sprengler 2009). They can be used in many ways—and with many nuances. Fashion history is filled with revivals, including the sartorial interest in the more recent pasts, which is assumed to be so typical of the phenomenon of retro, emerging in the 1960s (Guffey 2006: 10). For example, Mildred Adams writes in the *New York Times* in 1933 about the stylish woman who is "eclectic and capricious, rummaging in the ragbags of the recent past, trying on the old and pretending it is the new, mixing all sorts of things together in one grand show, for that is the mood of 1933" (Adams 1933, cited in Sprengler 2009: 26). While clearly a different historic context, the description itself does not sound much different from contemporary vintage-style practices, which are assembled from the clothes spilling over from varied decades, in part reversing fashion, by wearing the old, yet also being "timely."

As Lucy Norris notes, "ridding ourselves of stuff is not only central to our ability to formulate the self but also to reconfigure social relations established through consuming, exchanging, and living with things" (Norris 2012: 130). The prominent mode of consumption is the purchase of new clothes, rising with fast fashion to dwindling numbers of clothes that are being produced to bring "newness" to the market—often only by a small variation of what we already own. Kate Fletcher has called this system of fashion for its mode of overproduction— hinging on the impossibility of "up-to-dateness"—as out of date. With its limitless production of value-free clothing, she argues, it "creates an anachronistic form of fashion itself," that is completely out of time and out of line with "people, ecosystems and soil" (Fletcher 2014: 141). Rather than "fighting time" with the consumption of the ever new—the recycling and revaluing of the old and the reuse of the disposals of "modernity"—no matter if through selective sampling of vintage items or thriving for the "total look" of one decade—seem in light of such an anachronism of fashion no outmoded, or untimely, choices.

REFERENCES

Abrams, Lynn. (1997). "Freizeit, Konsum und Identität deutscher und britischer Arbeiter vor dem ersten Weltkrieg." In *Europäische Konsumgeschichte: Zur Gesellschafts- und Kulturgeschichte des Konsums*, edited by Hannes Siegrist, Hartmut Kaelble, Jürgen Kocka, 267–81. Frankfurt am Main: Campus.

Abrams, Mark. (1959). *The Teenage Consumer*. London: London Press Exchange.

Alford, Holly. (2004). "The Zoot Suit: Its History and Influence." *Fashion Theory* 8 (2): 225–36.

Allstädt, Gudrun. (2002). "Vintage: Schön Alt, Viel Wert." *Textilwirtschaft* 16: 18.

Amit, Vered. (2000). *Constructing the Field: Ethnographic Fieldwork in the Contemporary World*. London: Routledge.

Anderson, Benedict. (1991). *Imagined Communities: Reflections on the Origin and Spread of Nationalism*. London: Verso.

Appadurai, Arjun. (1996). *Modernity at Large: Cultural Dimensions of Globalization*. Minneapolis: University of Minnesota Press.

Ariès, Philippe. (1962). *Centuries of Childhood: A Social History of Family Life*. New York: Alfred A. Knopf.

Aronowsky Cronberg, Anja. (2009). "New Vintage: A Foray into Nostalgia and the Romanticising of the Past." *Vestoj: The Journal of Sartorial Matters* 1: 125–31.

Aronowsky Cronberg, Anja, ed. (2009). *Vestoj: The Journal of Sartorial Matters* 1: On Material Memories.

Ash, Juliet and Elizabeth Wilson, eds. (1992). *Chic Thrills: A Fashion Reader*. London: Pandora.

Ashmore, Sonia. (2006). "'I think they're all mad:' Shopping in Swinging London." In *Swinging Sixties*, edited by Christopher Breward, David Gilbert and Jenny Lister, 58–79. London: V&A Publications.

Ashmore, Sonia. (2010). "Hippies, Bohemians & Chintz." In *British Asian Style: Fashion and Textiles*, edited by Christopher Breward, 106–21. London: V&A Publishing.

Assmann, Alaida. (2011). "Canon and Archive." In *The Collective Memory Reader*, edited by Jeffrey K. Olick, Vered Vinitzky-Seroussi and Daniel Levi, 334–7. New York: Oxford University Press.

Assmann, Alaida. (2013). *Ist die Zeit aus den Fugen: Aufstieg und Fall des Zeitregimes der Moderne*. Munich: Carl Hanser Verlag.

Assmann, Jan. (1995). "Collective Memory and Cultural Identity." *New German Critique* 65: 125–33.

Austin, Guy. (1996). *Contemporary French Cinema: An Introduction*. Manchester: Manchester University Press.

Baacke, Dieter. (1972). *Beat: Die Sprachlose Opposition*. Munich: Juventa.

Baacke, Dieter. (1997). "Die Welt der Musik und die Jugend: Eine Einleitung." In *Handbuch der Jugendkulturen*, edited by Dieter Baake, 9–26. Opladen: Leske + Budrich.

Baacke, Dieter. (1999). *Jugend und Jugendkulturen: Darstellung und Deutung*. Weinheim: Juventa.

Bad Breisig Schwingend (2008). [Film] Dir. Nina Schermer. Available online: https://www.youtube.com/watch?v=toW1ivzWpoA (accessed January 10, 2015).

Badman, Keith and Terry Rawlings. (1997). *Empire Made: A Handy Parka Pocket Guide to All Things Mod!* London: I. P.

Baker, Sarah Elise. (2013). *Retro Style: Class, Gender and Design in the Home*. London and New York: Bloomsbury.

Bal, Mieke, Jonathan Crewe and Leo Spitzer, eds. (1999). *Acts of Memory: Cultural Recall in the Present*. Hanover and London: University Press of New England.

Barnard, Malcolm. (2001). *Fashion as Communication*. London: Routledge.

Barnes, Richard. (1991). *Mods!* London: Plexus Publishing.

Barthes, Roland. (1990). *The Fashion System*. Berkeley: University of California Press.

Baudelaire, Charles. (2004). "The Painter of Modern Life." In *The Rise of Fashion*, edited by Daniel Purdy, 213–21. Minneapolis: University of Minnesota Press.

Baudrillard, Jean. (1993). *Symbolic Exchange and Death*. London and Thousand Oaks: Sage.

Bauman, Zygmunt. (2007). *Consuming Life*. Cambridge: Polity.

Baxter-Wright, Emma. (2006). *Vintage Fashion: Collecting and Wearing Designer Classics*. New York: Collins Design.

Bayley, Stephen. (1991). *Taste: The Secret Meaning of Things*. London: Pantheon.

Benjamin, Walter. (1968). *Illuminations*. New York: Harcourt, Brace and World, Inc.

Benjamin, Walter. (1996). *Selected Writings*, Volume 1. Cambridge, MA: Belknap Press of Harvard University Press.

Benjamin, Walter. (2008). *The Work of Art in the Age of its Technological Reproducibility, and other Writings on Media*. Cambridge, MA: Belknap Press of Harvard University Press.

Benn DeLibero, Linda. (1994). "This Year's Girl: A Personal/Critical History of Twiggy." In *On Fashion*, edited by Shari Benstock and Suzanne Ferris, 41–57. New Brunswick: Rutgers University Press.

Bennett, Andy and Paul Hodkinson, eds. (2012). *Ageing and Youth Cultures: Music, Style and Identity*. London: Bloomsbury.

Bjälesjö, Jonas. (2002). "The Place in Music and Music in Place." *Ethnologia Scandinavica: A Journal for Nordic Ethnology* 22: 20–33.

Booker, Christopher. (1969). *The Neophiliacs: A Study of the Revolution in English Life in the Fifties and Sixties*. London: Collins.

Botticello, Julie. (2012). "Between Classification, Objectification, and Perception: Processing Secondhand Clothing for Recycling and Reuse." *Textile* 10 (2): 164–83.

Bourdieu, Pierre. (1984). *Distinction: A Social Critique of the Judgement of Taste*. Cambridge, MA: Harvard University Press.

Boyer, Bruce. (2012). "A Rift: Jazz Men Take on Ivy." In *Ivy Style: Radical Conformists*, edited by Patricia Mears, 137–46. New Haven and New York: Yale University Press.

Boym, Svetlana. (2001). *The Future of Nostalgia*. New York: Basic Books.

Breward, Christopher. (1995). *The Culture of Fashion*. Manchester: Manchester University Press.

Breward, Christopher. (1999). *The Hidden Consumer: Masculinities, Fashion and City Life 1860–1914*. Manchester: Manchester University Press.

Breward, Christopher. (2002). "Style and Subversion: Postwar Poses and the Neo-Edwardian Suit in Mid-Twentieth-Century Britain." *Gender and History* 14 (2): 560–83.

Breward, Christopher. (2003). *Fashion*. Oxford: Oxford University Press.

Breward, Christopher. (2004). *Fashioning London: Clothing and the Modern Metropolis*. Oxford: Berg/Bloomsbury.

Breward, Christopher. (2006). "Introduction." In *Swinging Sixties*, edited by Christopher Breward, David Gilbert and Jenny Lister, 8–21. London: V&A Publications.

Breward, Christopher, Edwina Ehrman and Caroline Evans. (2004). *The London Look: Fashion from Street to Catwalk*. London: Yale University Press.

Breward, Christopher and Caroline Evans, eds. (2005). *Fashion and Modernity*. Oxford: Berg/Bloomsbury.

Breward, Christopher and David Gilbert, eds. (2006). *Fashion's World Cities*. Oxford: Berg/Bloomsbury.

Breward, Christopher, David Gilbert and Jenny Lister, eds. (2006). *Swinging Sixties*. London: V&A Publications.

Brown, Stephen. (2001). *Marketing: The Retro-Revolution*. London, Thousand Oaks: Sage.

Bruzzi, Stella and Pamela Church Gibson, eds. (2000). *Fashion Cultures: Theories, Explorations and Analysis*. London: Routledge.

Buckley, Cheryl and Hazel Clark. (2012). "Conceptualizing Fashion in Everyday Lives." *Design Issues* 28 (4): 18–28.

Burman-Baines, Barbara. (1981). *Fashion Revivals: From the Elizabethan Age to the Present Day*. London: Harper Collins Distribution Services.

Buruma, Ian. (2000). *Anglomania: A European Love Affair*. New York: Vintage Books.

Busch, Bernd. (1995). *Belichtete Welt: Eine Wahrnehmungsgeschichte der Fotografie*. Frankfurt am Main: Fischer Taschenbuch.

Butler, Judith. (2007). "Performative Acts and Gender Constitution: An Essay in Phenomenology and Feminist Theory." In *The Performance Studies Reader*, edited by Henry Bial, 187–99. London and New York: Routledge.

Calefato, Patrizia. (2000). "Signs of Order, Signs of Disorder: The Other Uniforms." In *Uniform: Order and Disorder*, edited by Franceso Bonami, 195–204. Milan: Edizoni Charta.

Calefato, Patrizia. (2004). *The Clothed Body*. Oxford: Berg/Bloomsbury.

Carlyle, Thomas. (1991). *Sartor Resartus: Leben und Meinungen des Herrn Teufelsdröckh*. Zürich: Manesse.

Carlyle, Thomas. (2004). "'The Dandiacal Body' from Sartor Resartus." In *The Rise of Fashion*, edited by Daniel Purdy, 165–73. Minneapolis: University of Minnesota Press.

Carter, Angela. (1982). *Nothing Sacred: Selected Writings*. London: Virago.

Carter, Michael. (2003). *Fashion Classics: From Carlyle to Barthes*. Oxford: Berg/Bloomsbury.

Casey, Edward. (1996). "How to Get from Place to Place in a Fairly Short Stretch of Time: Phenomenological Prolegomena." In *Senses of Place*, edited by Steven Feld and Keith H. Basso, 13–52. Santa Fe: School of American Research Press.

Casey, Edward. (2000). *Remembering: A Phenomenological Study*. Bloomington: Indiana University Press.

Cassidy, Tracy Diane and Hannah Rose Bennett. (2012). "The Rise of Vintage and the Vintage Consumer." *Fashion Practice* 4 (2): 239–62.

Chenoune, Farid. (1995). *A History of Men's Fashion*. Manchester: Flammarion.

Childs, Peter and Mike Storry, eds. (1999). *Encyclopedia of Contemporary British Culture*. London and New York: Routledge.

Cicolini, Alice. (2005). "Vintage Fashion." In *Encyclopedia of Clothing and Fashion*, edited by Valerie Steele. Farmington Hills: Charles Scribner's Sons.

Clark, Hazel. (2008). "Slow + Fashion: An Oxymoron – or a Promise for the Future?" *Fashion Theory* 12 (4): 427–46.

Clarke, John. (2000). "Style." In *Resistance through Rituals: Youth Subcultures in Post-War Britain*, edited by Stuart Hall and Tony Jefferson, 175–91. London: Routledge.

Clarke, John, Stuart Hall, Tony Jefferson and Brian Roberts. (2000). "Subcultures and Class." In *Resistance through Rituals: Youth Subcultures in Post-War Britain*, edited by Stuart Hall and Tony Jefferson, 9–74. London: Routledge.

Clifford, James. (1995). "On Collecting Art and Culture". In *The Cultural Studies Reader*, edited by Simon During, 49–73. London and New York: Routledge.

Cohen, Adam. (2004). *Mein eBay: Geschichte und Geschichten vom Marktplatz der Welt*. Berlin: PLOT.

Cohen, Albert. (1955). *Delinquent Boys: The Culture of the Gang*. Glencoe: The Free Press.

Cohen, Stanley. (1973). *Folk Devils and Moral Panics: The Creation of the Mods and Rockers*. London: Harper Collins Distribution Services.

Cohn, Nik. (1971). *Today There Are No Gentlemen*. London: Littlehampton Book Services.

Collins, Jim, ed. (2002). *High-Pop: Making Culture into Popular Entertainment*. New York: Wiley-Blackwell.

Cooper, Cynthia. (1997). *Magnificent Entertainments: Fancy Dress Balls of Canada's Governors General 1876–1898*. New Brunswick: Goose Lane Editions.

Craik, Jennifer. (1994). *The Face of Fashion: Cultural Studies in Fashion*. London: Routledge.

Curtis, Barry. (2004). "A Highly Mobile and Plastic Environ." In *Art and the Sixties: This Was Tomorrow*, edited by Chris Stephens and Katharine Stout, 47–63. London: Tate Publishing.

Daniels, H. D. (1997). "Los Angeles Zoot Suit Race Riot, the Pachuco and Black Music Culture." *Journal of Negro History* 82 (2): 201–20.

Davey, Kevin. (1999). *English Imaginaries: Anglo-British Approaches to Modernity*. London: Lawrence & Wishart.

Davis, Fred. (1979). *Yearning for Yesterday: A Sociology of Nostalgia*. London and New York: Macmillan.

Davis, Fred. (1984). "Decade Labeling: The Play of Collective Memory and Narrative Plot." *Symbolic Interactionism* 7 (1): 15–24.

Debord, Guy. (2000). *The Society of the Spectacle*. Detroit: Black and Red.

DeLong, Marilyn, Barbara Heinemann and Kathryn Reiley. (2005). "Hooked on Vintage!" *Fashion Theory* 9 (1): 23–42.

Demossier, Marion. (2011). "Beyond Terroir: Territorial Construction, Hegemonic Discourses, and French Wine Culture." *Journal of the Royal Anthropological Institute* 17: 685–705.

Denzin, Norman K. (1997). *Interpretive Ethnography: Ethnographic Practices for the 21st Century*. Thousand Oaks: Sage.

Desjardins, Mary. (2006). "Ephemeral Culture/eBay Culture: Film Collectibles and Fan Investments." In *Everyday eBay: Culture, Collecting and Desire*, edited by Ken Hillis and Michael Petit, 31–43. London: Routledge.

Dubin, Tiffany and Anne E. Berman. (2000). *Vintage Style: Buying and Wearing Classic Vintage Clothes*. New York: HarperCollins World.

Eberlein, Undine. (2000). *Einzigartigkeit: Das romantische Individualitätskonzept der Moderne*. Frankfurt am Main: Campus.

Eicher, Joanne. (2010). "Introduction to Global Perspectives." In *Encyclopedia of World Dress and Fashion, Volume 10: Global Perspectives,* edited by Joanne Eicher, 3–10. Oxford: Oxford University Press.

Elias, Norbert. (1997). *Über die Zeit.* Frankfurt am Main: Suhrkamp.

Engelmann, Jan, ed. (1999). *Die Kleinen Unterschiede: Der Cultural Studies Reader.* Frankfurt am Main: Campus.

Entwistle, Joanne (2000). *The Fashioned Body: Fashion, Dress and Modern Social Theory.* Cambridge: Polity.

Entwistle, Joanne (2001). "The Dressed Body." In *Body Dressing,* edited by Joanne Entwistle and Elisabeth Wilson, 33–58. Oxford: Berg/Bloomsbury.

Entwistle, Joanne (2009). *The Aesthetic Economy of Fashion: Markets and Value in Clothing and Modelling.* Oxford: Berg/Bloomsbury.

Erbe, Günter. (2002). *Dandys: Virtuosen der Lebenskunst. Eine Geschichte des Mondänen Lebens.* Köln: Böhlau.

Erll, Astrid. (2010). "Cultural Memory Studies: An Introduction." In *A Companion to Cultural Memory Studies,* edited by Astrid Erll and Ansgar Nünning, 1–15. Berlin and New York: Walter de Gruyter.

Erll, Astrid and Ansgar Nünning, eds. (2010). *A Companion to Cultural Memory Studies.* Berlin and New York: Walter de Gruyter.

Erll, Astrid and Ann Rigney. (2009). "Introduction: Cultural Memory and its Dynamics." In *Mediation, Remediation and the Dynamics of Cultural Memory,* edited by Astrid Erll and Ann Rigney, 1–14. Berlin and New York: Walter de Gruyter.

Esposito, Elena. (2004). *Die Verbindlichkeit des Vorübergehenden: Paradoxien der Mode.* Frankfurt am Main: Suhrkamp.

Evans, Caroline. (1997). "Dreams That Only Money Can Buy … Or, The Shy Tribe In Flight From Discourse." *Fashion Theory* 1 (2): 169–88.

Evans, Caroline. (2000). "Yesterday's Emblems and Tomorrow's Commodities: The Return of the Repressed in Fashion Imagery Today." In *Fashion Cultures: Theories, Explorations and Analysis,* edited by Stella Bruzzi and Pamela Church Gibson, 93–113. London and New York: Routledge.

Evans, Caroline. (2003). *Fashion at the Edge: Spectacle, Modernity and Deathliness.* London and New Haven: Yale University Press.

Evans, Caroline. (2004). "Post-War Poses: 1955–75." In *The London Look: Fashion from Street to Catwalk,* edited by Christopher Breward, Edwina Ehrman and Caroline Evans, 117–38. London and New Haven: Yale University Press.

Evans, Caroline. (2010). "British Fashion." In *The Cambridge Companion to Modern British Culture,* edited by Michael Higgins, Clarissa Smith and John Storey, 208–24. Cambridge: Cambridge University Press.

Fabian, Johannes. (2002). *Time and the Other: How Anthropology Makes Its Object,* 2nd edn. New York: Columbia University Press.

Featherstone, Mike. (2000). *Undoing Culture: Globalization, Postmodernism and Identity.* London: Sage.

Feldman, Christine Jacqueline. (2009). *We are the Mods: A Transnational History of a Youth Culture.* New York: Peter Lang.

Fillin-Yeh, Susan. (2001). *Dandies: Fashion and Finesse in Art and Culture.* New York: NYU Press.

Fine, Ben and Ellen Leopold. (1993). *The World of Consumption.* London: Routledge.

Fischer, Volker. (1980). *Nostalgie: Geschichte und Kultur als Trödelmarkt.* Luzern and Frankfurt am Main: C. J. Bucher.

Fiske, John. (1997). "Die Kulturelle Ökonomie des Fantums." In *Kursbuch Jugendkultur: Stile, Szenen und Identitäten vor der Jahrtausendwende*, edited by SPoKK, 54–69. Mannheim: Bollmann Vlg.

Fletcher, Kate. (2014). *Sustainable Fashion and Textiles: Design Journeys*, 2nd edn. London and New York: Routledge.

Flusser, Vilem. (1990). *Ins Universum der technischen Bilder*. Göttingen: European Photography.

Flusser, Vilem. (1999). *The Shape of Things: A Philosophy of Design*. London: Reaktion Books.

Fogg, Marnie. (2003). *Boutique: A '60s Cultural Phenomenon*. London: Mitchell Beazley.

Follin, Frances. (2004). *Embodied Visions: Bridget Riley, Op Art and the Sixties*. London: Thames & Hudson.

Frank, Thomas. (1998). *The Conquest of Cool: Business Culture, Counterculture, and the Rise of Hip Consumerism*. Chicago: University Of Chicago Press.

Frese, Matthias and Julia Paulus. (2003). "Geschwindigkeiten und Faktoren des Wandels: Die 1960er Jahre in der Bundesrepublik." In *Demokratisierung und Gesellschaftlicher Aufbruch: Die Sechziger Jahre als Wendezeit in der Bundesrepublik*, edited by Matthias Frese, Julia Paulus and Karl Teppe, 1–23. Paderborn: Schöningh.

Frese, Matthias, Julia Paulus and Karl Teppe. (2003). *Demokratisierung und Gesellschaftlicher Aufbruch: Die sechziger Jahre als Wendezeit der Bundesrepublik*. Paderborn: Schöningh.

Frick, Carole Collier. (2005). "The Florentine 'Rigattiere:' Second Hand Clothing Dealers and The Circulation of Goods in the Renaissance." In *Old Clothes, New Looks*, edited by Alexandra Palmer and Hazel Clark, 13–28. Oxford: Berg/Bloomsbury.

Friedberg, Anne. (2002). "'… also bin ich': Der Käufer-Zuschauer und Transsubstantiation durch Erwerb." In *Shopping: 100 Jahre Kunst und Konsum*, edited by Max Hollein and Christoph Grunenberg, 62–7. Ostfildern: Hatje Cantz Verlag.

Friedl, Bettina. (2001). "Wearable Art: The Complication of Art through Fashion in the Sixties." In *The Sixties Revisited: Culture, Society and Politics*, edited by Jürgen Heideking, Jörg Helbig and Anke Ortlepp, 61–98. Heidelberg: Universitätsverlag Winter.

Früchtl, Josef and Jörg Zimmermann. (2001). "Ästhetik der Inszenierung: Dimensionen eines Gesellschaftlichen, Individuellen und Kulturellen Phänomens." In *Ästhetik der Inszenierung*, edited by Josef Früchtl and Jörg Zimmermann, 9–47. Frankfurt am Main: Suhrkamp.

Gebhardt, Winfried. (2000). "Feste, Feiern und Events: Zur Soziologie des Außergewöhnlichen." In *Events: Soziologie des Außergewöhnlichen*, edited by Winfried Gebhardt, Ronald Hitzler and Michaela Pfadenhauer, 17–32. Opladen: Leske + Budrich Verlag.

Gebhardt, Winfried, Ronald Hitzler and Michaela Pfadenhauer, eds. (2000). *Events: Soziologie des Außergewöhnlichen*. Opladen: Leske + Budrich.

Geertz, Clifford. (1987). "Dichte Beschreibung: Bemerkungen zu einer deutenden Theorie von Kultur." In *Dichte Beschreibung. Beiträge zum Verstehen Kultureller Systeme*, edited by Clifford Geertz, 7–44. Frankfurt am Main: Suhrkamp.

Geiger, Annette. (2011). "Fashion and Time: The Impossibility of the Present." In *Fashion out of Order: Disruption as Principle*, edited by Dorothea Mink, 148–57. Stuttgart: Arnoldsche Verlagsanstalt.

Ginsburg, Madeleine. (1980). "Rags to Riches: The Second-Hand Clothing Trade 1700–1978." *Costume* 14: 121–35.

Goodrum, Alison. (2005). *The National Fabric: Fashion, Britishness, Globalization.* Oxford: Berg/Bloomsbury.

Göttsch, Silke and Albrecht Lehmann, eds. (2001). *Methoden der Volkskunde: Positionen, Quellen, Arbeitsweisen der Europäischen Ethnologie.* Berlin: Dietrich Reimer.

Grainge, Paul. (2002). *Monochrome Memories: Nostalgia and Style in Retro America.* Westport: Praeger.

Granata, Francesca, ed. (2010). *Fashion Projects.* No. 3: On Fashion and Memory.

Green, Jonathon. (1998). *All Dressed Up: The Sixties and the Counter-Culture.* London: Jonathan Cape.

Gregson, Nicky, Kate Brooks and Louise Crewe. (2001). "Bjorn Again? Rethinking 70s Revivalism Through the Reappropriation of 70s Clothing." *Fashion Theory* 5 (1): 3–27.

Gregson, Nicky and Louise Crewe. (2003). *Second-Hand Cultures.* Oxford: Berg/Bloomsbury.

Gronow, Jukka. (1997). *The Sociology of Taste.* London: Routledge.

Grossberg, Lawrence. (1984). "Another Boring Day in Paradise: Rock and Roll and the Empowerment of Everyday Life." *Popular Music* 4: 225–51.

Grossberg, Lawrence. (1993). "The Media Economy of Rock Culture: Cinema, Post-Modernity and Authenticity." In *Sound and Vision: The Music Video Reader,* edited by Simon Frith, Andrew Goodwin and Lawrence Grossberg, 185–209. London: Routledge.

Grossberg, Lawrence. (2010). *Cultural Studies in the Future Tense.* Durham and London: Duke University Press.

Guffey, Elizabeth E. (2006). *Retro: The Culture of the Revival.* London: Reaktion Books.

Gumbrecht, Hans Ulrich and K. Ludwig Pfeiffer, eds. (1986). *Stil: Geschichten und Funktionen eines kulturwissenschaftlichen Diskurselements.* Frankfurt am Main: Suhrkamp.

Hackspiel-Mikosch, Elisabeth, ed. (2002). *Nach Rang und Stand: Deutsche Ziviluniformen im 9. Jahrhundert.* Krefeld: Deutsches Textilmuseum.

Halbwachs, Maurice. (1980). *The Collective Memory.* New York: Harper Colophon.

Halbwachs, Maurice. (1992). *On Collective Memory.* Chicago and London: University of Chicago Press.

Hall, Stuart. (1999). "Ethnizität. Identität und Differenz." In *Die kleinen Unterschiede: Der Cultural Studies Reader,* edited by Jan Engelmann, 84–98. Frankfurt am Main: Campus.

Hall, Stuart and Tony Jefferson, eds. (2000). *Resistance through Rituals: Youth Subcultures in Post-War Britain.* London: Routledge.

Hallaz, Piri. (1967). *A Swinger's Guide to London.* New York: Coward-McCann.

Hamilton, Richard. (1982). *Collected Words: 1953–1982.* London: Thames & Hudson.

Hannerz, Ulf. (1996). *Transnational Connections: Culture, People, Places.* London: Routledge.

Hansen, Karen Tranberg. (2000). *Salaula: The World of Secondhand Clothing and Zambia.* Chicago: Chicago University Press.

Hansen, Karen Tranberg. (2003). "Fashioning Zambian Moments." *Journal of Material Culture* 8 (3): 301–9.

Harvey, David. (1990). *The Condition of Postmodernity: An Enquiry into the Origins of Cultural Change.* Cambridge, MA: Blackwell.

Haubl, Rolf. (2000). "Be-dingte Emotionen: Über identitätsstiftende Objekt-Beziehungen." In *Von Menschen und Dingen: Funktion und Bedeutung materieller Kultur,* edited by Hans A. Hartmann and Rolf Haubl, 13–36. Wiesbaden: VS Verlag füer Sozialwissenschaften.

Hauser, Andrea. (1994). *Dinge des Alltags: Studien zur Historischen Sachkultur eines Schwäbischen Dorfes*. Tübingen: Tübinger Vereinigung für Volkskunde.

Hawley, Jana M. (2006). "Digging for Diamonds: A Conceptual Framework for Understanding Reclaimed Textile Products." *Clothing and Textiles Research Journal* 24 (3): 262–75.

Hebdige, Dick. (1974). "The Style of the Mods." *Stencilled Occasional Papers* (Centre for Contemporary Cultural Studies, University of Birmingham): 1–13.

Hebdige, Dick. (1979). *Subculture: The Meaning of Style*. London: Routledge.

Hebdige, Dick. (1988). *Hiding in the Light: On Images and Things*. London: Routledge.

Hebdige, Dick. (2000). "The Meaning of Mod." In *Resistance through Rituals: Youth Subcultures in Post-War Britain*, edited by Stuart Hall and Tony Jefferson, 87–96. London: Routledge.

Heidrich, Herman. (2001). "Von der Ästhetik zur Kontextualität: Sachkulturforschung." In *Methoden der Volkskunde: Positionen, Quellen, Arbeitsweisen der Europäischen Ethnologie*, edited by Silke Göttsch and Albrecht Lehmann, 33–65. Berlin: Dietrich Reimer.

Hepp, Andreas, Tanja Thomas and Carsten Winter. (2003). "Medienidentitäten: Eine Hinführung zu den Diskussionen." In *Medienidentitäten: Identität im Kontext von Globalisierung und Medienkultur*, edited by Carsten Winter, Tanja Thomas and Andreas Hepp, 7–26. Cologne: Herbert von Haleg.

Hewitt, Paolo, ed. (1999). *The Sharper Word: A Mod Anthology*. London: Helter Skelter Publishing.

Hewitt, Paolo. (2000). *The Soul Stylists: Forty Years of Modernism*. London: Random House.

Hillis, Ken. (2006). "Auctioning the Authentic: eBay, Narrative Effect, and the Superfluity of Memory." In *Everyday eBay: Culture, Collecting and Desire*, edited by Ken Hillis and Michael Petit, 167–84. London: Routledge.

Hillis, Ken, Michael Petit and Nathan Scott Eplay, eds (2006). *Everyday eBay: Culture, Collecting and Desire*. New York: Routledge.

Hitzler, Ronald, Thomas Bucher and Arne Niederbacher. (2001). *Leben in Szenen: Formen Jugendlicher Vergemeinschaftung Heute*. Opladen: Verlag für Sozialwissenschaften.

Hobsbawm, Eric. (1994). *The Age of Extremes: The History of the World, 1914–1991*. New York: Vintage.

Hobsbawm, Eric, ed. (1997). *The Invention of Tradition*. Cambridge: Cambridge University Press.

Hodkinson, Paul. (2002). *Goth: Identity, Style and Subculture*. Oxford: Berg/Bloomsbury.

Hofmann, Viola. (2009). "Their Own Teenage Look? Der Minirock als Gegenstand von Jugendmode, Modeindustrie und historischer Konstruktion." In *Mini & Mini: Ikonen der Popkultur zwischen Dekonstruktion und Rekonstruktion*, edited by Jürgen Kramer, Anette Pankratz and Claus-Ulrich Viol, 35–50. Bielefeld: Transcript.

Hollander, Anne. (1979). "People are Talking about ... Boom in Vintage Clothes." *Vogue* 169 (4): 273, 505.

Horx, Matthias. (1995). *Megatrends für die Späten Neunziger Jahre*. Düsseldorf: Econ.

Hume, Marion. (1996). "Tailoring." In *The Cutting Edge: 50 Years of British Fashion 1947–1997*, edited by Amy de la Haye, 36–61. London: V&A Publications.

Huyssen, Andreas. (1995). *Twilight Memories: Marking Time in a Culture of Amnesia*. New York and London: Routledge.

Huyssen, Andreas. (2003). *Present Pasts: Urban Palimpsests and the Politics of Memory*. Stanford: Stanford University Press.

"It's a Mod, Mod World." (1995). *Klenkes,* November: 24–6.

Jackson, Peter, Michelle Lowe, Daniel Miller and Frank Mort. (2000). *Commercial Cultures: Economies, Practices, Spaces*. Oxford: Berg/Bloomsbury.

Jameson, Frederic. (1984). "Postmodernism, or the Cultural Logic of Late Capitalism." *New Left Review* 146: 53–92.

Jenss, Heike. (2001). "Retro-Looks in Modedesign und Jugendkultur: Tom Ford (Gucci), Anna Sui und die Mods." In *Textil-Körper-Mode: Dortmunder Reihe zu kulturanthropologischen Studien des Textilen.* 1, zeit.schnitte, edited by Gabriele Mentges and Heide Nixdorff, 225–301. Dortmund and Berlin: Ebersbach.

Jenss, Heike. (2004). "Dressed in History: Retro-Styles and the Construction of Authenticity." *Fashion Theory* 8 (4): 387–403.

Jenss, Heike. (2005a). "Sixties Dress Only! The Consumption of the Past in a Retro Scene." In *Old Clothes, New Looks: Second-Hand Fashion*, edited by Alexandra Palmer and Hazel Clark, 177–96. Oxford: Berg/Bloomsbury.

Jenss, Heike. (2005b). "Ethnographische Modeforschung." In *Kulturanthropologie des Textilen: Ein einführendes Handbuch*, edited by Gabriele Mentges, 387–406. Berlin: Ebersbach.

Jenss, Heike. (2007). *Sixties Dress Only! Mode und Konsum in der Retro-Szene der Mods*. Frankfurt am Main: Campus.

Jenss, Heike. (2010). "Secondhand Clothing." In *Berg Encyclopedia of World Dress and Fashion, Volume 8: West Europe*, edited by Lise Skov and Joanne Eicher, 171–5. Oxford: Berg.

Jenss, Heike. (2013). "Cross-Temporal Explorations: Notes on Fashion and Nostalgia." *Critical Studies in Fashion and Beauty* 4 (1 & 2): 107–24.

Jones, Ann Rosalind and Peter Stallybrass. (2000). *Renaissance Clothing and the Materials of Memory*. Cambridge: Cambridge University Press.

Jones, Jennifer. (2007). *Sexing La Mode: Gender, Fashion and the Commercial Culture in Old Regime France*. Oxford: Berg/Bloomsbury.

Jones, Mark. (1992). "Do Fakes Matter?" In *Why Fakes Matter: Essays on Problems of Authenticity*, edited by Mark Jones, 7–12. London: Antique Collectors Club.

Kaelble, Hartmut. (1997). "Europäische Besonderheiten des Massenkonsums." In *Europäische Konsumgeschichte: Zur Gesellschafts- und Kulturgeschichte des Konsums*, edited by Hannes Siegrist, Hartmut Kaelble and Jürgen Kocka, 169–203. Frankfurt am Main: Campus.

Kaiser, Susan. (2012). *Fashion and Cultural Studies*. Oxford: Berg/Bloomsbury.

Kaschuba, Wolfgang. (1999). *Einführung in die Europäische Ethnologie*. Munich: C. H. Beck.

Kästner, Sabrina. (2003). "Hippiemode." In *Jugendkulturelle Moden: Von Hippie bis HipHop*, edited by Doris Schmidt, 1–16. Baltmannsweiler: Schneider Hohengehren.

Kawamura, Yuniya. (2005). *Fashion-ology: An Introduction to Fashion Studies*. Oxford: Berg/Bloomsbury.

Keenan, William J. F. (2001). "Dress Freedom: The Personal and the Political." In *Dress to Impress*, edited by William J. F. Keenan, 179–95. Oxford: Berg/Bloomsbury.

Keet, Philomena. "Making New Vintage Jeans in Japan: Relocating Authenticity." *Textile* 9 (1): 44–61.

Keightley, Emily. (2008). "Engaging with Memory." In *Research Methods for Cultural Studies*, edited by Michael Pickering, 175–92. Edinburgh: Edinburgh University Press.

Keightley, Emily, ed. (2012). *Time, Media and Modernity*. New York: Palgrave.

Keightley, Emily and Michael Pickering. (2012). *The Mnemonic Imagination: Remembering as Creative Practice*. London: Palgrave Macmillan.

Keller-Drescher, Lioba. (2003). *Die Ordnung der Kleidung: Ländliche Kleidung in Württemberg 1750–1850*. Tübingen: Tübinger Vereinigung für Volkskunde.

Kemper, Peter, Thomas Langhoff and Ulrich Sonnenschein, eds. (1999). *"alles so schön bunt hier." Die Geschichte der Popkultur von den Fünfzigern bis heute*. Stuttgart: Reclam.

Knoblauch, Hubert. (2000). "Das strategische Ritual der Kollektiven Einsamkeit: Zur Begrifflichkeit und Theorie des Events." In *Events: Soziologie des Außergewöhnlichen*, edited by Winfried Gebhardt, Ronald Hitzler and Michaela Pfadenhauer, 33–50. Opladen: Leske + Budrich.

Köhler, Ina. (2005). "Die Individualisierung der Globalisierer." *X-ray, Global Style & Fashion* (1): 73–7.

Kontopodis, Michael. (2009). "Editorial: Time. Matter. Multiplicity." *Memory Studies* 2 (1): 5–10.

Kopytoff, Igor. (1986). "The Cultural Biography of Things: Commodization as Process." In *The Social Life of Things: Commodities in Cultural Perspective*, edited by Arjun Appadurai, 64–94. Cambridge: Cambridge University Press.

Korff, Gottfried. (1991). "Umgang mit Dingen." In *Lebens-Formen. Alltagsobjekte als Darstellung von Lebensstilveränderungen am Beispiel der Wohnung und Bekleidung der "Neuen Mittelschichten,"* edited by Fächergruppe Designwissenschaft, 35–51. Berlin: Hochschule der Künste.

Korff, Gottfried and Martin Roth. (1990). "Einleitung." In *Das Historische Museum: Labor, Schaubühne, Identitätsfabrik*, edited by Gottfried Korff and Martin Roth, 9–40. Frankfurt am Main: Campus.

Koselleck, Reinhart. (2004). *Futures Past: On the Semantics of Historical Time*. New York: Columbia University Press.

Kraft, Jens. (1984). "Dandies der Achtziger: Mods." *Tango* 3: 20–3.

Kruse, H. (1993). "Subcultural Identity in Alternative Music Culture." *Popular Music* 12 (1): 31–43.

Kuhn, Annette. (2000). "A Journey through Memory." In *Memory and Methodology*, edited by Susannah Radstone, 179–96. Oxford: Berg/Bloomsbury.

Kwint, Marius. (1999). "The Physical Past." In *Material Memories*, edited by Marius Kwint, Christopher Breward and Jeremy Aysley, 1–16. Oxford: Berg/Bloomsbury.

Laing, Dave. (1969). *The Sound of our Time*. London: Quadrangle Books.

Landsberg, Alison. (2004). *Prosthetic Memory: The Transformation of American Remembrance in the Age of Mass Culture*. New York: Columbia University Press.

Lash, Scott. (1996). "Reflexivität und ihre Doppelungen: Struktur, Ästhetik und Gemeinschaft." In *Reflexive Modernisierung: Eine Kontroverse*, edited by Ulrich Beck, Anthony Giddens and Scott Lash, 195–285. Frankfurt am Main: Suhrkamp.

Laver, James. (1937). *Taste and Fashion: From the French Revolution until Today*. London: G. G. Harrap & Co.

Lefebvre, Henri. (1991). *The Production of Space*. Malden and Oxford: Blackwell Publishing.

Lehmann, Ulrich. (1999). "Tigersprung: Fashioning History." *Fashion Theory* 3 (3): 297–322.

Lehmann, Ulrich. (2000). *Tigersprung: Fashion and Modernity*. Cambridge, MA: MIT Press.

Lehnert, Gertrud. (1997). "Modische Inszenierungen: Mode, Puppen, Models." *Metis: Zeitschrift für historische Frauenforschung* 12: 44–54.

Lehnert, Gertrud, ed. (1998). *Mode, Weiblichkeit und Modernität*. Dortmund: Edition Ebersbach.

Lehnert, Gertrud. (2000). *Geschichte der Mode im 20: Jahrhundert*. Cologne: Ullmann Publishing.

Leiris, Michel. (1987). *Die Eigene und die Fremde Kultur*. Frankfurt am Main: Athenaeum.

Lemire, Beverly. (1997). *Dress, Culture and Commerce: The English Clothing Trade before the Factory, 1600–1800*. London: Palgrave Macmillan.

Lemire, Beverly. (2005). "Shifting Currency: The Culture and Economy of the Second Hand Trade in England, c.1600-1850." In *Old Clothes, New Looks: Second Hand Fashion*, edited by Alexandra Palmer and Hazel Clark, 29–47. Oxford: Berg/Bloomsbury.

Lemire, Beverly. (2012). "The Secondhand Clothing Trade in Europe and Beyond: Stages of Development and Enterprise in a Changing Material World *c*. 1600–1850." *Textile* 10 (2):144–63.

Lentz, Graham. (2002). *The Influential Factor*. Horsham: GEL Publishing.

Leopold, Ellen. (1992). "The Manufacture of the Fashion System." In *Chic Thrills: A Fashion Reader*, edited by Juliet Ash and Elizabeth Wilson, 101–17. London: University of California Press.

Leutner, Petra. (2004). "Oberflächen mit Körper: Haut und Frisur in den Minilooks." In *Haar Tragen: Eine Kulturwissenschaftliche Annäherung*, edited by Christian Janecke, 291–306. Cologne: Böhlau.

Liedeke, Plate and Anneke Smelik. (2013). "Performing Memory in Art and Popular Culture: An Introduction." In *Performing Memory in Art and Popular Culture*, edited by Liedeke Plate and Anneke Smelik, 1–22. London: Routledge.

Lindroth, L. and D. N. Tornello. (2002). *Virtual Vintage: The Insider's Guide to Buying and Selling Online*. New York: Random House.

Lischka, Gerhard Johann, ed. (2002). *Mode—Kult*. Cologne: Wienand.

Lister, Jenny. (2006). "Kaleidoscope: Fashion in Sixties London." In *Swinging Sixties*, edited by Christopher Breward, David Gilbert and Jenny Lister, 22–39. London: V&A Publications.

Livingstone, Marco, ed. (1994). *Pop Art*. Munich: Thames & Hudson.

Loschek, Ingrid. (1994). *Reclams Mode und Kostümlexikon*. Stuttgart: Reclam.

Lovasz, Katalin. (2006). "Playing Dress-Up: eBay's Vintage Clothing-Land." In *Everyday eBay: Culture, Collecting and Desire*, edited by Ken Hillis and Michael Petit, 283–94. London: Routledge.

Love, Harriet. (1982). *Harriet Love's Guide to Vintage Chic*. New York: Holt, Rinehart and Winston.

Lowenthal, David. (1985). *The Past is a Foreign Country*. Cambridge and New York: Cambridge University Press.

Lüders, Christian. (2000). "Beobachten im Feld und Ethnographie." In *Qualitative Forschung: Ein Handbuch*, edited by Uwe Flick, Ernst von Kardoff and Ines Steincke, 384–401. Reinbek bei Hamburg: Rowohlt.

Luger, Kurt. (1991). *Die konsumierte Rebellion: Geschichte der Jugendkultur 1945-1990*. Vienna: Österreichischer Kunst- u. Kulturvlg.

Lury, Celia. (2002). "Style and the Perfection of Things." In *High-Pop: Making Culture into Popular Entertainment*, edited by Jim Collins, 201–24. New York: Wiley-Blackwell.

Luvaas, Brent. (2012). *DIY Style: Fashion, Music and Global Digital Cultures*. Oxford: Berg/Bloomsbury.

McCracken, Grant. (1988). *Culture and Consumption: New Approaches to the Symbolic Character of Consumption*. Bloomington: Indiana University Press.

Macdonald, Sharon. (2013). *Memorylands: Heritage and Identity in Europe Today*. London: Routledge.

MacInnes, Colin. (1959). *Absolute Beginners*. London: Allison & Busby.

Mackinney-Valentin, Maria. (2010). "Snapshot: Vintage Dress." *The Berg Fashion Library*. Available online: http://www.bergfashionlibrary.com/view/bewdf/BEWDF-v10/EDch10033.xml (accessed March 17, 2014).

McRobbie, Angela, ed. (1989). *Zoot Suits and Second-Hand Dresses*. London: Routledge.

McRobbie, Angela. (1991). *Feminism and Youth Culture: From Jackie to Just Seventeen*. Basingstoke: Macmillan.

McRobbie, Angela. (1994). "Second-Hand Dresses and the Role of the Ragmarket." In *Postmodernism and Popular Culture*, edited by Angela McRobbie, 135–53. London and New York: Routledge.

McRobbie, Angela. (2009). "Postfeminist Popular Culture: Bridget Jones and the New Gender Regime." In *The Aftermath of Feminism: Gender, Culture and Social Change*, by Angela McRobbie, 11–23. London: Sage Publications.

McRobbie, Angela and Jenny Garber. (2000). "Girls in Subcultures." In *Resistance through Rituals*, edited by Stuart Hall and Tony Jefferson, 209–22. London: Routledge.

Maeder, Edward. (1987). *Hollywood and History: Costume Design in Film*. Los Angeles: Thames & Hudson.

Maffesoli, Michel. (1996). *The Time of the Tribes: The Decline of Individualism in Mass Society*. London: Sage.

Marsh, Madeleine. (1999). *Miller's Collecting the 1960s*. London: Bounty Books.

Martin, Richard and Harold Koda. (1989). *The Historical Mode*. New York: Rizzoli.

Marwick, Arthur. (1998). *The Sixties: Cultural Revolution in Britain, France, Italy and the United States*. Oxford: Oxford University Press.

Marwick, Arthur (2003). *British Society Since 1945*, 4th edn. London: Penguin Books.

Matt, Susan J. (2011). *Homesickness: An American History*. Oxford and New York: Oxford University Press.

Maynard, Margaret. (2013). "Fast Fashion and Sustainability." In *The Handbook of Fashion Studies*, edited by Sandy Black et al., 542–56. London and New York: Bloomsbury.

Mayring, Philipp. (1999). *Einführung in die Qualitative Sozialforschung*. Munich: Beltz.

Melly, George. ([1970] 1989). *Revolt into Style: The Pop Arts in the 50s and 60s*. Oxford: Oxford University Press.

Mentges, Gabriele. (2000). "Cold, Coldness, Coolness: Remarks on the Relationship of Dress, Body and Technology." *Fashion Theory* 4 (1): 27–48.

Mentges, Gabriele. (2002). "Fashion, Time and Consumption of a Renaissance Man in Germany: The Costume Book of Matthäus Schwarz of Augsburg, 1496–1564." *Gender and History* 14 (3): 382–402.

Mentges, Gabriele. (2004). "Überlegungen zu einer Kleidungsforschung aus Kulturanthropologischer Perspektive." In *Von Kopf bis Fuß: Ein Handbuch rund um Körper, Kleidung und Schmuck für die Interkulturelle Unterrichtspraxis*, edited by Birgitta Huse, 73–82. Münster: Waxmann Verlag.

Mentges, Gabriele. (2005a). "Die Angst vor der Uniformität." In *Schönheit der Uniformität: Körper, Kleidung, Medien*, edited by Gabriele Mentges and Birgit Richard, 17–42. Frankfurt am Main: Campus.

Mentges, Gabriele. (2005b). "Für eine Kulturanthropologie des Textilen." In *Kulturanthropologie des Textilen: Ein einführendes Handbuch*, edited by Gabriele Mentges, 11–56. Berlin: Edition Ebersbach.

Mentges, Gabriele, Dagmar Neuland-Kitzerow and Birgit Richard, eds. (2007). *Uniformierungen in Bewegung: Vestimentäre Praktiken zwischen Vereinheitlichung und Maskerade*. Münster: Waxmann.

Mentges Gabriele and Birgit Richard, eds. (2005). *Schönheit der Uniformität: Körper, Kleidung, Medien*. Frankfurt am Main: Campus.

Mentges, Gabriele and Gudrun M. König. (2010). "Modegeschichte als Mediengeschichte." In *Medien der Mode. Textil-Körper-Mode: Dortmunder Reihe zu kulturanthropologischen Studien des Textilon, 6*, edited by Gudrun M. König and Gabriele Mentges, vii–xx. Berlin: Ebersbach.

Miles, Steven. (1998). "'Fitting In and Sticking Out:' Consumption, Consumer Meanings and Construction of Young People's Identities." *Journal of Youth Studies* 1 (1): 81–6.

Milestone, Katie. (1997). "The Love Factory: The Sites, Practices and Media Relationships of Northern Soul." In *The Clubcultures Reader: Readings in Popular Cultural Studies*, edited by Steve Redhead, 134–49. Oxford: John Wiley & Sons.

Miller, Daniel, ed. (1995). *Acknowledging Consumption: A Review of New Studies*. London: Routledge.

Miller, Daniel. (2005). "Materiality: An Introduction." In *Materiality*, edited by Daniel Miller, 1–50. Durham, NC: Duke University Press.

Miller, Daniel. (2009a). *Stuff*. Cambridge and Malden, MA: Polity.

Miller, Daniel. (2009b). "Buying Time." In *Time, Consumption and Everyday Life: Practice, Materiality and Culture*, edited by Elizabeth Shove, Frank Trentmann and Richard Wilk, 157–69. Oxford: Berg/Bloomsbury.

Miller, Janice. (2011). *Fashion and Music*. Oxford, New York: Berg/Bloomsbury.

"Mods Today and Mods Tomorrow." (n.d.) *The Scene* No. 10.

Molfino, Allessandra M. (1986). "Antikomanie." In *Anziehungskräfte: Variété de la Mode 1786–1986*, edited by Münchner Stadtmuseum, 30–3. Munich: Stadtmuseum.

Moon, Christina. (2014). "The Secret World of Fast Fashion." *Pacific Standard*, March 17. Available online: http://www.psmag.com/navigation/business-economics/secret-world-slow-road-korea-los-angeles-behind-fast-fashion-73956/ (accessed August 26, 2014).

Moser, Johannes. (2000). "Kulturanthropologische Jugendforschung." In *Jugendkulturen: Recherchen in Frankfurt am Main und London*, edited by Johannes Moser. Frankfurt am Main: Universität Frankfurt Inst. f. Kulturanthropol.

Muggleton, David. (1997). "The Post-Subculturalist." In *The Clubcultures Reader: Readings in Popular Cultural Studies*, edited by S. Redhead, D. Wynne and J. O'Connor. Oxford: Blackwell.

Muggleton, David. (2000). *Inside Subculture: The Postmodern Meaning of Style*. Oxford: Berg/Bloomsbury.

Muggleton, David and Rupert Weinzierl. (2003). "What is 'Post-cultural Studies' Anyway?" In *The Post-Subcultures Reader*, edited by David Muggleton and Rupert Weinzierl, 3–26. Oxford: Berg/Bloomsbury.

Müller, Jürgen, ed. (2004). *Filme der 60er Jahre*. Cologne: Taschen.

Müller, Renate, Patrick Glogner, Stefanie Rhein and Jens Heim. (2002). "Zum sozialen Gebrauch von Musik und Medien durch Jugendliche: Überlegungen im Lichte Kultursoziologischer Theorien." In *Wozu Jugendliche Musik und Medien gebrauchen:*

Jugendliche Identität und musikalische Identitätsbildung, edited by Renate Müller, Patrick Glogner, Stefanie Rhein and Jens Heim, 9–26. Weinheim: Juventa.

Müller-Bachmann, Eckart. (2002). *Jugendkulturen Revisited: Musik- und Stilbezogene Vergemeinschaftungsformen (Post-)Adoleszenter im Modernisierungskontext*. Münster: Lit.

Müller-Doohm, Stefan and Klaus Neumann-Braun. (1995). "Kulturinszenierungen: Einleitende Betrachtungen über die Medien kultureller Sinnvermittlung." In *Kulturinszenierungen*, edited by Stefan Müller-Doohm and Klaus Neumann-Braun, 9–26. Frankfurt am Main: Suhrkamp.

Murugan, Meenasarani Linde. (2011). "Maidenform: Temporalities of Fashion, Feminity and Feminism." In *Analyzing Mad Men: Critical Essays on the Television Series*, edited by Scott F. Stoddard, 166–85. Jefferson: McFarland.

Musée du Louvre. (2015). "History of the Louvre: From Château to Museum." Available online: http://www.louvre.fr/en/history-louvre (accessed January 5, 2015).

Narumi, Hiroshi. (2010). "Street Style and its Meaning in Postwar Japan." *Fashion Theory* 14 (4): 415–38.

Niemczyk, Ralf. (1984). "Mods in Deutschland." *Spex*, January: 31–4, 52, 55.

Norris, Lucy. (2012). "Trade and Transformations of Secondhand Clothing: Introduction." *Textile* 10 (2): 128–43.

O'Hara, Georgina. (1986). *The Encyclopaedia of Fashion*. New York: Abrams.

O'Hara Callan, Georgina. (1998). *The Thames & Hudson Dictionary of Fashion and Fashion Designers*. London: Thames & Hudson.

O'Hara Callan, Georgina and Cat Glover. (2008). *The Thames & Hudson Dictionary of Fashion and Fashion Designers*. 2nd edn. London: Thames & Hudson.

Olick, Jeffrey, Vered Vinitzky-Seroussi and Daniel Levi. (2011). "Introduction." In *The Collective Memory Reader*, edited by Jeffrey K. Olick, Vered Vinitzky-Seroussi and Daniel Levi, 3–62. New York: Oxford University Press.

O'Neill, Alistair. (2000). "John Stephen: A Carnaby Street Presentation of Masculinity 1957–1975." *Fashion Theory* 4 (4): 487–506.

Ontrup, Rüdiger and Christian Schicha. (1999). "Die Transformation des Theatralischen." In *Medieninszenierungen im Wandel: Interdisziplinäre Zugänge*, edited by Rüdiger Ontrup and Christian Schicha, 7–18. Münster: LIT.

Osgerby, Bill. (1998). *Youth in Britain since 1945*. London: Wiley.

Osgerby, Bill. (2000). "'The Young Ones.' Youth, Consumption and Representations of the 'Teenager' in Post-War Britain." In *Youth Identities: Teens und Tweens in British Culture*, edited by Gerd Stratmann, Merle Tönnies and Claus-Ulrich Viol. Heidelberg: Universitätsverlag Winter GmbH Heidelberg.

Osterwold, Tilman. (1992). *Pop Art*. Cologne: Taschen.

Oxford English Dictionary. (2014). Oxford University Press. Available online: http://www.oed.com (accessed January 29, 2014).

Palmer, Alexandra. (1997). "New Directions: Fashion History Studies and Research in North America and England." *Fashion Theory* 1 (3): 297–312.

Palmer, Alexandra. (2005). "Vintage Whores and Vintage Virgins." In *Old Clothes, New Looks: Second-Hand Fashion*, edited by Alexandra Palmer and Hazel Clark, 197–213. Oxford and New York: Berg/Bloomsbury.

Palmer, Alexandra and Hazel Clark. (2005). *Old Clothes, New Looks: Second Hand Fashion*. Oxford and New York: Berg/Bloomsbury.

Pavitt, Jane. (2008). *Fear and Fashion in the Cold War*. London: V&A Publishing.

Peer, Aurelie van de. (2014). "So Last Season: The Production of the Fashion Present in the Politics of Time." *Fashion Theory* 18 (3): 317–39.

Pezzini, Isabelle. (1986). "Dandy." In *Anziehungskräfte: Variete de la Mode 1786–1986*, edited by Münchner Stadtmuseum, 92–7. Munich: Hanser.

Picard, Lil. (1965). "Op-report." *Kunstwerk*: 6.

Pink, Sarah. (2001). *Doing Visual Ethnography*. London: Sage.

Plessen, Marie Louise von, ed. (1992). *Die Nation und ihre Museen: Deutsches Historisches Museum*. Frankfurt am Main: Campus.

Plessner, Helmut. (1982). *Mit Anderen Augen: Aspekte Einer Philosophischen Anthropologie*. Stuttgart: Reclam.

Polhemus, Ted. (1994). *Streetstyle: From Sidewalk to Catwalk*. London: Thames & Hudson.

Polhemus, Ted. (1996). *Stylesurfing: What to Wear in the Third Millennium*. London: Thames & Hudson.

Postrel, Virginia. (2003). *The Substance of Style: How the Rise of Aesthetic Value is Remaking Commerce, Culture and Consciousness*. New York: HarperCollins.

Purdy, Daniel, ed. (2004). *The Rise of Fashion*. Minneapolis: University of Minnesota Press.

Purdy, Daniel. (2010). "Fashion Journals and the Education of Enlightened Consumers." In *The Fashion History Reader: Global Perspectives*, edited by Giorgio Riello and Peter McNeil, 238–56. London: Routledge.

Quant, Mary. (1965). *Quant on Quant*. London: Cassell.

Radner, Hilary. (2001). "Embodying the Single Girl in the 1960s." In *Body Dressing*, edited by Joanne Entwistle and Elizabeth Wilson, 183–97. Oxford: Berg/Bloomsbury.

Rawlings, Terry. (2000). *Mod: A Very British Phenomenon*. London: Omnibus Press.

Reiley, Kathryn and Marilyn DeLong. (2011). "A Consumer Vision for Sustainable Fashion Practice." *Fashion Practice* 3 (1): 63–84.

Reynolds, Simon. (2011a). *Retromania: Pop Culture's Addiction to Its Own Past*. New York: Faber and Faber.

Reynolds, Simon. (2011b). "Total Recall: Why Retromania is all the Rage." *Guardian*, June 1. Available online: http://www.guardian.co.uk/music/2011/jun/02/total-recall-retromania-all-rage (accessed March 25, 2013).

Ribeiro, Aileen. (1995). *The Art of Dress: Fashion in England and France, 1750–1820*. New Haven and London: Yale University Press.

Ribeiro, Aileen. (2002). "On Englishness in Dress." In *The Englishness of English Dress*, edited by Christopher Breward, Becky Conekin and Caroline Cox, 15–27. Oxford: Berg/Bloomsbury.

Richard, Birgit. (1998). "Die oberflächlichen Hüllen des Selbst: Mode als ästhetisch-medialer Komplex." *Kunstforum* 141: 49–93.

Riello, Giorgio and Peter McNeill, eds. (2010). *The Fashion History Reader: Global Perspectives*. London: Routledge.

Rocamora, Agnes. (2013). "New Fashion Times: Fashion and Digital Media." In *The Handbook of Fashion Studies*, edited by Sandy Black et al., 61–77. London and New York: Bloomsbury.

Roche, Daniel. (1994). *The Culture of Clothing: Dress and Fashion in the Ancien Regime*. Cambridge: Cambridge University Press.

Roller, Franziska. (1997). *Abba, Barbie, Cordsamthosen: Ein Wegweiser zum prima Geschmack*. Leipzig: Reclam.

Rublack, Ulinka. (2010). *Dressing Up: Cultural Identity in Renaissance Europe*. New York: Oxford University Press.

Samuel, Raphael. (2012). *Theatres of Memory: Past and Present in Contemporary Culture*. London: Verso.

Sander, Uwe. (1995). "'Good bye Epimetheus!' Der Abschied der Jugendkulturen vom Projekt einer besseren Welt." In *Jugendkulturen: Faszination und Ambivalenz: Einblicke in Jugendliche Lebenswelten*, edited by Wilfried Ferchhoff, Uwe Sander and Ralf Vollbrecht, 38–65. Munich: Juventa.

Savage, Jon. (2007). *Teenage: The Creation of Youth Culture*. New York: Viking.

Schepers, Wolfgang. (1988). "Die Fifties—Revival und Survival: Anonymes Design und Autorendesign." In *Jaegers Katalog der 1950er: Anonymes Design eines Jahrzehnts*, 86–90. Frankfurt am Main: Fricke.

Schepers, Wolfgang. (1998). "Back to the Sixties?" In *'68 Design und Alltagskultur zwischen Konsum und Konflikt*, edited by Wolfgang Schepers, 6–7. Cologne: DuMont.

Schickedanz, Hans-Joachim. (1980). *Der Dandy*. Dortmund: Harenberg.

Schmidt, Axel and Klaus Neumann-Braun. (2003). "Ethnografie der Musikrezeption Jugendlicher." In *Popvisionen: Links in die Zukunft*, edited by Klaus Neumann-Braun, 246–72. Frankfurt am Main: Suhrkamp.

Schouten, John M. and James H. Alexander. (1995). "Subcultures of Consumption: An Ethnography of the New Bikers." *Journal of Consumer Research* 22: 43–63.

Schulze, Gerhard. (1999). *Kulissen des Glücks: Streifzüge durch die Eventkultur*. Frankfurt am Main: Campus.

Schulze, Gerhard. (2000). *Die Erlebnisgesellschaft: Kultursoziologie der Gegenwart*. Frankfurt am Main: Campus.

Schwarz, Hillel. (2000). *Deja Vu: Die Welt im Zeitalter ihrer tatsächlichen Reproduzierbarkeit*. Berlin: Aufbau.

Seel, Martin. (2001). "Inszenieren als Erscheinenlassen: Thesen über die Reichweite eines Begriffs." In *Ästhetik der Inszenierung*, edited by Josef Früchtl and Jörg Zimmermann, 48–62. Frankfurt am Main: Suhrkamp.

Seeling, Charlotte. (1999). *Mode: Das Jahrhundert der Designer 1900-1999*. Cologne: Könemann.

Sennett, Richard. (1998). *Verfall und Ende des Öffentlichen Lebens: Die Tyrannei der Intimität*. Frankfurt am Main: Fischer.

Shove, Elizabeth, Frank Trentmann and Richard Wilk, eds. (2009). *Time, Consumption and Everyday Life: Practice, Materiality and Culture*. Oxford: Berg/Bloomsbury.

Siegrist, Hannes, Hartmut Kaelble and Jürgen Kocka, eds. (1997). *Europäische Konsumgeschichte: Zur Gesellschafts- und Kulturgeschichte des Konsums (18. bis 20. Jahrhundert)*. Frankfurt am Main: Campus.

Silverman, Kaja. (1994). "Fragments of a Fashionable Discourse." In *On Fashion*, edited by Shari Benstock and Suzanne Ferris, 183–95. New Brunswick: Rutgers University Press.

Simmel, Georg. ([1911] 1986), "Die Mode." In *Die Listen der Mode*, edited by Silvia Bovenschen, 179–207. Frankfurt am Main: Suhrkamp.

Simmel, Georg. ([1901] 2004). "Fashion." In *The Rise of Fashion*, edited by Daniel Purdy, 289–309. Minneapolis: University of Minnesota Press.

Slobin, Mark. (1993). *Subcultural Sounds: Micromusics of the West*. Hanover: Wesleyan.

Smallbone, Nicola. (1996). "A Girl in the Sixties: Mod, Rocker or Nobody? BA (Hons) diss., History of Design, University of Brighton.

Smart Martin, Ann. (1993). "Makers, Buyers, and Users: Consumerism as a Material Culture Framework." *Winterthur Portfolio* 28: 140–57.

"Smart Fashions for Limited Incomes." (1913). *Vogue* 42 (6): 47, 94, 96.

Soeffner, Hans-Georg. (1986). "Stil und Stilisierung: Punk oder die Überhöhung des Alltags." In *Stil: Geschichten und Funktionen eines kulturwissenschaftlichen*

Diskurselements, edited by Hans Ulrich Gumbrecht and K. Ludwig Pfeiffer, 317–431. Frankfurt am Main: Suhrkamp.

Sombart, Werner. (2004). "Economy and Fashion: A Theoretical Contribution on the Formation of Modern Consumer Demand." In *The Rise of Fashion*, edited by Daniel Purdy, 310–16. Minneapolis: University of Minnesota Press.

Sommer, Carlo Michael. (1997). "Stars als Mittel der Identitätskonstruktion." In *Der Star: Geschichte, Rezeption, Bedeutung*, edited by Werner Faulstich and Helmut Korte, 114–24. Munich: Fink.

Sonntag, Michael. (1999). *Das Verborgene des Herzens: Zur Geschichte der Individualität*. Hamburg: Rowohlt-Taschenbuch-Verlag.

Sontag, Susan. (1973). *On Photography*. New York: Farrar, Straus and Giroux.

SpoKK, ed. (1997). *Kursbuch Jugendkultur: Stile, Szenen und Identitäten vor der Jahrtausendwende*. Mannheim: Bollmann.

Sprengler, Christine. (2009). *Screening Nostalgia: Populuxe Props and Technicolor Aesthetics in Contemporary American Film*. New York and Oxford: Berghahn Books.

Starzinger, Anneli. (2000). *Kommunikationsraum Szenekneipe: Annäherung an ein Produkt der Erlebnisgesellschaft*. Wiesbaden: Deutscher Universitätsverlag.

Stauber, Barbara. (2001). "Übergänge Schaffen: Jugendkulturelle Zusammenhänge und ihre Bedeutung für das Erwachsen(?)werden am Beispiel Techno." In *Techno-Soziologie*, edited by Ronald Hitzler and Michaela Pfadenhauer, 119–35. Opladen: Leske + Budrich.

Steele, Valerie. (1997). *From New Look to Now: Fifty Years of Fashion*. New Haven: Yale University Press.

Steele, Valerie. (2005). "Fashion." In *Encyclopedia of Clothing and Fashion*, Volume 2, edited by Valerie Steele, 12–13. New York: Scribner.

Steinberg, Shirley, Priya Parmar and Birgit Richard, eds. (2005). *Encyclopedia of Youth Cultures*. New York: Greenwood Press.

Stellrecht, Irmtraud. (1993). *Interpretative Ethnologie: Eine Orientierung*. In *Handbuch der Ethnologie*, edited by Thomas Schweizer and Margarete Schweizer, 29–79. Berlin: Dietrich Reimer.

Stephens, Chris and Katharine Stout, eds. (2004). *Art and the 60s: This Was Tomorrow*. London: Tate.

Stern, Jane and Michael Stern. (1990). *Sixties People*. London: Knopf.

Stoddard, Scott F., ed. (2011). *Analyzing Mad Men: Critical Essays on the Television Series*. Jefferson: McFarland.

Stratmann, Gerd. (2000). "'Absolute Beginners' and Their Heirs in Contemporary British Novels." In *Youth Identities: Teens und Twens in British Culture*, edited by Gerd Stratmann, Merle Tönnies and Claus-Ulrich Viol, 125–34. Heidelberg: Isd.

Straw, Will. (1997). "Sizing Up Record Collections: Gender and Connoisseurship in Rock Music Culture." In *Sexing the Groove: Popular Music and Gender*, edited by Sheila Whiteley, 3–16. London: Routledge.

Synnott, Anthony. (1993). *The Body Social: Symbolism, Self and Society*. London: Routledge.

Tarlo, Emma. (2007). "Islamic Cosmopolitanism: The Sartorial Biographies of Three Muslim Women in London." *Fashion Theory* 11 (2–3): 143–72.

Taylor, Lou. (2002). *The Study of Dress History*. Manchester: Manchester University Press.

Taylor, Lou. (2004). *Establishing Dress History*. Manchester: Manchester University Press.

Terdiman, Richard. (1993). *Present Past: Modernity and the Memory Crisis*. Ithaca and London: Cornell University Press.

The New Faces (2010). [Film] Dir. Dean Chalkley. Available online: http://showstudio. com/project/the_new_faces (accessed September 4, 2014).

The Vogue Archive. 1892–Present. Available from: Proquest.

Thornton, Sarah. (1995). *Club Cultures: Music, Media, Subcultural Capital.* Cambridge, MA: Wesleyan.

Thrift, Nigel. (2010). "Understanding the Material Practices of Glamour." In *The Affect Theory Reader*, edited by Melissa Gregg and Gregory J. Seigworth, 289–308. Durham and London: Duke University Press.

Til, Barbara. (1998). "Mode '68: Anarchie und Kleiderwirbel." In *'68 Design und Alltagskultur zwischen Konsum und Konflikt*, edited by Wolfgang Schepers, 105–15. Cologne: DuMont.

Titton, Monica. (2010). "Fashion in the City: Street-Style-Blogs and the Limits of Fashion's Democratization."*Texte zur Kunst* 78. Available online: http://www. textezurkunst.de/78/mode-der-stadt/ (accessed August 26, 2014).

Tolkien, Tracy. (2000). *Dressing Up Vintage.* New York: Rizzoli.

Trosse, Sabine. (1999). *Geschichten im Anzug: Über den Retro-Trend im Bekleidungsdesign.* Münster: Waxmann.

Tulloch, Carol. (1992). "Rebel without a Pause: Black Street Style and Black Designers." In *Chic Thrills*, edited by Juliette Ash and Elizabeth Wilson, 84–98. London: University of California Press.

Tulloch, Carol. (2010). "Style-Fashion-Dress: From Black to Post-Black." *Fashion Theory* 14 (3): 361–86.

Turkle, Sherry. (2007). *Evocative Objects: Things We Think With.* Cambridge, MA: MIT Press.

Twigg, Julia. (2013). "Fashion, the Body and Age." In *The Handbook of Fashion Studies*, edited by Sandy Black et al., 78–94. London and New York: Bloomsbury.

Ulin, Robert C. (1995). "Invention and Representation as Cultural Capital: Southwest French Winegrowing History." *American Anthropologist* 97 (3): 519–27.

Ullmaier, Johannes. (2002). "Subkultur im Widerstreit: Mods Gegen Rocker—und Gegen Sich Selbst." In *"Alles so Schön Bunt Hier:" Die Geschichte der Popkultur von den Fünfzigern bis Heute*, edited by Peter Kemper, Thomas Langhoff and Ulrich Sonnenschein, 61–75. Leipzig: Reclam.

Urry, John. (2000). "Sociology of Time and Space." In *The Blackwell Companion to Social Theory*, edited by Bryan Turner, 416–43. Malden, MA and Oxford: Blackwell.

Veblen, Thorstein. (2004). "Dress as an Expression of a Pecuniary Culture. The Theory of the Leisure Class." In *The Rise of Fashion*, edited by Daniel Purdy, 261–88. Minneapolis: University of Minnesota Press.

Victoria & Albert Museum. (2006). "Interview with Robert Orbach." Available online: http://www.vam.ac.uk/content/articles/i/robert-orbach/ (accessed January 8, 2015).

Vinken, Barbara. (1993). *Mode nach der Mode: Kleid und Geist am Ende des 20. Jahrhunderts.* Frankfurt am Main: Fischer Taschenbuch.

Vinken, Barbara. (2005). *Fashion Zeitgeist: Trends and Cycles in the Fashion System.* Oxford: Berg/Bloomsbury.

Vollbrecht, Ralf. (1997). "Von Subkulturen zu Lebensstilen: Jugendkulturen im Wandel." In *Kursbuch Jugendkultur: Stile, Szenen und Identitäten vor der Jahrtausendwende*, edited by SPoKK, 22–31. Mannheim: Bollmann.

Vulliamy, Ed. (2007). "Absolute MacInnes." *The Guardian*, April 14. Available online: http://www.guardian.co.uk/uk/2007/apr/15/britishidentity.fiction (accessed March 14, 2013).

Waetzold, Stephan and Alfred A. Schmid. (1979). *Echtheitsfetischismus? Zur Wahrhaftigkeit des Originalen*. Munich: Selbstverlag.

Walter, Klaus. (1999). "The Kids are not Alright: Skins Gegen Links und Rechts." In *"Alles so schön bunt hier:" Die Geschichte der Popkultur von den Fünfzigern bis Heute*, edited by Peter Kemper, Thomas Langhoff and Ulrich Sonnenschein, 197–208. Stuttgart: Reclam.

Warner, Helen. (2014). *Fashion on Television: Identity and Celebrity Culture*. London and New York: Bloomsbury.

Weight, Richard. (2013). *Mod! A Very British Style*. London: The Bodley Head.

Weinzierl, Rupert. (2000). *Fight the Power! Eine Geheimgeschichte der Popkultur und die Formierung neuer Substreams*. Vienna: Passagen.

Weller, Paul. (1981). "The Sixties: The Total Look." In *Cool Cats: 25 years of Rock 'n' Roll Style*, edited by Tony Stewart. London: Delilah Books.

Welters, Linda. (2008). "The Fashion of Sustainability." In *Sustainable Fashion: Why Now? A Conversation about Issues, Practices, and Possibilities*, edited by Janet Hethorn and Connie Ulasewicz, 7–29. New York: Fairchild.

West, Nancy Martha. (2000). *Kodak and the Lens of Nostalgia*. Charlottesville: University of Virginia Press.

West-Pavlov, Russell. (2013). *Temporalities*. London: Routledge.

White, Nicola and Ian Griffiths. (2000). *The Fashion Business: Theory, Practice, Image*. Oxford: Berg/Bloomsbury.

Whiteley, Nigel. (1987). *Pop Design: Modernism to Mod*. London: Design Council Books.

Whiteley, Sheila, ed. (1997). *Sexing the Groove: Popular Music and Gender*. London: Routledge.

Wicke, Peter. (1987). *Rockmusik: Zur Ästhetik und Soziologie eines Massenmediums*. Leipzig: Reclam.

Wildt, Michael. (1997). "Die Kunst der Wahl." In *Europäische Konsumgeschichte: Zur Gesellschafts- und Kulturgeschichte des Konsums (18. bis 20. Jahrhundert)*, edited by Hannes Siegrist, Hartmut Kaelble and Jürgen Kocka, 307–25. Frankfurt am Main: Campus.

Willems, Herbert and Martin Jurga. (1998). *Inszenierungsgesellschaft: Ein einführendes Handbuch*. Opladen and Wiesbaden: Verlag für Sozialwissenschaften.

Willingmann, Heike. (2001). "Kleid auf Zeit: Über den Umgang mit der Vergänglichkeit von Bekleidung." *Textil–Körper, Mode: Dortmunder Reihe zu kulturanthropologischen Studien des Textilen* 1: zeit.schnitte 141–223.

Wilson, Elizabeth. (1990). "These New Components of the Spectacle: Fashion and Postmodernism." In *Postmodernism and Society*, edited by Roy Boyne and Ali Rattansi, 209–36. Basingstoke: Palgrave Macmillan.

Wilson, Elizabeth. (2005a). *Adorned in Dreams: Fashion and Modernity*. London: I. B. Tauris.

Wilson, Elizabeth. (2005b). "Fashion and Modernity." In *Fashion and Modernity*, edited by Christopher Breward and Caroline Evans, 9–14. Oxford: Berg/Bloomsbury.

Wilson, Elizabeth. (2013). *Cultural Passions: Fans, Aesthetes and Tarot Readers*. London: I. B. Tauris.

Wilson, Elizabeth and Lou Taylor. (1989). *Through the Looking Glass*. London: BBC Publications.

Winter, Carsten, Tanja Thomas and Andreas Hepp, eds. (2003). *Medienidentitäten: Identität im Kontext von Globalisierung und Medienkultur*. Cologne: Halem.

Winter, Rainer. (1997). "Medien und Fans: Zur Konstitution von Fan-Kulturen." In *Kursbuch Jugendkultur: Stile, Szenen und Identitäten vor der Jahrtausendwende*, edited by SPoKK, 40–53. Mannheim: Bollmann.

Winter, Rainer and R. Eckert. (1990). *Mediengeschichte und Kulturelle Differenzierung: Zur Entstehung und Funktion von Wahlnachbarschaften.* Opladen: Leske und Budrich.

Woodward, Sophie. (2007). *Why Women Wear What They Wear.* Oxford: Berg/ Bloomsbury.

Woodward, Sophie. (forthcoming). "Humble Blue Jeans: Material Culture Approaches to Understanding the Ordinary, Global and the Personal." In *Fashion Studies: Research Methods, Sites and Practices*, edited by Heike Jenss. London and New York: Bloomsbury.

Wyneken, Gustav. (1914). *Was ist Jugendkultur?* Munich: Steinicke.

Wyrwa, Ulrich. (1997). "Consumption, Konsum, Konsumgesellschaft: Ein Beitrag zur Begriffsgeschichte." In *Europäische Gesellschafts- und Kulturgeschichte des Konsums (18. bis 20. Jahrhundert)*, edited by Hannes Siegrist, Hartmut Kaelble and Jürgen Kocka, 747–62. Frankfurt am Main: Campus.

York, Peter. (1980). "Recycling the Sixties." In *Style Wars*, edited by Peter York, 178–92. London: Sidgwick & Jackson.

Zierold, Martin. (2010). "Memory and Media Cultures." In *A Companion to Cultural Memory Studies*, edited by Astrid Erll and Ansgar Nünning, 399–407. Berlin and New York: Walter de Gruyter.

INDEX

www.ingramcontent.com/pod-product-compliance
Lightning Source LLC
Chambersburg PA
CBHW062031270326
41929CB00014B/2398